**Praise for Corey Mitchell
and His Masterful True-Crime Thrillers**

"Corey Mitchell's life experiences made him a writer who could empathize with crime victims in a unique and personal way. That empathy is evident in every true crime book he wrote and is what makes his books heartfelt, compelling reads to this very day."

—**Suzy Spencer**, New York Times bestselling author of *Wasted*

"No one faces evil head on like Corey Mitchell."

—**Gregg Olsen**, *New York Times* bestselling author of *A Killing in Amish Country*

Strangler

"Incredibly intelligent, attractive, and charismatic, Tony Shore seemed to have it all. Corey Mitchell unmasks this beguiling character to reveal a self-centered monster bent on destruction. A must-read, cautionary tale of manipulation, control, and murder."

—**Diane Fanning**, author of *Written in Blood*

"*Strangler* reads like a horror movie. It was such a frightening story that I held my breath from the very beginning and didn't breathe again until it was finally over!"

—**Dale Hudson**, author of *Die, Grandpa, Die*

"Corey Mitchell's fast-paced book literally sizzles with his portrayal of dastardly deeds in my hometown. It is true-crime storytelling at its chilling best."

—**Steve Long**, author of *Every Woman's Nightmare*

"In *Strangler*, Corey Mitchell takes you into the heart of a gripping mystery set in Houston, Texas. The more you learn about the charming Tony Shore, the more the truth behind the deception will haunt you."

—**Sue Russell,** author of *Lethal Intent*

"The taut, cool writing of Corey Mitchell is the perfect counterpoint to the strangling humid heat that envelops the Houston crime spree. Parents, keep your children indoors and read this with the knowledge that it could happen anywhere."

—**Del Howison**, editor of *Dark Delicacies*

"Corey Mitchell provides a fascinating and educational insight into the crimes and thought process of a narcissistic serial killer. Having interacted with such offenders, I appreciated the accurate depiction of the personality traits displayed by Tony Shore. Highly recommended!"

—**Roy Hazelwood**, former FBI profiler and author of *Dark Dreams*

"Corey Mitchell has done it again. *Strangler* is provocatively chilling and delivered with a compassionate respect for the justice that trumped perceived criminal superiority."

—**Joyce King**, author of *Hate Crime: The Story of a Dragging in Jaspar, Texas*

"*Strangler* is a chilling account of the investigation, case history, and subsequent courtroom drama about convicted serial murderer and pedophile Anthony Allen Shore. For police detectives, it is a primer about the machinations of a sexual predator who preys on young girls. For prosecutors, it outlines some great courtroom tactics and legal truths. For female readers, this story demonstrates that relationships should be looked at from all angles and constantly reevaluated. For parents, the advice rings loud and clear: know, warn, and monitor your daughter's whereabouts—one of his victims was age nine!"

—**Andrea Campbell**, forensic artist and author

"Anyone addicted to TV's *CSI* owes it to themselves to read *Strangler*. In fact, *Strangler* could launch *CSI: Houston*. Are you paying attention, Mr. Bruckheimer?"

—**Dennis McDougal**, *LA Times* bestselling author of *Blood Cold* and *The Yosemite Murders*

Murdered Innocents

"A gory, yet sensitive, true crime tale that will scare the hell out of you."

—**Poppy Z. Brite**, bestselling author of *The Exquisite Corpse*

"Corey Mitchell uncovers yet another level of the insanity behind the world of youth and violence."

—**Aphrodite Jones,** bestselling author of *The Red Zone* and *A Perfect Husband*

Also by Corey Mitchell*

Dead and Buried

Murdered Innocents

Strangler

Pure Murder

Savage Son

*Available from Kensington Publishing Corp.

EVIL EYES

COREY MITCHELL

PINNACLE BOOKS
Kensington Publishing Corp.
http://www.kensingtonbooks.com

For Carol and Don Mitchell,
your example of love and strength
goes beyond inspirational

Some names have been changed to protect the privacy of individuals connected to this story.

PINNACLE BOOKS are published by

Kensington Publishing Corp.
119 West 40th Street
New York, NY 10018

All Kensington Titles, Imprints, and Distributed Lines are available at special quantity discounts for bulk purchases for sales promotions, premiums, fund-raising, and educational or institutional use. Special book excerpts or customized printings can also be created to fit specific needs. For details, write or phone the office of the Kensington special sales manager: Kensington Publishing Corp., 119 West 40th Street, New York, NY 10018, attn: Special Sales Department, Phone: 1-800-221-2647.

Pinnacle and the P logo Reg. U.S. Pat. & TM Off.

ISBN-13: 978-0-7860-4264-7
ISBN-10: 0-7860-4264-8
First Kensington Mass Market Edition: April 2006

eISBN-13: 978-0-7860-3780-3
eISBN-10: 0-7860-3780-6
First Kensington Electronic Edition: April 2006

10 9 8 7 6 5 4 3

Printed in the United States of America

Justice will only be achieved when those who have not been injured by crime are as indignant as those who have.
—King Solomon

In Memory

Dick Yarbrough
Gene Williford
Max

ACKNOWLEDGMENTS

Two people in particular helped make this book come to life. Harriett Semander and Andy Kahan provided the heart and grit of this story for me. They are beacons in a dense fog.

I also would like to thank Melinda Aguilar, Jane Montgomery, Keri Whitlow, JoAnna Nicolaou, Joseph Foy, Sandra Carlsen, Doug Bostock, Sharon Watts, Mike Cox, Alison Pierce, Paul Bunten, Tom Wine, Don Grove, Denise Domain, Dianne Clements, Scott Durfee, Lynn Erickson, Richard Kuhn, Gavin Routt, Michael Guarino, Virginia Gibbons, Elias Melendrez, and my anonymous sources.

Also Richard Curtis, Michaela Hamilton, He Who Shall Remain Nameless, Stephanie Finnegan, and everyone at Kensington/Pinnacle.

Special thanks to Michelle Hartmann for the use of her photos.

For my friends Ray Seggern and Kelly Nugent, Peter and Kathryn Soria, Lupe Garcia, Mike and Lynette Sheppard, Knox and Heather Williams, Ricky and Shirin Butler, Kevin and Shana Fowler, Trey and Missy Chase, Clint and Cathy Stephen, Phil and Karen Savoie, Chris and Beverly Goldrup, Kirk and Teresa Morris, Dennis McDougal, Aphrodite Jones, Poppy Z. Brite, Adam Grossman, Letty and John Espinosa, Drew and Sarah Stride, Irma Guerrero, Bobbie Stephens, Bertha Gutierrez, Dale Heath, and Ruby Tristan.

For my in-laws Dennis and Margaret Burke, Denise Burke, and my Chi-niece, Leah Burke.

For my family Don and Carol Mitchell, Kyle and Ramona Mitchell, Darrin and DeDe Mitchell, and all of my wonderful nieces, Julie, Kaylee, and Madison, and my awesome nephew, Ronnie. Also to Bill and Renee Runyan, Todd Solomon, and Jeremy Frey. Also, Lucas and Dallas.

For my late wife, Lisa. I always miss you and love you.

For my wife Audra. From copyediting to counseling, thank you for always being there for me. Your love and support mean everything to me. You are beyond compare. My love, forever.

For Emma, our daughter. Here's to a safe and happy life. We love you.

PROLOGUE

*May 23, 1982, Hammerly Walk Apartments,
Houston, Texas, 6:30 A.M.*

The man watched as the young pretty white girl glided out of her car. He thought about the woman he killed earlier that morning.

He didn't know her name—as usual. The one from the morning, that is. Or this one, for that matter. Or the three women he killed in April.

The man stood quietly in the bushes of the apartment complex. The slim white girl had smooth skin, just the way he liked. She also had pretty hair. He eyed her as she walked toward him. The man slid out from the bushes and directly behind the young woman. He grabbed her just as she began her ascent up the staircase. The strong black man placed his large hands around the woman's throat and began to squeeze. Caught off guard, the woman's face was panic-stricken. The man continued the death grip as he dragged her onto her neighbor's patio.

"Where do you live?" he asked the young woman.

She pointed up at the apartment on the second floor.

"Is there anyone else inside?"

Lying, she shook her head furiously. Her roommate was probably inside.

The man continued to strangle the woman. She began to lose consciousness and sagged to the ground like a rag doll. The man trotted up the stairs to the woman's apartment. He opened the door, which was not locked, and walked inside. The room was dark. The man felt along the inside of the wall for a light switch. When the room was illuminated, it was time for the man to be surprised. An attractive eighteen-year-old Hispanic woman, Melinda Aguilar, stood directly in front of him.

Melinda had been getting ready for the 10:45 A.M. church service, where she and her roommate, Lori Lister, taught Sunday school. Dressed only in a terry cloth bathrobe, she was terrified. She froze in her tracks and stared at the muscular man. She did not scream; she did not run. She could only stare at the intruder. The man seemed dumbfounded as well.

Aguilar yelled out for her roommate, snapping the intruder out of his reverie. He approached her, grabbed her, and forced her into one of the rooms in the modest-sized apartment. It was the roommates' bedroom. He began to choke the pretty Hispanic girl.

"If you scream, I'll kill you," he threatened in a hushed tone. He forced the girl to her knees next to her own bed. Her head lay on the sheets. She kept her mouth shut, but he continued choking her. Aguilar knew she had to do something to save herself; however, she knew there was no way she could defend herself physically against this man. So she feigned unconsciousness. Apparently, the ruse worked as the man let go of her and let her body slump on the side of the bed. He searched the room for something with which to tie the girl up. There on the bed were belts and a wire coat hanger. He used the belts to tie her arms behind her back and her ankles. He then unraveled the hanger and used it to tie her wrists. After he secured Aguilar, he left the bedroom and shut the door halfway closed.

The man went back outside. Aguilar heard a loud *thump-thump-thump-thump-thump-thump*. The man was dragging her roommate up the concrete stairs by her hair.

The man peeked into the bedroom to check up on Aguilar. She watched her attacker through squinted eyes. She noticed that he seemed extremely pleased with himself. She could not believe when he literally jumped for joy and began clapping his hands like a demonic mechanical monkey doll. After the man's macabre dance, he retreated to the front room and grabbed Lister, who was still unconscious. He grabbed some more of Aguilar's belts and used them as restraints on Lister. He dragged his hapless victim into the bathroom, just like he had done earlier that morning with the pretty brunette whom he killed by drowning her in her own bathtub.

He liked that method. It was a new one for him. One that he had never used before.

He began to fill up Lori Lister's bathtub with steaming hot water. As the water rose in the tub, the man went back to the bedroom to check up on Aguilar. She appeared to be unconscious, so he returned to the bathroom.

When Aguilar heard the running water, she knew that her friend was in trouble. She also knew that they were both going to die unless she did something. Somehow, the five-foot-tall, eighty-six-pound Aguilar, with her ankles bound and her wrists confined behind her back, stood up and backed up to the sliding glass door in her bedroom. She managed to lift up the latch to the door and unlock it. Instead of trying to open it right away, however, she went back to her spot on the floor next to the bed and resumed playing possum.

Indeed, the amped-up man returned to the bedroom to check on her. Aguilar could still hear the water cascading from the bathroom. Luckily, the man did not approach her, but returned to Lister. Aguilar heard Lister scream. She realized this was her one and only chance to escape. She stated later that if she was "going to die, [she] would rather kill herself than to have him kill [her]."

The eighteen-year-old stood up and backed toward the bedroom door. She managed to lock the door. She then quietly walked to the sliding glass door. She slowly slid the door open a few inches and squeezed out onto the second-floor balcony. The wooden railing to the balcony stood four feet tall. There was no simple way out for Aguilar, but she had to do something immediately or her friend would die, so she backed up, took two steps, and propelled herself, headfirst, over the railing. Her feet hit the railing and caused her to somersault headfirst. She hit her head on the bottom of the wooden patio balcony and landed hard on her shoulder onto the concrete thirteen feet below. Full of adrenaline, she popped right up, hands still bound, and began to run until she spotted one of her neighbors outside drinking her early-morning coffee. The neighbor listened to her calmly describe what had happened and that her roommate was still inside. The neighbor immediately picked up the phone, clumsily dialed 911, and comforted her calm but frightened neighbor.

Houston police officers Donnie Schmidt and Luther Domain responded to a "family disturbance" call at the apartment complex. The officers knocked on the wrong apartment door. They were greeted by twenty-three-year-old Patricia Kay McDonald, the downstairs neighbor of Lister and Aguilar. Schmidt and Domain began to question McDonald about the commotion. McDonald told them that everything was taking place upstairs. Schmidt and Domain heard what sounded like an explosion upstairs. Apparently, the man had discovered that Aguilar locked herself in the bedroom. He had kicked the door in and discovered that she was missing. The man noticed the open sliding glass door and peered outside. He saw two police cars. He took off running through the front door.

Schmidt and Domain stepped off McDonald's porch only to see a black man "storm" out of the upstairs apartment. The man leaped halfway down the staircase and took off running. Schmidt, the younger of the two officers, took off on foot after the man. Domain, fifty, ran to his police cruiser to request backup. He was afraid that the man would run into the woods surrounding the apartment complex. "We've lost four or five prisoners in those woods," he recalled.

At the same time the chase commenced, Patricia Kay McDonald darted upstairs to check on her neighbors. She looked around the small apartment and eventually saw Lister submerged in the bathtub. Her neighbor, with whom she had only expressed the occasional "Hello, how are you," was on her back and unconscious. Her hands had also been bound with a wire coat hanger behind her back. The water from the tub's faucet was still running. McDonald thought she was dead.

As McDonald discovered Lister, Officer Schmidt raced after the man through the apartment courtyard area. The man suddenly turned around and headed for the back side of the apartment complex. He was headed for his car, a brown 1978 Pontiac Grand Prix. It just so happened to be parked near the police cruisers. As the man headed for his vehicle, he spotted Domain by his patrol car. Again he hightailed it in another direction and ran into a small area in the apartment complex.

It was a dead end.

Schmidt pulled his service revolver and told him to hit the pavement. The man immediately fell to the ground on his stomach. As Schmidt knelt down to restrain the suspect, one of the apartment residents helped handcuff the man.

Suddenly another neighbor began to scream, "She's dying! She's dying!" Schmidt and Domain had no idea what had happened in the apartment. Domain took control of the prisoner while Schmidt returned to the upstairs apartment where the man had just fled. The subdued man acted calm as Domain watched over him.

Inside the apartment bathroom, McDonald realized that her neighbor was in serious trouble. She described Lister's look as "deadly" and that she was turning blue. McDonald grabbed the young woman and pulled her out of the bathtub. She first removed the gag from her mouth, but Lister was not breathing. She wasn't sure what to do.

"I couldn't remember any CPR, any lifesaving method," so she began to pound on Lister's back. Eventually the crude method of resuscitation worked as Lister began to cough up water and blood. She gasped violently for air as she came to. Officer Schmidt scooted inside and only then realized that something bigger than a domestic disturbance had taken place here.

He would have no idea just how much bigger it really was.

* * *

August 10, 1982, Harris County District Attorney's
Office, Special Crimes Unit, Houston, Texas

Carl "Coral" Eugene Watts leaned forward in his sturdy wooden chair with his elbows on the long, dark brown conference table. The handsome man placed his chin on his fists. With him were his court-appointed attorneys, Zinetta Burney and Don Caggins, of the law firm of Burney, Caggins and Hartsfield. Watts's twenty-one-year-old girlfriend, Sheila Williams, whom he met at church, knew Caggins, who taught a paralegal course she had taken. Caggins specialized in civil rights issues. His partner, Burney, handled criminal matters. The three sat and waited.

The five-foot-eleven-inch, 160-pound, African American Watts looked bored.

After several minutes, the door opened. In walked a cadre of Houston police detectives, including Tom Ladd, his younger brother, Jim Ladd, Kenny Williamson, and Mike Kardatzke. They were joined by Harris County assistant district attorneys (ADA) Ira L. Jones II and Jack Frels. The six men took their places around the rectangular table.

They were not there just simply to talk about Watts's attack on Lori Lister and Melinda Aguilar. Watts had many more stories to tell. Thirteen years earlier to the day, in Los Angeles, California, Charles Manson's band of followers brutally massacred seven people, including actress Sharon Tate, in a crime that shocked the world and was splashed all over the headlines. The story Coral Eugene Watts began to tell was even more astounding and frightening.

Tom Ladd took charge of the questioning during the videotaped proceedings.

"Okay, Coral, we're gonna start this off. You understand,

at this point, during this interview, we're only gonna talk about cases that fall under the Harris County District Attorney's Office jurisdiction." Watts solemnly nodded his head. "We've decided that a good way to start this was, we're gonna go over the ones we talked about yesterday. All right?"

"Uh-huh," Watts muttered.

PART I

MICHIGAN

CHAPTER 1

Carl Eugene Watts was born in Killeen, Texas, on November 7, 1953, to parents Richard and Dorothy Mae. One year prior to his birth, his parents were married in Coalwood, West Virginia, located in the southernmost portion of the state. Richard Watts, who was several years older than Dorothy Mae, was also a private in the army. He had been transferred in 1953 to Fort Hood in Killeen, a town almost directly between Austin and Waco—an area that later would be known as the "Texas Bermuda Triangle," with such outlandish crimes as the Charles Whitman University of Texas tower shooting of fifteen people on August 1, 1966, the massacre of eighty-two Branch Davidians, led by David Koresh, at Mt. Carmel, just outside of Waco, on April 19, 1993, and the country's most notorious mass murder by a single individual, George Hennard, who killed twenty-two diners at a Luby's Cafeteria (a twenty-third person died later) in Killeen, Texas, on October 16, 1991.

Before Hennard's rampage, Killeen was known as the home to Fort Hood. On January 15, 1942, the United States War Department selected the tiny town, located sixty miles northeast of Austin, as the location for its Tank

Destroyer Tactical and Firing Center. At that time the base was known as Camp Hood. After the acquisition of more than 108,000 acres of land and the infusion of nearly $23,000,000, Camp Hood opened its gates on September 18, 1942. Within half a year, there were nearly ninety-five thousand troops and more than four thousand prisoners of war on-site.

Within two years, at the end of World War II, the base was stripped down, equipment was removed off-site, and the troops dwindled to eleven thousand, along with just under two thousand POWs. By 1950, Camp Hood had been renamed Fort Hood.

By the time Richard Watts was assigned to Fort Hood, the camp had been transformed into a permanent installation for troop training during the Korean War. Many grunts from Fort Hood were shipped out to the Far East to face combat.

Allegedly, the Watts family packed up their belongings and relocated back to Coalwood just three days after Carl's birth. One year later, the Watts family welcomed a daughter, Sharon Yvonne, into the family.

By 1955, the idyllic structure of the Watts clan had been ripped apart. Richard left Dorothy and the kids forever. No specific reason was ever given for his departure.

Dorothy once again packed up her meager belongings, dressed up her two children, and hopped into her car and drove straight through to the tiny town of Inkster, Michigan, located just fifteen miles west of Detroit.

Dorothy Mae Watts took a job as an art teacher at a nearby Detroit high school. Somehow, she managed to cope raising her children while maintaining her job.

Dorothy often returned to Coalwood, West Virginia, to visit her mama, Lula Mae Young. Coalwood is best-known as the home to author and budding scientist Homer

Hickam, who wrote about the small town in his bestselling book, *Rocket Boys*, which was later made into a popular movie starring Jake Gyllenhaal, renamed *October Sky*. Hickam may have even encountered Watts at the time when Watts would visit his grandmother.

Hickam described Coalwood as a town that "was built for the purpose of extracting the millions of tons of rich bituminous coal that lay beneath it." The two thousand residents of Coalwood all worked for the local mining company, Carter Coal Company, which eventually became Olga Coal Company, and lived in company-owned homes. Most workers were known as "bone pickers," the men who separated the rock from the coal.

Carl loved to visit his West Virginia grandmother, who lived in a house on a hill with nothing but the forest behind it. While he was there, Carl adapted the thick Appalachian drawl common to the area and prevalent among his cousins. They would draw out the letters in Carl's name until it sounded like coral, like a coral reef—a beautiful organism that lives beneath the surface and is dangerous to the touch. Carl liked the Coalwood-ized sound of his name, so he asked his mother to change it for him.

Carl Watts was now known as Coral.

It would be the first of several dramatic changes in his life.

Coral loved the backwoods of the Appalachian countryside. He and his sister, Sharon, used to enjoy playing in the creek behind their grandmother's home. That is, until Lula Mae found out what they were doing and had a fit. She warned the children that the creek was full of snakes and they were putting themselves in danger by playing out there.

The West Virginia forests held a plethora of trophies for Coral to hunt. His favorite prey was the jackrabbit. He enjoyed hunting down the beautiful creatures with his grandfather. He also enjoyed the touch of their soft pelts. He also learned how to skin the li'l critters.

According to *Houston Chronicle* reporter Evan Moore, Watts's grandmother believed that Coral "was always a good little boy." He enjoyed being close to women. "He was always around me or his mother. Even when the children got older and some of the boys would be goin' out at night, maybe drinkin' or chasin' women or gettin' in trouble, he stayed right up here with me. He wasn't interested in that sort of thing."

Back in Inkster, Michigan, Watts struggled in school. According to Moore, he had difficulty with school but put in long hours for his homework. The extra effort paid off as Watts earned good grades.

In 1961, however, Watts suffered a major setback. He was stricken with meningitis, an inflammation of the membrane that surrounds the brain and spinal cord, caused by a viral infection. Actually, he and Sharon both were stricken. Dorothy took both of her children to Detroit General Hospital, which took in Sharon but refused to see Coral. No reason was given.

Sharon had contracted bacterial meningitis and was given a clean bill of health.

Coral, on the other hand, was not so lucky. He suffered from a debilitating fever and was forced into an extended hospital stay at Herman Keifer Hospital. It turned out that not only did he have a severe bout of meningitis, but he was also diagnosed with polio. While in the hospital, Coral was subjected to numerous painful spinal taps and was often isolated from the rest of the patients.

The combination of meningitis and polio kept Watts down so much physically that he missed the entire third grade of school. His attention span dropped after that point and his studies suffered as a result. Watts used to complain that after the bout of meningitis his memory often failed him.

In 1962, Dorothy Mae Watts met a mechanic's assistant from Detroit named Norman Ceaser. Coral's stepfather had six children of his own before he married Dorothy. Together, the couple had two more children, which made for an extremely crowded household. Also, a household in which it was very easy to get lost in the mix if you did not attempt to get noticed.

According to Coral's younger sister, Sharon, Coral did not stand out. "He was always real quiet and almost shy. He was just very introverted." She also discussed his temper. "He was actually very even-tempered, mainly because he used to just hold everything in. It would take a lot to get under his skin or to upset him." Apparently, when he did get upset, he was quite volatile.

According to Sharon, Watts was not violent or abusive to her or anyone else in the family. She also stressed that neither their mother nor their stepfather ever abused any of the kids. In fact, they doted on Coral at her expense. She stated if anyone picked on anyone, it was she who picked on him.

Despite Watts's personal and mental setbacks, he seemed to be growing up and becoming a normal kid, with a strong love of sports. Sharon Watts also recalled he worked through his frustrations in life with sports. Coral was an excellent baseball player, football player, and track star, who specialized in the one-hundred-yard high hurdles. He was quite the star athlete at Northeastern High School and seemed to be calmer when competing.

Watts was also a successful boxer, who won a Golden Gloves boxing title in the middleweight division. He eventually quit boxing. He told his sister he quit "because he couldn't take a punch." He had always landed the punches and scored the knockouts; but the first time he got knocked down, he gave up on the sport.

Unfortunately, Watts's walk on the right side of life was short-lived. His academics took a beating. By the time he was fifteen years old, he was only reading at a fourth-grade level. He just did not seem to care anymore.

Watts's first run-in with the law occurred around 7:30 A.M. on June 25, 1969, at age fifteen. He had been earning spending money as a paper delivery boy in nearby Detroit. One morning, as he delivered papers to an apartment complex in Detroit, he attacked a twenty-six-year-old white woman, Joan Gave, one of his regular customers.

Watts knocked on Gave's door. As she opened it, he reared back his arm and punched her square in the face, completely unprovoked. He continued to punch her in the face. Gave eventually bellowed out a scream. Watts took off. Instead of fleeing the scene, however, Watts returned to complete the delivery of his papers. When he was done, he went home.

Four days later, several police officers showed up at the Ceaser household doorstep. They were there to arrest the minor Coral. When they cuffed him, he did not seem too concerned. When asked why he did it, Watts replied, "I just felt like beating someone up."

CHAPTER 2

Instead of being held in juvenile detention, Watts was taken to the Lafayette Mental Clinic, a forensic psychiatry center located in Detroit, on September 2, 1969. While in Lafayette, Watts admitted that he first had sex at fourteen. He did not, however, have much interest in girls. He also claimed that he was raised to believe that sex equaled "wicked behavior."

According to Watts's patient evaluation, he also experienced some disturbing dreams of beating up women and even killing them. When asked how he felt after such a dream, he responded, "I feel better after I have one."

After several weeks of evaluation and treatment, Watts still did not express remorse for his attack on Gave. His mother and stepfather were at a loss for his unpredictable behavior. Dorothy Ceaser did tell Dr. Gary M. Ainsworth, her son's mental clinician, that Coral would often make his sister cry with his bullying behavior.

Though Coral's parents were clueless, Dr. Ainsworth understood exactly what was happening. The doctor believed that Coral was "an impulsive individual who has a passive-aggressive orientation to life. There is no evidence of psychosis in the examination, although there

[is] some confusion in thinking when the situation becomes overly complex."

Dr. Ainsworth concluded by stating that Watts "is a paranoid young man who is struggling for control of strong homicidal impulses. His behavior controls are faulty, and there is a high potential for violent acting out. This individual is considered dangerous."

The clinic's recommendation for Watts was outpatient treatment.

He was free to go.

Coral Eugene Watts was released from Lafayette Mental Clinic on November 7, 1969. It was his sixteenth birthday.

CHAPTER 3

Over the next five years, from 1969 to 1974, Watts reported back to the Lafayette Mental Clinic for outpatient treatment less than ten times. He also began to dabble in drugs, including marijuana, methamphetamine, and a variety of pills. He started to withdraw from his friends. He also got into trouble at school for his behavior with girls.

Coral's lone source of enjoyment seemed to come from sports. He continued to excel in football and boxing. He received All-City honors as a tailback for Northeastern High School in Detroit. On the football field or in the boxing ring were the only times he could take out his frustrations on another human being and not worry about getting into trouble with the law. He claimed that it was his way of dealing with abusive parents. Coral later stated that his mother was verbally abusive and that his stepfather, when he was not drunk, was mean and physically abusive. Claims that everyone else in Watts's family has denied.

Watts claimed that his mother "beat him, hollered at him, didn't act as if she liked me," and that she also "struck him several times with a switch about the face."

Despite Coral's protestations that his mother abused

him, it is true that she helped him with his studies. With his mother's help, Coral was able to overcome his academic struggles and graduate from Northeastern High School in 1973 at the age of nineteen.

Watts received a scholarship that same year to play football for Lane College, a predominately black college located in Jackson, Tennessee. He would play running back for the Lane Dragons. Unfortunately, he never hit the playing field due to a severe knee injury. Watts dropped out of Lane three months into his first semester when it was determined that he could no longer play football. Coral moved back to Detroit and moved in with his mother and stepfather. He stayed in Detroit for approximately six months, where he worked as a mechanic for a wheel company called E&L Transport.

In early 1974, Watts returned to the Lafayette Mental Clinic for a checkup. He stated that not much had changed for him and that he was still suffering from the same problems. The psychological evaluation conducted on Watts indicated that he may have had problems with his sexuality and that there may have been hints of homosexuality. Much was made of "primitive thoughts" and "fantasies" that "threaten to break through." It was also noted on Watts's evaluation that he had a "strong impulse to beat up women."

Watts seemed to keep his impulses in check—for a while.

According to Michael J. Matthews, former director of information services at Western Michigan University (WMU), Watts enrolled in college courses on July 2, 1974. He was accepted under the Martin Luther King grant program, exclusively for minority students. He moved into Vandercook Hall, a student dormitory on campus, and shared a room with two roommates. Records indicate that Watts attended WMU to study engineering. Watts also secured a paying job in the university cafeteria for the Student Center Food Services Department.

The freedom accorded Watts did not help his desires. He slacked off in class and would instead spend his time in the dorm playing Ping-Pong and perfecting his couch potato skills. He also had plenty of time to sit and stew. His intense hatred for females only grew while in college.

On October 11, 1974, Watts got into trouble. He was caught stealing plywood from the WMU campus. School police arrested him but eventually let him go and did not press charges. He never gave any explanation as to why he stole the lumber.

On October 25, 1974, WMU student Lenore Knizacky sat in her apartment on the 100 block of Catherine Street, near campus. The time was 10:45 A.M. She heard a knock on her door, which she answered by opening her chained door slightly. A well-groomed, handsome black man stood in front of her and asked "Is Charles home?" (Charles just happens to be the name of one of Watts's many siblings.)

Knizacky informed the young man that there was no one by that name that lived in her apartment. "You might want to try some of my neighbors," she offered helpfully.

The man turned away from her and left. Approximately ten minutes later, he returned. Again he knocked. Again Knizacky partially opened her door.

"Is Charles there?" His voice was a bit more urgent.

"Would you like to leave a note for Charles?" the coed asked. Before she turned away from the door to retrieve a pencil and paper, she removed the chain from its slot, which left the door open. The man seized the opportunity and forced his way inside her apartment. Instantly he pounced on Knizacky.

"He got on top of me and he put his knee on my chest and his hands around my throat," she later recalled. He began to fondle her crotch. Knizacky let out a bloodcurdling scream for help. She kicked at her attacker with all her might.

"He was choking me. It was difficult to breathe." The man choked her until she passed out. "I blacked out, but I vividly remember a shadow of him getting up and walking away."

Just like that, the man was gone.

Four days later, Watts was spotted loitering around the Stadium Drive Apartments, at the 1900 block of Howard Street, at the southernmost tip of WMU. Several tenants complained that he had knocked on their doors and that he was looking for Charles.

The following day, at 1:44 P.M., October 30, 1974, nineteen-year-old WMU student, and mother, Gloria Steele was found dead in her apartment at the Stadium Drive Apartments complex. The psychology student had been stabbed thirty-three times in the chest and had a crushed windpipe. Apparently, she had been stabbed to death with a wooden carving tool. The weapon was broken and lodged into her spine. Steele had not been raped, nor was anything taken from her apartment.

There were also no witnesses, except for an apartment resident who passed a black man heading up her apartment staircase. She watched the man as he knocked on one of the apartment doors. The woman called out to him and asked what he needed.

"I'm looking for Charles," came the reply.

"Why are you here?" she asked.

"I don't know," came his forlorn reply. He then turned away from the door and left.

Mayola Steele, Gloria's mother, had no clue as to why anyone would hurt her young daughter.

"She was very quiet, she was kind, and she wasn't the real talkative type. I never had any problems with her going out to party . . . because she was always studying and she had a little girl to take care of," referring to Gloria's daughter, Chamice. Mayola also stated that her daughter, who graduated from Loy Norrix High School, on East Kilgore Road in Kalamazoo, had to study hard to maintain her grades.

"She didn't really bother anybody."

Gloria Steele shared her apartment with a bad man. Sam Waller, her boyfriend, had a serious drug problem. He admitted that he purchased heroin the night before Steele's murder, but he added that he carried out his addiction in secret.

"Gloria was naive," he later recalled. "She never messed with any drugs."

Mayola recalled that her daughter had come back from a job interview that day. The interview with the Upjohn Company was a success and she had been given a job offer.

Twenty-year veteran WMU police chief John Cease believed Watts murdered Steele. It was almost impossible for him to prove, however, because Steele's friends and family members, including her boyfriend, upon discovering her body, cleaned up the crime scene and, in essence, destroyed much of the evidence, such as hair, fingerprints, or footprints. There was speculation that they also moved Steele's body. They claimed it was not done to "impede the investigation."

Gloria's mother denied that anyone in her family messed with the crime scene. Mayola Steele insisted that "none of the family was up there." She added that the police had arrived at the scene before her family did. "It sure wasn't none of the family who went in there and moved everything."

The medical examiner was the first authority figure to view the body and estimated Steele's time of death between 11:30 A.M. and 1:30 P.M. Her body must have been moved from the time of the murder up until 1:44 P.M. when the medical examiner arrived.

"They did it and unfortunately kinked us in investigating for physical evidence," stated an incredulous Cease. The police chief believed they could have solved the murder within seventy-two hours, but any evidence he might have been able to collect may not have been admissible in court. Police officers, however, did recover the murder weapon at the scene.

It was lodged in Gloria Steele's spine.

Cease, who worked on more than 150 homicides throughout his career, described the Steele murder scene as "the most violent one I've ever seen. She was stabbed over and over and over again."

On November 12, 1974, twenty-three-year-old Diane K. Williams, an apartment resident manager, noticed a black man absentmindedly walking around her apartment complex located at the 1600 block of Gull Road in Kalamazoo Township. The man was wandering aimlessly while "looking for Charles." Apparently, it was not the first time the man had loitered on the property.

At 12:12 P.M., the man knocked on Williams's door and asked her if she knew where Charles was. Like Knizacky before her, Williams gave the man a piece of paper to write on. The man grabbed the paper out of her hand and forced open her door. He then grabbed her by the throat and dragged her deeper into her apartment. He threw her onto the living-room couch and then to her floor. Again, as with Knizacky, the woman fought back. "I fought as hard as I could," Williams admitted.

As the strangers struggled, Williams's telephone began to ring. Thinking quickly, Williams managed to knock the telephone off the hook and began to scream for help. Her husband's secretary was on the other line and could hear Williams's bloody cry for help. The man panicked and took off.

"It was like my life flashed before my eyes," the frightened yet resourceful manager recalled. After her attacker was gone, Williams stood up and looked out the window. She saw the man get into a tan Pontiac Grand Prix and speed off.

Williams called the police. She was able to identify the intruder's vehicle. From that information police put together a lineup of eight black males who drove the same car. Both Williams and Knizacky were able to pick Coral Eugene Watts out of a lineup.

On November 16, 1974, Watts was arrested and charged with assault and battery in both the Lenore Knizacky case and the Diane Williams case.

Two days later, Watts admitted he was at the Stadium Drive Apartments on October 29, 1974, the day before Gloria Steele was murdered. He denied killing Steele and offered to submit to a polygraph test. He then demanded a lawyer. (Official police records indicate that Watts was released that same day.)

Watts was arrested again, on November 21, 1974—this time for stealing the plywood from WMU. Watts kept his mouth shut and refused to speak to police. He was soon released on bond with no charges.

On December 6, 1974, Watts was interviewed by Ninth District Court presentence investigator Ronald Freemire. The twenty-one-year-old Watts admitted to Freemire that he had attacked at least fifteen other young women—mostly thin, attractive white women. He also claimed to have averaged nearly two attacks a week. Eventually, however, he clammed up and demanded a lawyer. Roman T. Plaszcak represented Watts and spoke with him for over thirty minutes to discuss his options. After conferring with his client, Plaszcak stated that Watts would like to commit himself voluntarily to the Kalamazoo Mental Hospital. Plaszcak also stated that "Watts should not be allowed back on the streets."

On December 12, 1974, Detroit police officers executed a search warrant for Watts's home on the 2200 block of Parker Street. They uncovered several carving tools, but nothing to tie Watts to the murder of Gloria Steele.

Less than one week later, on December 18, 1974, Watts was sentenced by the Ninth District Court to forty-five days in jail or the Kalamazoo Mental Hospital on larceny charges for the plywood thievery. Watts opted for the hospital stay.

Watts began to learn something about the legal system in Michigan: the mental hospital was his friend. His second extended stay at the hospital was practically a vacation. He enjoyed the luxuries of shooting pool and playing basketball. He also was examined by a slew of doctors.

Dr. James Katilius noted that Watts "has no special pre-occupations. He doesn't believe in God. He has never heard any voices. No delusions. He doesn't believe in ESP [extrasensory perception]. No suspiciousness. Nobody is against him. No gross psychotic symptoms noticed and all mental facilities are intact."

Katilius was aware of Watts's visits to the Lafayette Mental Clinic before the attacks. He was also aware that Watts believed he may have killed one or two of his victims. Katilius concluded that Watts suffered from antisocial personality disorder. "[Watts] is impulsive and unable to learn from previous experience. He blames others for his criminal acts."

On the contrary, Watts was learning plenty from his previous experiences.

A few days later, on January 8, 1975, Watts attempted to kill himself. At least, that is what he wanted the doctors to believe. He grabbed a small cord from a laundry bag and hung himself. He was discovered by a nurse and cut down. The feeble attempt did not even render him unconscious. Watts was eventually released from the Kalamazoo Mental Hospital and received gainful employment sweeping up a local church.

By late May 1975, the Gloria Steele murder still had not been solved. Captain R. J. Slater, of the Western Michigan University Campus Police, however, believed he knew exactly who killed Steele. He wrote, "As of 5/21/75 this case has been investigated to the point that this department has knowledge that one 'Watts, Coral E.,' a black male person, is the person that in fact killed Steele. This, however, cannot be proven with any type of physical evidence at this time."

* * *

Watts would make another visit to a mental hospital for another examination. This time it was leading up to his trial for the assault and battery charges against Lenore Knizacky and Diane Williams. In June 1975, Watts was admitted to the Center for Forensic Psychiatry in Ann Arbor, Michigan. He was examined by Dr. Elissa Benedek, who noted that Watts usually "feels good" after he beat up women. Dr. Benedek, like Dr. Katilius before her, did not believe Watts suffered from any form of mental illness. She confidently stated that he was competent to stand trial. She also noted that "this patient is quite clearly dangerous and his potential for recidivistic behavior is great." In other words, it was more than likely that Watts would continue to attack women if set free.

Watts spoke with various staff members during his stay at the center. He even sought out help, but not for his mental state. Rather, he sought legal advice. He wanted to know what he needed to do to assure that he would not go to prison.

Dr. Benedek asked Watts if it bothered him that he attacked women.

"No," he replied. "Getting caught bothers me."

"Aren't you concerned about what you did to these women?"

"No."

Watts's trial for the assault and battery of Knizacky and Williams took place on December 19, 1975. He pleaded "no contest" to the two attacks and received a one-year jail sentence in the county jail.

He was not charged with the murder of Gloria Steele.

CHAPTER 4

Watts was released from the Kalamazoo County Jail on August 24, 1976. He returned to Inkster, where he moved in with his mother and stepfather. He seemingly stayed out of trouble for the next few years. Watts hooked up with a childhood friend, high-school student Deloris Howard, and got her pregnant. Their relationship was rather subdued, according to Howard's brother and friend of Watts, Fred Braggs.

"From what she has told me, I wouldn't call him a Casanova. He wasn't no romantic," Braggs recalled, but Watts treated Howard well.

The couple did share enough affection to create a daughter, Nakisha Watts, who was born on February 3, 1979. Coral and Deloris had a seemingly healthy relationship, but, in reality, Watts turned into a deadbeat dad. He would not even claim Nakisha as his own flesh and blood; he took off.

Later that year, Deloris filed a claim in Wayne County Circuit Court against Watts and requested that he pay her $70 a week for child support. On January 25, 1980, Judge Horace Gilmore ruled that Watts was indeed the girl's father and that he must make restitution of $40 a week.

Howard claimed that she would not have filed a claim against her lover if he had not dropped a bombshell on her. She found out by reading the local paper that Coral had run off and got married to another woman.

Before Nakisha was born, Watts had met at a discotheque a young black woman by the name of Valeria Goodwill. This was the post–*Saturday Night Fever* era. Watts and Goodwill dated and were married on August 17, 1979. The happy couple moved in together into his house on the 2200 block of Parker Street in Detroit.

Apparently, Coral's mother was not a fan of Valeria.

Valeria was not a big fan of Coral, once she got to know him.

"One thing that bothered me," Valeria stated in an interview with Michigan police, "he would go to sleep at night and either have nightmares or something. I don't know what it was, but he would wake up suddenly and start fighting in his sleep . . . with his fists or something, like he was fighting somebody in his sleep.

"He wouldn't say anything," Valeria continued. "Sometimes he would fall out of the bed. One night I woke up and he was on the floor.

"He was still asleep. One night I woke up and he was kneeling outside the bed with his arms up on the bed and him kneeling down on the floor. I've seen him fall asleep on the couch and fall off the couch asleep and get back up on the couch and never wake up."

Valeria continued the bizarre reminiscence. "I'd have to be very careful waking him up. If I would touch him waking up, he would almost jump out of the bed. I had to get out of the way.

"He said he was nervous over his job, but I knew there was something the matter."

Goodwill had no idea what was truly the matter with her husband.

Soon after their marriage, Goodwill reported that Watts's behavior became erratic and unpredictable. First, he lost his mechanic job at a trucking company due to sloppy work. Instead of going out and looking for a new job, Watts would stay home and become fidgety and bored. His compulsive behavior began to surface when he would constantly rearrange the furniture. His once impeccably neat habits dropped by the wayside. He acted slovenly and apathetic. It started out normally enough for a man in his early twenties—leaving clothes on the floor. It escalated to food wrappers and napkins left on the floor, to actual garbage dumped on the carpet. He refused to clean up after himself. His behavior became more bizarre each day. He took to chopping up the house-plants with a kitchen knife. He would slice up candle-sticks and then melt the pieces onto the kitchen table.

According to Goodwill, Watts began to display even more unusual behavior. Out of the blue he claimed he no longer believed in God. He got upset with her when she told him she wanted to put up a Christmas tree in their house. He also forbade her from wearing any beauty products, such as makeup or wigs. He even flushed one of her wigs down the toilet in a bout of frustration.

Goodwill did not know what to make of her newlywed spouse. She became furious, however, when he started leaving the house at night without a word as to where he was going. He would often venture out without telling her anything, be gone for several hours at a time, and then return, often in a state of disarray. Sometimes his clothes would be rumpled or even torn.

Goodwill did notice that most of her husband's late-night jaunts took place after they had sex. After an intimate encounter with her husband, he would get up and walk out of the house.

"He would just get in the car and go. He'd be gone [for] hours and hours," she recalled.

On one of Watts's midnight excursions, on October 17, 1979, he was arrested for "disorderly prowling" outside a woman's home in Southfield, a suburb fifteen miles northeast of Detroit. Someone spotted him and called the cops, who arrived and actually chased him down in a quick getaway attempt. Watts was arrested, but the charges were eventually dropped. He did, however, pay $25 in fines for driving tickets for careless driving and driving without headlights, which occurred during the chase.

The arrest of Watts placed him squarely on the radar screen of the Detroit police. There had been approximately five attacks on young women in the Southfield area the year before, from June until October 1978. The attacker's modus operandi seemed to be the same every time. He would break into the women's homes and the women would wake up to a man standing over them with his hands either on their mouths, breasts, or genitals. No one victim could positively identify Watts as their attacker, but each victim's description seemed to resemble him closely.

Watts had been honing his skills. Things would get much worse after the birth of his daughter and the demise of his marriage.

CHAPTER 5

On October 8, 1979, a twenty-two-year-old white female, Peggy Pochmara, an employee at the Detroit Metro Airport, was found strangled in the front yard of a neighbor of her boyfriend in Detroit. She had not been sexually assaulted, nor had she been robbed.

On Halloween night forty-four-year-old former *Detroit News* food reporter Jeanne Clyne was killed after having been stabbed thirteen times outside her home in the upscale neighborhood of Grosse Pointe Farms, northeast of Detroit. The time was approximately 6:45 P.M. Again the victim had not been sexually assaulted, nor had she been robbed. Halloween revelers passed by Clyne's bloody dead body without a second glance as they thought she was a Halloween prank.

Neighborhood residents described a well-built African American male as a potential suspect.

On December 1, 1979, thirty-six-year-old Helen Mae Dutcher was stabbed twelve times outside of H&M Cleaners, near East Eight Mile Road and Woodward Avenue, just north of Woodlawn Cemetery. Dutcher's murder was even witnessed by a man named Joseph Foy, who gave a police sketch artist a description of an African American male who looked strikingly similar to Coral Watts.

Two other women's bodies were discovered in late 1979. Dawn Jerome's asphyxiated corpse was located less than eighteen miles away in nearby Taylor. On September 21, 1979, thirty-two-year-old Malak "Mimi" Haddad's headless body was discovered in Allen Park. She had apparently gotten out of her car and was heading home. Her head has never been recovered.

On March 10, 1980, Hazel Conniff, twenty-three, was strangled in Detroit. Conniff, who worked for the local telephone company, was found in the driveway of her boyfriend's home tied to a chain-link fence with her own belt cinched around her petite neck. The eerie sight was punctuated by the position of her body, which was seated and facing forward. Conniff had not been raped or robbed.

Three weeks later, at 4:15 A.M. on March 31, 1980, twenty-six-year-old Denise Dunmore's strangled body was found in a Detroit parking lot. She had not been raped or robbed.

Seventeen-year-old high-school student Shirley Small's dead body was discovered at 6:54 A.M. on April 20, 1980, on a sidewalk seventy feet away from her family's Georgetown Townhouse complex, between Packard Street and Page Avenue. She and her family lived on the southeast side of Ann Arbor, Michigan, approximately twenty miles from Inkster and forty-two miles west of Detroit.

Small had always enjoyed spending her weekend nights at the local skating rink. Small and her boyfriend had been in a rocky on-again, off-again relationship. This particular night, it appeared to be off-again. The couple got into an argument while at the skating rink and the young lady left in a huff to go home. It was a four-to-five-mile walk.

Small's boyfriend drove off after her at approximately 4:00 A.M. He found her walking on the sidewalk and tried to coax her into his car. She would have nothing to do with him and continued on. The boyfriend gave up and drove off. She was seen by some neighbors at 4:30 A.M.

When Small's body was discovered, it was determined that she bled to death because of two stab wounds to the heart with a scalpel-like instrument. According to her autopsy report, it was actually one stab wound between the second and third ribs that was retracted and plunged back in without ever leaving her heart. Small also had six deep slices on her face: two on each of her cheeks, including one three-and-a-half-inch wound described as looking like a "hockey stick," one over her right eyebrow, and one on her upper lip.

Small's purse was lying on the ground next to her body. She also had not been robbed or raped.

One of Small's neighbors, Dennis Casselberry, believed her murderer was probably someone she knew. "We were concerned, but figured it was a fluke—probably a personal thing."

By May of 1980, Valeria Goodwill had had enough. She filed for divorce from Coral Eugene Watts.

On May 31, 1980, twenty-seven-year-old Linda Monteiro was found strangled outside her home in Detroit. She had just returned from a meeting for her church choir. Her body was found just four blocks from where Hazel Conniff's had been discovered. As with the other women,

Monteiro's body showed no signs of sexual assault. It also did not appear as if she had been robbed.

Things seemed to slow down in June and the first half of July. By the middle of the month, however, they picked up with a vengeance.

On July 13, 1980, twenty-six-year-old Brown Jug Restaurant night manager Glenda Richmond was found dead just twenty-seven feet from her apartment door on East Ellsworth Road and Braeburn Circle, next to Ellsworth Park in Ann Arbor. She had been stabbed twenty-eight times in her left breast with a screwdriver.

According to police reports, Richmond, an Eastern Michigan University student, left work at 4:00 A.M. She dropped off a fellow coworker at home and would have arrived at her own residence between 4:20 and 4:30 A.M. At 5:17 A.M., her body was discovered lying on her back. She wore blue jeans, a blouse, bra, and panties. Her blouse had been lifted up to expose her stomach.

Richmond had parked her car in the apartment complex parking lot and was walking toward her apartment. Her keys were found lying next to her corpse and her purse was still slung over her shoulder. Everything was still inside her purse. She had not been robbed or raped.

On July 31, at 3:00 A.M., aspiring model Lilli Dunn, twenty-eight, was abducted from her driveway on Agnes Street in Southgate, near Wyandotte and the northwest upper portion of Lake Erie. Dunn, like Jeanne Clyne, worked for the *Detroit News*, but as an accounting clerk. Two witnesses spotted the married mother fight, kick, and scream at her assailant as he dragged her into his car. The witnesses were unable to reach the car before it bolted out of there. Police later discovered her purse, a pair of high-heeled shoes, and a brush. They did not, however, find Dunn's body.

Later that same day, at 3:43 A.M., twenty-two-year-old, Windsor, Ontario, Canada, resident Irene Kondratowitz was grabbed from behind by a man and had her throat slashed as she walked to her home after a night of barhopping. She survived the attack but was unable to identify her assailant. According to the United States Customs authorities, Coral Watts's 1978 brown Grand Prix was photographed crossing the border from Windsor into Detroit at 4:16 A.M., soon after the reported time of the attack on Kondratowitz.

Less than two months later, at around 4:00 A.M. on September 14, 1980, twenty-year-old University of Michigan Business School graduate student Rebecca Greer Huff was found dead outside her Walden Hills apartment, off Pauline Boulevard and South Maple Road. She had been stabbed fifty-four times with a screwdriver with a quarter-inch shaft.

Huff had a deep love for Ann Arbor and the University of Michigan. She had recently been elected to the student government. Her father, William Huff, stated that his daughter worked for Delta Airlines. "She got to see the world when she worked for Delta." He also knew that his daughter would succeed in whatever she did. "I think she would have been quite successful. She was very attractive, intelligent, and considerate."

The popular Huff had been out late with some friends. She left one of her friends' apartment at 3:45 A.M. to return to her own apartment. She drove home, parked her car in the apartment parking lot, and walked at least one hundred feet from her car to her apartment door when she was attacked.

Huff's autopsy report indicated that her death was brutal. She had been stabbed fifteen times in the heart, four times in the left lung, and six times in the liver. She had a total of twenty-eight cuts through her blouse.

* * *

The Ann Arbor press noticed a pattern among the local murders: all white women attacked outside of apartments at or around 4:00 A.M. on Sunday mornings. Thus was born the "Sunday Morning Slasher."

The Ann Arbor Police Department also took notice. They created a task force to put a stop to the brutal murders. Word got out immediately and spread to Detroit.

When Sergeant James Arthurs, of the Detroit Police Department, heard about the Sunday Morning Slasher murders, he could not help but recall a similar attack back in 1969, which he had dubbed the "Paperboy Attacks." It was an attack by a fifteen-year-old newspaper delivery boy who assaulted a young white woman by the name of Joan Gave, who lived on Van Dyke Street. Arthurs immediately contacted the Ann Arbor Police Department to inform them of the attacker, Coral Watts. Ann Arbor detectives added Watts's name to an already extensive list of suspects.

Early the next month, on October 6, 1980, at 10:00 P.M., twenty-year-old Sandra "Sandy" Dalpe, of Windsor, Ontario, was attacked and stabbed by an unknown black male on Lincoln Avenue. Somehow, she survived the attack.

Dalpe described the attack.

"I was walking home from a night-school class and I was across the street and two houses back from where I lived," she recalled. "I heard two footsteps behind me, and as I was about to cross the street, I was stabbed in the back and the knife went through my left shoulder blade."

The blow was so forceful that she received broken ribs, a punctured lung, and a three-inch-wide wound.

"Apparently, the knife was one-half inch from my heart." Dalpe also received a four-inch cut on the right side of her neck, as well as a two-inch stab wound on her left shoulder. She also received two large parallel slices on the left side of her face that she described as looking like "long letter *J*'s."

These *J*'s were particularly brutal. "One goes from my mouth to my ear," she recalled, "and the other one [is] one inch below. It completely severed my external jugular vein, the sternocleidomastoid muscle, and the muscles beneath it."

The damage did not end there. "The spinal assessory nerve and facial nerve [were] severed. I have paralyzed muscles and extremely weak muscles and muscles that have wasted away."

The attack also made it difficult for her to eat. She also had problems with raising her arms and moving her head.

Dalpe claimed that she saw the man who attacked her. "I did see this evil person that morning waiting across the street at a bus stop. He was sitting in it. I thought that was odd and I wondered if he was hurt. I actually felt guilty not seeing if he was okay before I got on my bus to go to work."

Dalpe also described her attacker's method of operation. "I also saw his car in front of the school that night. He drove away as soon as I walked past the car. I saw him crouched beside the bushes. I saw a shiny thing and thought someone was looking for something."

Dalpe believed the man thought he killed her and had left her for dead. Miraculously, somehow, she survived.

According to the United States Customs, Coral Watts's

brown Grand Prix was photographed crossing over the U.S.-Canadian border at 2:15 A.M. the following day.

On November 1, 1980, thirty-year-old Mary Angus, also from Windsor, managed to evade Watts. She arrived at her home at 1:30 A.M. after returning from a Halloween party. When she got out of her car, she noticed a well-built black man wearing a gray hooded sweatshirt. She kept an eye on the man as she walked up to her front door. As she took out her key chain, she noticed that the man had stopped to kneel down and tie his shoe. He immediately switched directions and made a beeline for Angus. The young woman screamed at the top of her lungs and bolted for her front door. Her actions startled the man, who took off running. Later, she would be presented with a photographic lineup by the police, wherein she immediately pointed to a picture of Coral Eugene Watts. Unfortunately, she added that she was not 100 percent sure that he was her potential attacker due to the poorly lit conditions.

Once again, U.S. Customs had records that indicated Watts's Grand Prix was seen crossing over the border from Windsor into Detroit at 2:07 A.M., shortly after the near attack.

Five days later, on November 6, 1980, sixty-three-year-old waitress Lena "Joyce" Bennett's naked body was discovered hanging by a black trench coat belt from a wooden beam in her Van Antwerp Street garage in Harper Woods, Michigan.

Bennett had driven home from her late-night shift at a nearby restaurant. Unlike the other women discovered in Michigan, Bennett had been sexually assaulted. Allegedly, a broomstick had been inserted into her vagina.

CHAPTER 6

Fellow Ann Arbor Homicide detectives Paul Bunten and Dale Heath believed they knew who was responsible for the assaults and murders in Ann Arbor: Coral Eugene Watts.

On November 15, 1980, fifteen-year veteran Bunten was informed by two beat patrol officers that they spotted Watts as he stalked a young woman at 4:50 A.M. down Main Street in Ann Arbor. It would be the first and only time that any authority figures witnessed Watts's elaborate game of cat and mouse.

Watts cruised Main Street in his Grand Prix. He honed his sights in on a young woman coming home late that night. He would drive past the woman slowly and pull over a block or so ahead of her. The woman soon became aware that someone was following her. She darted around a corner and headed off in a different direction. Watts doubled back the car and continued to stalk her.

The woman became increasingly frightened. She continued to duck into corners and into apartment doorways to evade the man. The interminable dance lasted for more than nine blocks.

The two officers witnessed the entire ordeal.

Finally the woman darted around one corner too many for Watts, who lost her in the shadows. She managed to get inside her apartment on the 200 block of North Main Street. Watts was furious.

"He almost went nuts," Bunten recalled to the *Houston Chronicle.* "The police who were watching him said he got frantic, started craning his head around in the car, trying to see where she'd gone. He even got agitated and ran around trying to see her."

He excitedly forced open his car door and literally jumped out of his seat. He began to search along the sidewalk and in the apartment doorways to find her. She was nowhere to be found.

Dejected, Watts turned around and headed back to his Grand Prix, only to be confronted by the two officers. With athletic grace and speed, he slipped the cops. The officers pursued him on foot; however, Watts's All-City running-back credentials helped him make it to his vehicle and blaze out of there. Unfortunately for Watts, his driving skills were no match for his athletic prowess. The officers caught up to him in their police cruiser and arrested him for driving with a suspended license and expired license tags.

A search of his vehicle led to the discovery of something quite unusual. Watts had an oversized dictionary in the backseat of his Grand Prix. Upon closer inspection the officers could see something scratched on the cover. It said, "Rebecca is a lover." Detective Bunten could not help but be reminded later of the recent murder of Rebecca Huff. The search also turned up blood evidence as well as some wood-carving tools.

The two officers brought Watts in for an interrogation at the Ann Arbor Police Department. "I was certain I had a prime suspect," Bunten remembered. "What struck me was how normal he seemed," he said of the soft-spoken twenty-seven-year-old Watts. Bunten observed his perp's calm demeanor. He did notice that Watts's hands twitched slightly, his only sign of nervousness.

Watts knew that Bunten was not there to talk to him about the vehicular infractions.

"I know what you've been up to," Bunten declared. "I can't prove it yet, but I will."

Watts merely looked up at Bunten and said, "I want a lawyer."

Bunten stopped talking and allowed the suspect to make his phone call. Bunten had no evidence against Watts, so there was no justification in holding him any longer.

Watts was free to go.

That did not, however, prevent Bunten from pursuing his man. In essence, he became Watts's stalker.

Bunten was relentless in his endeavors. He began by calling other police jurisdictions and finding everything he could to tie Watts to the Sunday Morning Slasher killings. Bunten spoke with the Kalamazoo Police Department about the murder of Gloria Steele. Apparently, the wound patterns inflicted on Steele were reminiscent of the stab wounds on Glenda Richmond. Kalamazoo detectives informed Bunten that Watts was a key suspect in the Steele murder; however, they could not secure any evidence to pin it on him.

Bunten discovered information about Watts's various stints in mental institutions. He also found out that Watts may have been terrorizing the city of Detroit as well.

Finally, Watts's former psychiatrist and former attorney warned Bunten that he had probably found his killer.

All of these factors led Bunten to round up several

officers and begin a 24/7 surveillance of Coral Eugene Watts. "We turned into insomniacs," he stated.

Apparently, at first, Watts was unaware of the watching eyes. Only five days after his arrest, at 7:00 P.M. on November 20, 1980, he allegedly attempted to attack sixty-year-old Rita Pardo in an apartment complex laundry room in Windsor, Ontario. A man wearing a dress shirt, dark pants, and a light brown trench coat grabbed Pardo from behind and began to choke her with his hands. She screamed and the man hightailed it out of there. Watts's Grand Prix was not tracked crossing the border from Canada to the United States later that night; however, he was seen the next day wearing clothing that was similar to what Pardo described.

The pressure of the surveillance was increased substantially the following day. According to Bunten, a meeting was held at the Detroit Police Department that included Bunten, Sergeant James Arthurs, Detroit Police Internal Affairs, the state of Michigan police force, Windsor, Ontario authorities, and Homicide Squad Seven. Their purpose: somehow try and find a way to stop Coral Eugene Watts before he killed again.

They all followed Watts's every move. They followed him to work at E&L Transport, the trucking company, located on the 21000 block of Hayden Road in Woodhaven; they followed him to the grocery stores; they followed him as he went to visit his girlfriend Beverly Frye's house.

"He knew we were watching him," Bunten recalled with relish. "He'd get out at a traffic light and yell at private citizens, thinking they were cops."

Watts would occasionally jump in his car and head out of the Detroit area. Sometimes he would drive for more than three hundred miles, stop, turn around, and head back home. He was always on the go, always on the prowl, and always on the lookout.

Bunten turned up the pressure when he secured a search warrant for Watts's Inskter apartment and the Ceaser household as well. Officers did not find anything in his apartment. They did, however, find a tennis shoe with blood on it in his mother's house. The blood could not be traced.

The main reason for searching Watts's various premises had been established. Bunten was trying to get under his suspected murderer's skin.

Bunten continued to be a nuisance for Watts. A few days later, on November 26, 1980, Bunten secured a warrant for a tracking device for Watts's Grand Prix. Four days later, the detective secretly attached the bugging device, a "beeper type transmitter," to the undercarriage of Watts's ride.

"He got paranoid," Bunten said of Watts. "He knew we were watching him and the longer we watched him, the less he'd move around. He got to where he almost couldn't leave his neighborhood."

Indeed, the killings in the greater Detroit Metropolitan area and Ann Arbor area came to a halt over the next two months.

The warrant for the tracking device ended on January 29, 1981.

That same day, Bunten moved in for the kill. He corralled Watts at the Ceaser home on the 28000 block of Avondale Street and brought him into the Detroit Police Department Homicide Section for questioning.

The interrogation lasted more than five hours. Despite Bunten's seasoned ability at getting suspects to talk, he could not crack Watts.

"I used every means I know to get somebody to confess. . . . He's so streetwise, nothing would work."

Again Bunten was surprised by how easygoing Watts was. "He was nice. He was polite. If you can forget what he does, he's seems like a soft-spoken, timid, but personable, pleasant person."

Watts, however, refused to answer most of Bunten's questions. At one point in the interview, he did admit to Bunten that he was "possibly emotionally ill." He did not elaborate.

Bunten believed he knew how to break through Watts's steely exterior. "I not only know you did these, I know 'how' you did them," he assured Watts.

The detective rose from the interrogation-room table, walked up directly behind Watts, and thrust his left arm around the man's neck. He was attempting to emulate what he believed was Watts's preferred method of attack.

"We knew the women had been attacked from behind. The killer had wrapped his left arm around their throat, then reached over their right shoulder and stabbed them," Bunten recalled. "The blouses were pulled up at the front, and marks on the throat of one, just under the chin, came from a man's wristwatch on a left arm.

"I got up and walked behind him and said, 'You grabbed them like this. Then you pulled their heads back like this'"—as he jerked back the African American's head—"'and you reached over with your right arm and stabbed them like this!'"

Watts began to cry. Bunten had finally struck a nerve.

"He started crying," Bunten stated incredulously. "Just broke down and started crying. It was the first real emotion we'd seen from him. I thought he might break for a minute, but he didn't."

Watts wanted to see his mother. Bunten, somewhat

taken aback by the regressive emotions on display, decided to go along with it. He suspected that if Watts got to see his mommy, he would confess. He agreed.

"That was probably a mistake. After that, he wouldn't say a word. It was all over."

Coral Eugene Watts was no longer talking.

Officers had also drawn blood from Watts at the Detroit Receiving Hospital. The blood work failed to tie Watts to any of the crimes.

With no confession and no blood tie-ins, Bunten had no choice but to resume the campaign of antagonism. The officer would "accidentally" bump into Watts on a more-than-regular basis. He would walk up to Watts and blurt out, "I want to talk to you, Coral" in front of other people. He would follow him to the grocery store and when Watts would walk out of the store, Bunten would be there waiting for him ready to have him "answer a few questions."

On March 10, 1981, Bunten was inside the Washtenaw County Courthouse when he noticed Watts chatting on a pay phone. Bunten decided to pay his favorite suspect a visit. He walked up to Watts and said, "Hi, Coral. You want to come talk to me?"

Watts looked up at his tormentor and said, "I am not interested in talking to the police no more." He then dropped the phone and took off.

The pay phone swung from its metallic cord.

It was the last anyone saw of Coral Eugene Watts . . . for a while.

PART II

TEXAS

CHAPTER 7

Paul Bunten drove Coral Watts out of Michigan. The suspected murderer packed up his bags and headed out of state the same day as the encounter at the courthouse.

He didn't even let his mother know.

Watts's first stop was Coalwood, West Virginia. He ran to his grandmother Lula Mae Young. His stay was brief, as he needed money, so he packed up and headed back to his original home: Texas. Somehow, he managed to scrape up enough money to buy a plane ticket.

Watts had asked some of his coworkers where the best place to get a job would be. They all told him Houston, Texas. Once again he drove off to get away from everything that haunted him, especially Paul Bunten.

Watts flew to Houston. He made plans to be picked up by a friend of his, forty-one-year-old Garland Silcox and his wife, Pat, who lived at the 7600 block of Lemma Drive on the northwestern side of Harris County, in the Chimney Hills subdivision. Silcox and Watts knew each other from working together at E&L Transport Company in Michigan five years earlier.

Silcox offered to let Watts stay with him until he got

himself situated with a job and a place to live. Watts, however, declined because he did not want to impose. Subsequently, he slept in Silcox's car for the first few weeks in Houston. Silcox also let Watts use his house as a location to retrieve his mail.

Watts began to look for work. He first went to United Transport, located on the 6500 block of Homestead Road, to find work as a mechanic and a parts man. One of his buddies from Michigan, Jerry Brock, worked there, and Watts hoped their friendship might open some doors for him at United. According to assistant manager Woody Meyers and maintenance superintendent Jerry Mooty, Watts applied for the job on March 23, 1981. He came to the company wearing a backpack. Meyers and Mooty did not hire him.

Watts next went for a job as a diesel mechanic at Coastal Transport Co., a Houston trucking firm, located on the 8600 block of Wallisville Road. Jerry Brock's brother, William Brock, worked there, as did Watts's friend Garland Silcox. Watts secured the shift of 4:00 P.M. to midnight. Afterward, he moved into the Liberty Courts motel, off Highway 90 and Interstate 10. A few days later, he trekked back up to Michigan to pick up his trusty brown 1978 Grand Prix.

He felt safe.

In Ann Arbor, Michigan, Officer Paul Bunten continued his search for the elusive Coral Watts. He continued to call Watts's family and friends to see if they had any idea where he went, but they all claimed not to have a clue. Bunten contacted his former employer at E&L Transport and found out that Watts had left a forwarding address to receive his final paycheck. The 7600 block of Lemma Drive in Houston, Texas.

He finally found his man.

Bunten knew he needed to act quickly. He created a nineteen-page dossier, or case history, on Watts that detailed his suspicions of Watts. On April 8, 1981, Bunten mailed out the package to the Houston Police Department's homicide division, where it was received by Detective Doug Bostock. Bunten added a letter that stated his belief that Watts was a serial killer—but he had no physical evidence to prove his theory.

The Houston Police Department (HPD) initially acted on the tip from Bunten. On April 15, 1981, forty-one-year-old Detective Bostock dropped in on Watts's new job at Coastal Transport and began to ask terminal superintendent Jim Coats about his newest employee. The detective informed Coats that Watts was a suspect in several murders in Michigan.

Coats believed Watts was a decent employee when he first started to work at Coastal. He tended to keep to himself, put his head down, and work. In short order, however, he began to make many mistakes. His focus was lacking. The boss was ready to fire Watts.

Detective Bostock needed a favor from Coats. He asked him to keep Watts on board so police could keep track of his movements. Coats acquiesced to the officer's wishes.

After two months on the job and with no progress made on the police's behalf, Coats went ahead and fired Watts, who informed his boss that he could forward his last paycheck to Dallas. He claimed he already landed a job at J-R Trucking and would move in with friends from Dallas. Coats informed Bostock, who, in turn, mailed out a copy of Bunten's dossier on Watts to the Dallas Homicide Division.

Watts, however, did not move to Dallas. Instead, Watts continually moved all over Houston, using Silcox's home address on all of his job applications. He would move more than six times. Watts's nomadic nature threw the Houston police officers off his scent. They were never able to locate him again.

By the summer of 1981, Watts had settled into the blink-and-you'll-miss-it town of Columbus, Texas, about seventy-three miles west of downtown Houston. Columbus is mainly considered a gassing up point for travelers coming into Houston from San Antonio or Austin. The tiny town resides "west of a lazy horseshoe bend in the Colorado River" and is also the former location of the legendary Indian village of Montezuma.

Watts found a decent job, with the help of two former coworkers from Michigan, at a company called Welltech, Inc., located just east of town on Farm Road 949. It was here that Watts worked as a mechanic and helped overhaul well service rigs. He started his new job on May 26, 1981.

According to former Columbus police chief Tom Wine, Watts liked to hang out at the local bars at night and on the weekends. Wine also stated that Watts wasted no time in hooking up with a young lady.

Wine could not tell that Watts was a bad man.

"If you met him, you would like him," the affable police chief stated. "He was always a real gentleman. He would see you in the streets and say 'Hi' all the time." Watts would even approach the chief and speak to him frequently.

"You would never have known what he was up to."

* * *

Eventually the Houston Police Department did not know what Watts was up to either and pulled back on their search for him. Detective Doug Bostock, however, made it a point to continue his search for Watts on his own time, often when he was off-duty. He was determined to find his man.

Watts, despite living and working in Columbus, did not stay away from Houston. He would often drive into the city on his days off—Fridays and Saturdays. He once drove into the big city on June 18, 1981, to attend the Kool Jazz Festival at the Astrodome. He even got several speeding tickets on his many trips to Houston.

Watts stayed in an apartment in Columbus for two months. He then moved into another apartment in nearby Eagle Lake while maintaining his job at Welltech.

Police did finally learn that he had relocated to Columbus, but no further moves were made to follow up on the suspected serial killer.

One of the reasons why nothing was done was due to political unrest in the nation's fourth largest city. Lack of police officers, severe underfunding, and a general malaise from the Houston Police Department and City Hall contributed to a lethal time in Houston.

It was an unfortunate time to suffer from so many difficulties. Houston had recently gained the unsavory title of "Murder Capital of the World," a title it unwillingly tussled over back and forth with—ironically enough—Detroit, Michigan. In 1980, there were 633 homicides. In 1981, Houston saw an increase of 68 homicides and raised its total to 701.

The city was a prime killing field perfect for a mobile, hard-to-pin-down individual with blood lust in his soul.

Perfect for a man like Coral Eugene Watts.

CHAPTER 8

By August 25, 1981, Watts was hired to work for the city of Houston's Metro bus system as a mechanic at the Milby Maintenance Facility. He would work the graveyard shift from 11:00 P.M. to 8:00 A.M., with Fridays and Saturdays off. He still lived in Eagle Lake and would commute to work every day in his reliable companion, the 1978 brown Grand Prix.

During that summer Detective Bostock still continued to follow Watts. He was even able to place a tracking device on Watts's vehicle, just like Detective Bunten had done earlier that year in Michigan. Bostock was able to pinpoint where Watts was at all times.

When not working, Watts still hung out in the local Columbus bars. On the weekends he continued to cruise the city streets of Houston, usually with a good buzz brought on by copious amounts of alcohol consumption, especially his favorite, straight Tennessee whiskey.

The following month, on September 5, 1981, Watts had a good buzz and was aimlessly driving around Houston when he spotted a young woman in her car. The attractive white woman appeared to be headed west out of the city. Watts decided to follow her. Indeed, he followed her all the way, over 160 miles, to the state capital of Austin, Texas. When he arrived in the city, he got distracted, lost the car that he had been following, and then found it again. He followed the young woman to an apartment complex on the 4500 block of Speedway, just nineteen blocks north of the University of Texas campus.

Linda Katherine Tilley was born on March 30, 1959, and raised in Arlington, Texas, near Dallas, by her parents, Joe and Carol. Linda was a very loving, relaxed child who enjoyed drawing and creating. She grew up into an excellent student and an excellent artist.

Her education took her to the University of Texas in Austin, where she majored in art. By 1981, her senior year, the twenty-two-year-old student spent the summer in New York, where she participated in a specialized art class at the Parsons School for Design. When she returned for the fall semester at Texas, in the last week of August, she moved into the apartments on Speedway.

Watts followed Tilley into her apartment complex. He silently crept up behind her and snatched her from behind. Tilley did not back down. She struggled with her attacker and flung both of them into the complex's swimming pool. The former Golden Glove boxing champion was too strong for her as he held her head underwater until she drowned. Once he determined she was dead, he quietly exited the swimming pool, got back into his car, and drove all the way back to Eagle Lake.

The following morning, Austin Homicide sergeant Bob Jasek stated that Tilley's completely clothed body was found floating in the swimming pool. There were no indications of struggle, no cuts or bruises, and no witnesses. No one heard anything. No one saw anything.

The Austin medical examiner declared that Tilley's death was accidental. Toxicology reports determined that she was intoxicated. The assessment was the young woman likely had tripped, fallen into the pool, and drowned.

Two days later, on September 7, 1981, Coral Watts began his new job working for the city of Houston. He also kept his job at Welltech and would continuously drive back and forth between Columbus and Houston. He also maintained his residence in Eagle Lake during this time.

Three days later, on September 10, 1981, Watts attended the St. Paul's Temple Church of God in Christ, located on the 400 block of Massachusetts Street, where he met Sheila Williams. Watts had been invited to the church earlier in the year and was introduced to Williams by a mutual friend during a homecoming dinner the month before.

"We sat at the same table and a church member introduced us," Williams fondly remembered. "We started dating about a month later. He'd go to church regularly and sometime[s] he'd pick me up for church."

St. Paul's was an interesting little church, where the parishioners sang and even spoke in tongues. According to the Reverend Paul Ellis, Watts did not participate in the speaking of tongues.

CHAPTER 9

She flies, she rests confused, she seeks understanding within herself—and is once again alright—in glory.
> —Elizabeth Ann Montgomery's journal

Elizabeth Ann Montgomery always seemed to be in a hurry. It started when she was born. She rushed headlong into this world on September 17, 1955, at 1:05 A.M., five-and-a-half weeks premature at Mount Auburn Hospital in Cambridge, Massachusetts. Her parents, Jane and Eugene, worried about their daughter from day one. Their tiny three-pound seven-ounce baby seemed fragile.

Her doctor, George McCormick, quickly dispelled their concerns.

"Mrs. Montgomery, your baby has strength and intelligence," the doctor reported to the relieved mother.

"You don't have to tell me about my daughter," the headstrong Jane Montgomery informed the doctor. "My Elizabeth is mine. I love her regardless."

The doctor looked at her and said, "Your baby is turning over in her incubator."

"What difference is that?" she queried.

"Mrs. Montgomery, even ten-pound babies do not

turn over." The doctor was amazed at this tiny treasure. "She is a gifted child. She not only has strength, but the intelligence to go far in life."

Jane Montgomery, still worried over the health of her daughter, wondered. "I hesitated to believe it," she stated in regard to the doctor's prognostication, "but as time went by, she proved her ability."

By the age of three, Elizabeth displayed several abilities. One of those was reading the Sunday newspaper. Jane Montgomery marveled at how her daughter would ask her questions about current events, like the time she wanted to understand the conflict differences between the United Kingdom and Hong Kong.

"I'm trying to explain to a three-year-old that Hong Kong belongs to the British government," her mother recalled with a sense of exasperation and exhilaration.

Jane was one of six Montgomery children. The family lived a fun, carefree life of family get-togethers, outdoor barbecues, and sporting activities. As Elizabeth grew older, she began to develop into a beautiful young woman. She parlayed her beauty into several modeling jobs in and around Massachusetts. She also became an accomplished athlete. Her specialty was long-distance running.

At the age of seventeen, Elizabeth had learned to speak French fluently. She hoped that one day she would be able to study in Paris.

Elizabeth Montgomery always set high standards for herself. She never seemed satisfied. She was not disappointed with herself; she just always seemed to want more.

Elizabeth was an excellent student. After high school, she was accepted to Wesleyan University. At the same time, she began to date Paul Cronin Jr., son of the Cronin family who owned the Massachusetts-based Grover-Cronin retail chain stores. The stores were hugely successful clothing and general stores that made the Cronins very wealthy. Paul junior was in line to take over the company one day. He asked Elizabeth to marry him, and she agreed.

After graduation from college, Elizabeth and Paul moved to Houston, Texas, in late 1979. The plan was to take jobs working for the Houston-based clothing store Palais Royal so they could learn the ropes of running a major successful business and then return home to Massachusetts and run the family business. Paul also allegedly offered to purchase a horse ranch for Elizabeth as an enticement to travel halfway across the country.

Once they arrived, Elizabeth learned that the horse ranch deal had fallen through. Instead, she simply was hired at Palais Royal and also enrolled in graduate school at the University of Houston.

Elizabeth spoke with her mother every week. During one phone conversation, after she had been in Texas for a while, she told her mother, "Texas is great! Texas is wonderful! I love it here!"

Her mother, a tried-and-true Bostonian, asked her in a gruff manner, "What the hell is so great about Texas?"

Elizabeth, with a hint of a smile in her voice, replied, "A Texan stands tall in his boots!"

Not long after Elizabeth and Paul arrived in Texas, Elizabeth knew something was wrong. Official police reports indicate that Paul had a severe drinking problem. It was so bad that Elizabeth broke off the engagement and kicked her fiancé out of their apartment. Paul eventually packed up his bags and returned to Massachusetts. He checked himself into a rehabilitation clinic in an attempt to sober up.

By 1981, twenty-five-year-old Elizabeth Montgomery was finally starting to realize that things in her life were all right. She met another man, and much to her mother's chagrin, she got engaged to him as well. She and her fiancé, thirty-two-year-old truck driver Willis "Bill" Daigle, shared an apartment together at the Pasada del Rey Apartments on the 6200 block of Marinette Drive, near Sharpstown Mall. They were engaged to be married the following summer. While it would be Montgomery's first marriage, it would be Daigle's third.

According to Elizabeth's coworker, Elizabeth and Bill's relationship was a tempestuous one. Elizabeth believed that Bill had cheated on her several times while he was out on the road. In retaliation, Elizabeth allegedly slept with three or four men while Bill was away. It was not the healthiest of relationships.

On Saturday, September 12, 1981, Elizabeth was at her apartment with Bill. She decided to slip outside and walk her two white dogs. She had the larger dog on an eighty-five-inch leash. The smaller dog was not restrained.

It was just after midnight.

She spoke with a neighbor in the parking lot, who complained about her letting the dogs take care of their business in the apartment courtyard. Daigle heard the encounter and stepped outside. He told Montgomery to take her pets over to a nearby grassy knoll near the street.

Daigle walked back inside and left the door open. He wanted to get ready for a good night's sleep. Suddenly he was startled by a shrill noise of "Bill! Oh God, Bill!" Then he heard a piercing screech of "He's got a knife!"

"I heard her scream when she got into the courtyard and I ran out there," Daigle recalled. Montgomery stumbled toward him. At first Daigle noticed she did not have the smaller dog with her. The next thing he noticed was the color red. Elizabeth clutched her throat as blood seeped through her lithe fingers. He grabbed her and pulled her into their apartment. The large white dog and Daigle's weimaraner began to attack each other. Daigle separated the dogs but stopped when Montgomery slumped onto him.

"She finished bleeding to death in my arms."

Elizabeth Montgomery had been stabbed in the heart with a knife. The single infliction killed her.

Suzi Wolf, born in 1959, was the third of four daughters born to parents John and Romaine. Her father, John, was an attractive, outgoing man who had been a star athlete at Bay City Central High School. He even landed a temporary career as a semipro football player. Romaine loved to play cards with the men in the Wolf family when they gathered together in Suzi's grandmother's old wooden white house.

Two years after Suzi was born, disaster struck. Soon after giving birth to her fourth daughter, Michelle, Romaine Wolf suffered a severe stroke. The debilitating attack left Romaine severely disabled with immobility and slurred speech. In essence, Romaine lost most of her motor skills.

Suzi's oldest sister, Judy, who was ten years older than Suzi, took over the maternal role in the Wolf family. Judy took care of Suzi, Michelle, and their other sister, Barb. In addition, she also became the housekeeper for her father. Her father developed an unusual habit of sleeping all day and sometimes not waking up until six o'clock on certain nights. It was not because of work either.

Despite the heavy workload, Judy relished the opportunity to help the family. She had a special affinity for Suzi.

"She was my baby," Judy told her cousin and *Minnesota Star-Tribune* reporter, Larry Werner. "She'd take one of those little fat hands of hers and she'd put them on my face when I'd cry because I was feeling sorry for myself and she'd say, 'Don't cry, Judy, don't cry.' She was really just a delightful child."

Suzi developed a voracious appetite for life and exploration at an early age. She started with vicarious travels through books. Oftentimes she would head over to the public library and grab piles and piles of reading material.

As she got older, she would live out several of the adventures she read about.

"She was kind of a crazy kid," her sister Judy recalled. "She was sweet. Rarely difficult. She was kind of a people person."

Two of the people she became closest to were her best friends, Keri Murphy and Lori Bukowski. Lori recalled that Suzi loved to dance and loved the Rolling Stones. Suzi and Keri definitely gathered no moss.

After high-school graduation, Suzi headed out west to California with a friend of hers. Suzi marveled at the Pacific Ocean. She told Keri that she loved standing in the sand looking out upon the vast expanse of the ocean on one side, then turning around and seeing the beautiful, lush green mountains behind her. Suzi loved California, but was not such a big fan of the state's inhabitants. She came back to Michigan.

Suzi and Keri were ready for something more. The two free spirits set out to see the country. Their first stop was Ypsilanti, Michigan, just six-and-a-half miles southeast of Ann Arbor. It was the first time that either girl had their own apartment; the first time they were responsible for their own well-being; the first time they were on their own.

And they loved it.

Keri Murphy recalled their first Thanksgiving meal together that year. Neither girl could cook. They traded ideas about how to fix the turkey, including putting it into a plastic bag and cooking it in the dishwasher. They opted for the turkey in the brown-bag trick. They placed the festive bird in a brown grocery bag and placed it into the oven at 335°. Only problem was, it was already 11:00 A.M. and the girls had no idea how long it took to cook a turkey. After a few hours of waiting, Suzi declared that she was already hungry. To alleviate this problem, she pulled a chicken pot pie out of the freezer, placed it in the oven alongside the turkey, and turned the temperature up to 450°. The increase in temperature ignited the paper bag which, in turn, ignited the turkey. The girls realized they needed to put the fire out, grabbed the nearest container—of salt. They poured the contents of the salt dispenser all over the flaming bird. In the process, they created turkey jerky for their holiday celebration.

The girls also got fired for the first time in their lives while in Ypsilanti. They both secured jobs at the small local airport as part of a nighttime cleaning crew. They were assigned to clean the outside windows of the control tower, as well as at least thirty offices every night. Keri enjoyed freaking out the air traffic controllers, who were already a little high-strung as it was, by wrapping her legs around the tower pole, instead of using a secured wire, while cleaning the windows. The windows were at least four stories high.

One night while Keri cleaned the tower windows, Suzi called up to Keri to give her the keys. Keri reached in her pocket, grabbed the keys, and dropped them down to Suzi, not quite understanding distance, weight, and velocity. Suzi failed to catch the keys, which rocketed to the concrete below. They were bent in the process. Subsequently the girls could not get into the offices to clean them that night. They called their boss up at home and explained the situation to him. He drove to the airport, and instead of giving them backup keys, he gave them their walking papers.

Suzi and Keri took their pink slips and converted them into travel vouchers. They were restless and eager to leave their home state. They heard from friends that Houston, Texas, was the place to be. Jobs were plentiful and the weather was much better than in Michigan. In February 1981, they took off in an old beat-up van.

Instead of making the 1,330-mile trek in two or three days, the girls decided to venture onward. They made a stop in the Great Smoky Mountains National Park, where they camped out under the stars. They eventually made their way down to the beaches of Florida, where they camped out and slept on the beach for a week.

Suzi was determined to sleep underneath the stars with the sound of waves crashing at her feet. She informed Keri that she was going to sleep in her sleeping bag.

The following morning Keri was startled awake by screams coming from Suzi. When Keri ran to her to find out what had happened, she stopped, stared at her friend, and began to burst into laughter. Suzi was covered with hundreds of snails, which had sought out the warmth of her sleeping bag. The freaked-out Suzi could not help but join her best friend in laughing.

They made it all the way to Houston. "Just kind of an adventure led us down here. No plans," Keri recalled.

They moved in together into the Louisville Apartments on the 9200 block of Clarewood Street, one block north of Bellaire Boulevard. The girls immediately landed jobs as waitresses at Pizza Hut. The free spirits resumed their partying ways, but they quickly fell on hard times. Despite what they had heard, President Ronald Reagan's trickle-down economic theory seemed to bypass the girls and most other middle- and lower-class Houstonites. The girls bickered about bills. Mainly, Keri was mad because Suzi was not contributing. It got so bad that Suzi moved out and moved in with her boyfriend, Michael Bogh, in the same apartment complex. Eventually that did not work out because, according to another friend, Karen Mankiewicz, Bogh allegedly hit her. Wolf moved in with Mankiewicz, who also lived in the Louisville Apartments complex, on September 5, 1981. By this time Suzi and Keri no longer spoke to one another.

Over time, Suzi decided she wanted her best friend back in her life. She also decided she wanted to move again—to California. Through a mutual friend, Suzi let Keri know of her desires; however, Keri wanted nothing to do with her. Suzi decided to stay put. She also continued to party with Karen as her sidekick and landed a job at a nearby Kroger grocery store as a grocery clerk.

On September 13, 1981, less than fifteen minutes after Elizabeth Montgomery collapsed into the arms of her fiancé on Marinette Drive, and less than two-and-a-half miles away, Suzi Wolf walked into a Safeway grocery store. She and Karen had been to a party that evening at the Falls Apartments, off Bellaire Boulevard and Corporate Drive. They had arrived at the party at 9:00 P.M. and returned home at approximately 1:15 A.M. Suzi drove her ex-boyfriend Bogh's car to and from the party. Bogh had lent it to her because he did not feel like hanging out. When Suzi and Karen arrived at their apartment, Karen was ready to call it a night. Suzi, on the other hand, still had some energy left. She told Karen that she was going to spend the night with ex-boyfriend Bogh, but first she wanted some Blue Bell vanilla ice cream. She drove to the Safeway grocery store on the 8700 block of Bellaire Boulevard, which was closer than her Kroger's.

Unbeknownst to her, a man in a brown Grand Prix followed her to Safeway. He watched Suzi as she entered the store.

He waited.

He remained calm, even though he had just murdered another woman.

Suzi Wolf exited Safeway just after 1:40 A.M. with her half gallon of ice cream. She also purchased a half gallon of milk, a package of doughnuts, and a pack of Benson & Hedges cigarettes, all for just $5.11. She opened the door to her 1974 tan-and-brown Oldsmobile Cutlass, sat down inside, fired up the engine, and drove home to her apartment. Suzi parked her car in the south parking lot and stepped out of her vehicle and into the large phalanx of apartments. She walked approximately 125 feet from where she had parked the car up to the concrete sidewalk that led to her front door. As she reached for her keys, the man who had been following her sneaked up behind her and stabbed her in the arm and chest. He stabbed her nine times with a single-edge knife, possibly a butcher knife. The majority of wounds were in the left breast area. Apparently, Wolf's attacker got down on his knees and straddled her as he continued to stab. He stabbed her with such force that one of the deathblows was six-and-a-half inches deep.

As quickly as he had appeared, he was gone into the night.

Wolf's upstairs neighbor Chuck Christopher had heard a scream and stepped out onto his overhanging balcony to inspect. He saw Wolf's still body sprawled out with her lower half across the sidewalk and her torso in the grass with a white man standing over her. Christopher dashed downstairs to help. He noticed the white man standing inside a wooden patio area.

"I saw his hair pop up," Christopher recalled. "His hair was standing on end. He looked kinda like Dagwood," the comic-strip character. He described the white man as between the ages of twenty and thirty, with straight blond hair and a moustache. The man had no shirt on and was wearing cutoff denim shorts.

Christopher also stated that the white man took off running once he was spotted. The man even looked back at Christopher and made eye contact. "He looked at me and I looked at him," he remembered. Christopher, however, did not see the fleeing man holding a knife or weapon of any kind.

At 2:00 A.M., early on Sunday, Keri Murphy was awoken from a deep sleep by the ringing of her telephone. It was the Houston Police Department. They wanted family contact information for her best friend. Murphy sprinted out of bed and over to Suzi's apartment, where she saw her best friend's dead body on the sidewalk. "Suzi was there on the ground, lying with her shirt open and the melting ice cream. There was a box of Oreo cookies next to the ice cream." According to the police report, the undisturbed brown grocery bag sat upright twenty to twenty-five feet away from Wolf's corpse.

Murphy described the murder scene of her friend as something very different from what television dramas portray. "No one was controlling the scene. I was able to kneel down to Suzi and hold her for at least ten minutes. I touched the grocery bag she had been carrying. No one stopped me. No one was too concerned about what was going on."

Murphy recalled that the police brought in giant klieg lights to spotlight the murder scene. The lights shone on

Wolf's exposed chest. "Her blouse was open and her breasts were exposed. I didn't really think much about it because I was used to seeing Suzi walk around naked all the time. It was no big deal."

Suzi's dead body lay motionless in her H.I.S. Chic blue jeans. She wore a short-sleeved white Andrea blouse, a long-sleeved Gardenia brown shirt, a pair of black Playboy bikini panties, a pair of size-5 beige pants, and a pair of brown Wild Pair strapped heels on her feet. Her right arm was bent at the elbow and her hand appeared as if it were resting on her right hip. She was clutching her set of keys in that same hand.

Suzi Wolf's body was eventually claimed by her family and flown back to Michigan, where she was buried. Murphy chose not to return to her home state for the funeral. She felt she would cause too much of a disruption amongst Suzi's family if she were to return, since she and Suzi had been fighting.

September 13, 1981, the day that Elizabeth Ann Montgomery and Suzi Wolf were murdered, also just so happened to be Coral Watts's last day at Welltech.

CHAPTER 10

As the murders began in Houston, most officials failed to take notice. The reason being: the big mayoral campaign season was in high gear. Mayor Jim McConn was running for reelection against Harris County sheriff Jack Heard and city controller Kathy Whitmire. The race was a contentious one. Most people did not want McConn back in office due to some allegedly shady business dealing and "insider deals," according to Richard Murray in his book *Power in the City: Mayoral Elections and Patterns of Influence in Houston, Texas*.

That left Heard and Whitmire.

The contenders split the police ranks down the middle. The Patrolman's Union, or the rank-and-file street beat cops, supported Whitmire, while the Policeman's Association backed Sheriff Heard. The division was a distraction. Many officials believed that the Houston Police Department lost its focus during the 1981 to 1982 mayoral campaign and took its collective eye off its number one responsibility: the safety of its citizens.

One Houston police officer, however, did not lose sight of his major objective. Detective Doug Bostock had been doing his best to locate and track Watts. Bostock received information that Watts was spotted in Houston wearing a Metropolitan Transit Authority, or Metro, work uniform.

Watts got a new job as a mechanic working on the city's buses. He had the pre-graveyard shift from 7:00 P.M. to 3:00 A.M. As a result, Watts moved from his apartment on Eagle Lake to the Idylwood Apartments on Houston's seedier southeast side at the 6600 block of Sylvan Road, near the Gulf Freeway and Wayside Drive. It was not unusual for Watts to work twelve-hour shifts with Metro.

Watts did well enough that he was able to purchase a second vehicle. On October 21, 1981, he paid $1,960 in cash for a 1976 blue Dodge van from the Fair Deal Auto Sales car lot, located on the 2000 block of Broadway Street. According to one of the Fair Deal employees, Watts definitely made an impulse buy. He apparently came to the car lot, spotted the van, and told the salesman that he wanted it and would be right back. He returned four hours later with the cash in hand. He drove the van off the parking lot soon thereafter.

On November 2, 1981, Kathy Whitmire and Sheriff Jack Heard won the runoff spots for the mayoral election. Mayor Jim McConn would not be reinstated into office. The rift between the Houston Police Department's rank-and-file and management became even more strained. The focus of the police department continued to drift away from its citizenry as each side looked to score deals from the next prospective mayor.

Meanwhile, Detective Bostock continued to pursue the ever-elusive Watts. He sent a team of surveillance officers to the address provided on Watts's Metro application, but it turned out to belong to Garland Silcox, Watts's friend who let Watts use his address as a mail drop-off. Bostock also circulated more photographs of Watts to area police officers.

On November 19, 1981, Bostock was finally able to track down Watts. The detective and two police officers headed over to the bus barn where Watts worked on Milby Street, where they were able to attach a tracking device to Watts's Pontiac Grand Prix.

The following morning the Houston Police Department communication specialists were able to track Watts's location. The car was located at the 6600 block of Sylvan Road at the Idylwood Apartments. Bostock went out to the complex to confirm.

Unfortunately, the modern spy technology would prove to be unsuccessful. Watts discovered the tracking device and took his car to a garage to have it removed. Once again he had eluded the authorities. It would be several months before Houston authorities were able to catch up with him.

A few days later, in December 1981, Kathy Whitmire was named the new mayor of Houston. The rank-and-file police officers were ecstatic. Their candidate had won. They were more excited because they believed Whitmire's election afforded them certain political capital. Namely, a new police chief.

From January 1982 to March 1982, Interim Chief John Bales took over the reins of police chief. His tenure was short-lived.

Mayor Whitmire selected Lee P. Brown, who had just served as the commissioner of public safety for the city of Atlanta, Georgia, to step in as the official police chief.

While in Atlanta, Brown oversaw the city's police, fire, corrections, and civil defense departments. He also helped ease the city during the infamous "Atlanta Child Murders" by alleged serial killer Wayne Williams. Brown became Houston's first black police chief.

One of Chief Brown's main objectives was to right the ship known as HPD that had gone astray. He noted that several divisions were severely understaffed and those that had enough people were not being paid enough. Officers and detectives were not receiving overtime pay; therefore, fewer investigations were undertaken and more crime continued on unabated and uninterrupted. Poor pay opportunities led to less applicants for positions; which led to lower-quality employees; which led to much poorer protection of the citizenry.

Fertile ground for a streetwise serial killer.

Fertile ground for a new mayor and police chief to step in and make a difference.

CHAPTER 11

Phyllis Ellen Tamm—or Ellen, as she was commonly known by her friends and family, since her mother was also named Phyllis—was a tough cookie. Five years earlier, she left a relationship with a man in Memphis, Tennessee, that she felt was going nowhere. She packed her bags and headed southwest for Houston, Texas.

When Ellen arrived in Houston, she quickly found a place on the 4800 block of Montrose, two blocks south of Highway 59 and five blocks north of Bissonnet Street in the Montrose area that *Texas Monthly* dubbed "the strangest neighborhood in Texas."

Twenty-seven-year-old Ellen Tamm never had a shortage of dates. She actually was dating several men at one time. One of her male companions, John Eugene Hill, was actually more of a "brother-sister" relationship, since he was a self-proclaimed homosexual. Hill and Tamm had been close friends for four years. They shared their most intimate secrets with one another, but they did not have a sexual relationship. Tamm often vented with Hill about her man problems and the stress of her work situation.

Tamm had another man in her life, with the last name of Elbert, from Memphis. Tamm's relationship with

Elbert was considered quite shaky. Indeed, Hill later reported that Tamm often confided in him all of the problems she and Elbert were going through.

Yet another man in Tamm's life was Nash Baker from Houston. They dated on and off for the past four years, but they were not having a sexual relationship.

Tamm allegedly "dated" another homosexual, Randy Rudy. Again, their relationship was strictly platonic.

Since her love life was less than stellar, one of Tamm's goals in Houston was to advance her career as an art director. She started out doing freelance work for various advertising agencies around the city. It was not long before she landed a steady job as a senior art director for Rives Smith Baldwin Carlberg advertising agency.

Ellen's boss and the ad agency's creative business manager, Peggy Oehmig, thought the world of Tamm. "She was competent . . . very organized, very conscientious, never late . . . even a little pushy at times."

According to police reports, Tamm was not very satisfied with her job. She informed her coworker Diane Vergouven that she was not happy. She had made several unsuccessful attempts to get transferred to the company's New York office. She was also in the process of taking job interviews with other advertising agencies in Houston.

Tamm's love life was not in much better shape. According to Hill, Tamm returned to Memphis to spend time with Elbert for the Christmas holidays. One week later, she met Hill in New York, where she complained that her relationship with Elbert was on its last breath. She informed Hill that Elbert yelled at her because he believed she was constantly harassing him. Tamm also told Hill that she had not had sex in a long time, but she was okay with that.

Tamm returned to Houston on January 3, 1982, at 7:00 P.M.

Her tough exterior gave her an air of confidence. It also may have gotten her into trouble. Peggy Oehmig claimed that Tamm was not concerned with crime in the least. Oehmig admired Tamm's tenacity.

"Ellen Tamm is a survivor. Don't worry about her."

On Monday morning, January 4, 1982, at 7:45 A.M., however, there was reason to worry. A passerby discovered the body of Ellen Tamm.

Ellen usually started each morning off with a three-mile jog around the Rice University campus with Hill. This particular morning, a fellow jogger, Donna Morris, spotted Tamm out running by herself on Sunset Boulevard and Main Street at approximately six-fifteen.

Tamm's death scene was a grotesque vision. She had been hung with her own brown tube top from a low-slung branch of a ten-foot-tall bush off the 1600 block of Bissonnet Street. The branch was just under four feet off the ground. The five-foot-ten-inch, 160-pound Tamm wore white shorts, brown tights, white socks and tennis shoes, gray sweatshirt and gray jogging jacket. She was found sitting in the lotus position, as if in the midst of heavy meditation. The only problem was that her body was suspended two inches off the ground. Her feet were on the sidewalk. Her behind hung below the bush from which she hung.

Tamm was fully clothed. Her body was not bruised or cut in any way. Also, her clothes did not have any tears or stains on them.

Police were not quite sure what to make of Ellen Tamm's death. There were no signs of struggle, either on Tamm's body or at the scene. No drag marks, no disturbed grass, no broken tree limbs.

Indeed, the medical examiner Joseph Jachimczyk, who had previously worked on Houston's most notorious case—the serial killing trio Dean Corll, Elmer Wayne Henley, and David Brooks, who sexually assaulted and murdered at least twenty-seven young men and buried many of the bodies in a Houston boat shed—ruled her death a suicide.

No one in Ellen's family believed she would have committed suicide. Attorney Melton Picard, Tamm's uncle, even flew in from Tennessee. Picard worked with Dr. Jachimczyk to reconsider the mode of death. The medical examiner's office spent more than one hundred hours on Tamm's case. Jachimczyk subsequently changed his ruling in the cause of death.

"The available evidence indicates her death was either a freak accident or a clever, cunning, opportunistic homicide," the medical examiner reported.

CHAPTER 12

Margaret "Meg" Fossi was born Margaret Everson to Marjory and Leonard Everson. As a child Meg suffered from scoliosis, but she never let it drag her down. Her loving parents watched out for her and showered her with love and affection. She also learned the value of hard work through her father, who was a corporate attorney for the National Can Company. Meg learned well. She excelled in all her academic endeavors and had big plans for her future.

In 1975, Meg Everson enrolled in Rice University, located in Houston, Texas. Rice is historically ranked in the top twenty best colleges in *U.S. News & World Report*'s annual college roundup and is considered the most prestigious institution in Texas. One of Meg's good friends, Mary Beth Herlihy, described Everson as "brilliant" and "wild." She mentioned that Meg liked to smoke marijuana.

Rice associate architecture professor John Casbarian sang Everson's academic praises. "Meg was a good student who had remarkable potential," he stated, "and she was a sweet, warm person." Casbarian believed Everson would succeed in her chosen profession. "It is one thing for a student to do well in school, but often they do not, initially, have the technical skill required in the workplace." He believed Everson did.

Meg spent her summers working for Skidmore, Owings and Merrill, a prestigious architectural firm located in Chicago, with offices in Houston. During the school year, Everson would work part-time in the company's Houston offices. Craig Hartman, associate partner with the firm, described her as "a meticulous worker who did excellent work."

Meg graduated with a Bachelor of Arts in architecture in 1979. That same year, she met fellow student Larry Fossi.

The following year after graduation, Meg and Larry married on March 1, 1980. Meg's gold wedding band was inscribed "LJF to ME 3-1-80." They celebrated with a belated summer-long honeymoon trip to Italy, where they subsisted on $2 a day. "It was wonderful," Larry recalled.

The following year the newlyweds agreed to focus their attention on completing their education to further their careers. Meg reenrolled at Rice to attend graduate courses in architecture, while Larry was accepted to Yale Law School in New Haven, Connecticut. The intention was for Larry to graduate from law school and move back to Houston. The couple believed that Houston was rife with opportunity. Meg's father said that the couple believed Houston to be the "city of the future for architecture and law." It was where the couple planned to thrive in the working world and to raise a family together.

Meg moved in with Larry's sister Kathy and her husband, Wayne Gregory, into a cozy brown wooden home on the 4600 block of Kinglet Street in the southwestern side of town while Larry attended Yale. Larry noted that Meg was coming into her own as an architect. He described her work at the time as "gorgeous" and "incredible."

"She was at the peak of her powers," he later described his wife's abilities.

On Saturday night, January 16, 1982, Meg went out to dinner with a study group of fourteen friends to the Athens Bar & Grill on the 8000 block of Clinton Drive. The purpose of the gathering was for the students to get to know one another.

After dinner one of the study group members went home, while the remaining thirteen students went to the nearby town of Pasadena and the infamous Gilley's. The country-and-western bar, owned by country music superstar Mickey Gilley, was made internationally famous less than two years earlier in the movie *Urban Cowboy*. Fossi and her twelve classmates stayed until closing time, at 2:00 A.M.

Afterward, Fossi rode back to the campus of Rice University with classmates Roberto Roca, Roca's girlfriend, Janie Harrison, Kim Doty, and Bill Gilliland. Meg fell asleep in the back of Roca's car. She had knocked back quite a few beers while at Gilley's. Roca pulled up to the school parking lot and woke her up. The time was somewhere between 2:30 and 2:40 A.M.

Roca first dropped Doty off at her car. He then dropped off Fossi and Gilliland at the architectural building, where Fossi had parked her brother-in-law's 1973 green Mercury Caprice. Doty got into her car and drove off while Fossi and Gilliland went inside the classroom building to retrieve a roll of drawings and a pencil box. They then returned to the parking lot, said "good night" to one another, and got into their separate vehicles.

Fossi sat down inside the car, which had a broken

driver's seat that could neither move forward nor backward. She grabbed a small pillow, which she placed behind the small of her back. It helped prop her up and made it easier for her to see. She began to drive home.

She did not notice the brown Grand Prix that followed her.

As she got closer to home, the Grand Prix closed in on her. Fossi noticed headlights glaring in her rearview mirror and was temporarily blinded. She overcorrected and drove into the concrete curb; in the process she punctured both tires on her car's left side. The man who forced her into the curb stopped his car behind her. He got out of his vehicle and quietly approached her car. He walked up to Fossi's window, which she rolled down, stuck his fist through, and punched her in the throat.

He killed her instantly.

The strong man pulled Meg Fossi's five-foot-four-inch, 118-pound limp body out of the front seat of the car. He grabbed her car keys, carried her to the back of the car, opened the trunk, and tossed her body inside. He then closed the trunk with an audible click. He turned around and walked back to his car. The silent killer started his Grand Prix, kicked it into gear, and drove away.

Later that same Sunday morning, Wayne Gregory and his son stopped by Gregory's office to pick up some space heaters. They also picked up some breakfast at Shipley Do-Nuts. As they returned home, Gregory spotted his Caprice just one block away on the 4500 block of Kinglet Street. He spotted the two flat tires and noted that Meg was nowhere to be seen. Gregory returned home and called the police.

Kathy Gregory gave the officers permission to open the trunk of the car to search for any clues to her sister-in-law's disappearance, but, inexplicably, they did not look inside. Upon the direction of Homicide police detective B. E. Frank, police instead towed the Caprice to the central police station to search for evidence into the whereabouts of Meg Fossi.

On the following day, Monday, January 18, 1982, after having no luck locating Fossi, and receiving permission from Larry Fossi to open the trunk forcibly if necessary, police decided to open the trunk of her car.

Officer C. O. Flowers managed to remove the trunk lock from the vehicle.

Inside he found the body of Meg Fossi. She was lying facedown. Her legs were bent back at the knees with her feet pointing toward the back of her head. She had on all of her clothes, except for her pair of purple socks. She wore pink painter's-type pants and a purple long-sleeved sweatshirt over a multicolored blouse. She also wore a cranberry-shaded scarf, which had been carefully knotted. Interestingly, she wore silver razor blade–style earrings. She also had on a beige bra and panties. Upon even closer inspection it was evident that Fossi had died from a crushed larynx. Her windpipe had closed, which caused her to suffocate to death.

Upon hearing the news of his wife's death, Larry Fossi immediately flew to Houston. He was quickly ushered into the Houston Police Department and was not impressed. "I remember an office in utter disarray," he told the *Houston Chronicle*, "stuffed with files and worn-out furniture and broken equipment, and I wondered, 'How can they function here?'"

Fossi's opinion changed once he actually met the man who would work his wife's murder. He described Detective Tom Ladd as a "tough, hardened, yet caring, human being." He felt as if his wife's last moments would now be in the hands of a competent individual.

* * *

The man who attacked Meg Fossi was not done that morning. After he killed the graduate student and stuffed her body into the trunk of her car, he continued to look for more victims. He found his next one on the South Loop West Freeway, also known as Loop 610, at the Stella Link exit, near the Astrodome and Astroworld, pulled over to the shoulder of the highway. The woman was fixing a flat tire on her car. The time was 6:45 A.M.

The man was not driving his car, however; he was walking on the freeway. He walked up behind her, grabbed her head, pulled it back, and slit her throat twice. The woman managed to escape, ran into traffic, and was picked up by a man in a car.

The man who had slit her throat calmly continued walking on the freeway and headed out of sight.

He assumed he had his second kill for the evening.

CHAPTER 13

On January 21, 1982, three days after the discovery of Meg Fossi's body, Kathy Whitmire arrived at her inauguration ceremony in downtown Houston. When the soon-to-be-inducted mayor drove up, she was embarrassed to discover that there was no police presence there for her protection. The mayor-to-be immediately returned to her vehicle and demanded that security be put into place before she continued. The police officers claimed it was a misunderstanding and that Whitmire showed up too early.

As young women were being slaughtered, Houston's authority figures were engaged in petty games of one-upmanship.

Just over one week later, on January 29, 1982, nineteen-year-old Seabrook resident Alice Martell drove up to her Seaway Apartments trapezoid-shaped residence on the 700 block of Gale Street in Seabrook, Texas, right off Galveston Bay, and into a living nightmare. As she got out of her white car and walked toward her apartment, she was attacked without warning. She remembered nothing of her attacker. Indeed, she woke up in a hospital bed.

"I didn't even know I was stabbed until I woke up in a hospital." She had been stabbed two times in the upper left chest area and once on the chin with what appeared to be an ice pick. "He grabbed me by the neck from behind and choked me. That's why I didn't know he stabbed me."

Apparently, Martell's attacker also stole her purse.

Martell was unable to identify her attacker.

The following night, on January 30, 1982, in nearby Galveston, Texas, nineteen-year-old bartender Patty Johnson was coming home from her job in the early-morning hours. She was attacked by a black man as she got out of her car to head into her residence located at Fourteenth Street and Avenue M. The man tackled her to the ground, straddled her chest, and slashed her throat with a knife. Another man, in a second-floor apartment, heard the commotion, stepped out onto his balcony, and saw the melee before him. The man from the apartment yelled at the attacker to get off the woman. The attacker stopped what he was doing, looked up, and casually strolled away, leaving the young woman for dead.

Patty Johnson, however, survived.

She described her attacker as a black man, about five feet eleven inches, and weighing between 160 to 170 pounds. She was eventually presented a photographic lineup of several suspects. After much consideration, she picked the man she believed to be her assailant: Howard Mosley.

Mosley was a piece of work. The twenty-five-year-old Mosley worked as a warehouseman for the Lipton Tea Company in Galveston. The two-time loser was trying to keep his nose clean. He had been busted six years before for "unauthorized use of a motor vehicle"—he stole a car.

The following year, in 1977, he was charged and sentenced with a ten-year prison term for aggravated robbery.

Like so many other offenders in Texas prisons, Mosley received an early release. He did, however, stay out of trouble; but trouble apparently came looking for him.

On February 16, 1982, Galveston police arrested Mosley and charged him with the assault of Patty Johnson.

The six-foot-seven-inch Mosley was in serious trouble. Under the habitual criminal provision, any person in the state of Texas with three criminal convictions would be deemed a "habitual criminal" and sentenced to a life behind bars, regardless of the severity of the third felony conviction. It was the precursor to what is now more commonly known as the "Three Strikes Law," which was passed in California in 1994 after the abduction and murder of Polly Klaas by three-time loser and early parolee Richard "Rick" Allen Davis.

CHAPTER 14

Elena Semander was born on February 16, 1961, to parents Zaharias and Harriett, in Houston, Texas. Elena was the oldest of four children. She had two younger sisters, Maria and JoAnna, and a younger brother, John. The Semander clan was a tight-knit Greek family who not only believed in the concept of family, but actually lived it.

Elena graduated from Kincaid in 1979. The successful athlete received a full athletic scholarship to play field hockey at the University of Denver in Colorado. She led her team to the national championship, but was disheartened when the girls' athletic teams never received any improvements on their facilities while the inferior men's teams received new gymnasiums, new lockers, and more. Elena, long before the Title IX era of college athletics, voiced her disgust by leaving the University of Denver and transferring to the University of Houston (UH) in the fall of 1980.

Elena, always close to her family, moved back in with her parents in their comfortable home in northwestern Houston. She registered to attend school at UH, where she majored in physical education and coached local youth sporting teams. She broke her leg during her second semester at UH and instead focused her energy on her family, academics, and church.

On February 6, 1982, Elena decided to spend some time with her cousin and friend, Karen Pappas. Her sister JoAnna remembered Elena getting ready that evening. Elena dressed stylishly in purple corduroy pants, a black silk shirt, navy blue shoes, gold belt, gold Seiko watch, and a gray rabbit fur coat, which she playfully stole out of her sister Maria's closet. Elena bopped into her brown 1979 Chevrolet Monza and drove about six miles to the Galleria, which was, at the time, Houston's upscale shopping mall. She pulled her vehicle into the Bennigan's parking lot at approximately 7:30 P.M., walked inside the restaurant, and spotted Karen. The cousins sat down at a table, ordered dinner, as well as a few drinks. After getting their bellies full and downing a few adult beverages, the girls left the restaurant, in Karen's Pontiac Sunbird. The time was 9:20 P.M.

From Bennigan's, Karen drove over to a nearby night-club called Judge's. Once inside the club, the girls met up, unintentionally, with one of Karen's friends from work, Blake Blazer. The young women also ran into a friend of Elena's named Paul Jahne. After several hours of dancing, cavorting, and consuming alcohol, the four decided to call it a night. They left Judge's at approximately 2:15 A.M., early Sunday.

According to Karen, Elena wanted to eat breakfast at JoJo's diner. Neither Karen nor Blake was up for it, but Paul offered to take Elena for breakfast and then drop her off at her car at the Galleria. The cousins said their good-byes and Paul and Elena took off.

Paul drove his car to the JoJo's located at Richmond Avenue, near Hillcroft Street. As they pulled up to the restaurant and looked inside the glass of the front door, they could see they would be waiting awhile. The post–bar-and-nightclub crowd had beaten them to the punch. They decided to test their luck and walked inside anyway.

Once inside, Elena and Paul were informed by the hostess that there was a long waiting list. They both decided to pass on an early breakfast and Paul took Elena to her car.

In the parking lot of the Galleria, Paul got out of his car and walked Elena to her car. They said their "good nights" and Elena drove off. Paul saw the smoke puff out of the Monza's tailpipe. The time was just after 2:30 A.M.

Instead of driving home to her parents' house, Elena decided to pay a visit to some friends who lived in a nearby apartment complex. Barry Elson, Timothy Stasinoulias, and Nicholas Anton all shared a tiny apartment at the West Hollow Apartments, located at the 10000 block of Fondren Road. Semander met Anton a few weeks earlier at church, where they both coached basketball teams. Anton introduced Elena to Elson and Stasinoulias soon thereafter.

Stasinoulias noted that Elena had dropped by to visit Anton at least three or four times since they met, but she had never stayed the night.

At approximately 2:45 A.M., Gregory Rhodes, who had fallen asleep inside his parked car behind the West Hollow Apartments, arose. His car was parked next to a gray Dumpster. When he looked up, he saw Elena step out of her brown Monza. Rhodes watched Elena as a black man walked up to her, put his arm around her, and pulled her back behind the Dumpster, out of his line of vision. Rhodes did not think much of it and fell back asleep. A few minutes later, he was awoken by the sound of a low moan that emanated from behind the Dumpster. The next sound he heard was a *thud,* as if something had been tossed inside the Dumpster. Rhodes stirred momentarily, then fell back asleep.

Several hours later, on Sunday, at 11:05 A.M., Guillermo Shaw backed up his 1981 orange Ford refuse truck to the same Dumpster. Shaw worked as a garbageman for Brehm's Disposal Service B#4, Inc. He hooked the large metal bin to the back of his truck and activated the mechanism that grabs the bin, lifts it in the air, and dumps the trash inside the vehicle.

After he disposed of the trash, Shaw activated another switch, which began the compacting process. Shaw went about his normal routine until something he saw out of the corner of his eye caught his attention.

A human leg.

Shaw immediately deactivated the compactor and looked inside. There he saw what looked like mangled female legs. He could tell that one leg had been broken. It was later determined that this was a direct result of the compaction. Shaw stepped away from the vehicle, ran to a pay phone, and called police.

Once police arrived, they scoured the scene and found a brown Chevy Monza parked twenty feet away from the Dumpster. One of the officers searched the car and found a woman's brown purse inside. After rifling through its contents, the officer discovered the driver's license of Elena Semander.

Inside the garbage truck, Elena Semander lay face-down. Her body was covered with trash. Officers, led by Detective Paul Motard, eventually removed the body from the back of the garbage truck and placed her on a stretcher. Elena was clad only in white cotton panties and nylon stockings. Even more disturbing was her black shirt had been used as a gag in her mouth and was tied in with her hair in the back. She had blood on her mouth and nose.

A West Hollow Apartments resident, Carlos Nava, informed the officers that he knew Elena. He was also friends with Stasinoulias and Anton and went to retrieve them. The two young men had the unenviable task of identifying their dead friend's body. As one of the officers pulled back the sheet that covered Elena Semander's beautiful face, they recoiled in horror.

The following day, a police officer located several of Elena's personal items in a Dumpster on the 12200 block of Fondren Road, behind the Cobbleston Village Apartments. Among the items located were Elena's purple pants, her car keys, her gold belt, three rings, and her sister Maria's rabbit fur coat.

One month later, on March 19, 1982, Coral Watts moved out of his apartment on Sylvan Road and into a new apartment complex located at the 300 block of Sunnyside Street. He listed a "Sheila D. Watts," or Shelia Williams, as his wife and roommate. Williams had a daughter whom Watts listed as a resident as well.

CHAPTER 15

At fourteen, Emily Elizabeth LaQua was more mature than people twice her age. Or so she thought. Like most teenagers, Emily believed she was older than she really was. Or at least she wanted to be older.

Emily was born on October 4, 1967, in Moscow, Idaho, originally known as Paradise Valley, located just northwest of the Nez Perce National Historical Park, also on the border of the state of Washington, to parents Frank and Elizabeth. She was the second of three children, including her older sister, Geraldine, and a younger brother, Franklin junior.

The family moved to Seattle, Washington, when Emily was two. When they arrived at their new home, Emily's mother was stricken with pneumonia. Even as a two-year-old, Emily was a caregiver as she helped while her mother lay prone in bed.

Five years later, when her sister, Geraldine, had thirteen various surgeries, Emily participated fully in her recovery by cleaning up around the house and cooking. She seemed destined to try and make other people feel comfortable.

Emily was also very creative. When she was four years

old, she won first prize at the county fair for a floral arrangement.

As Emily grew up, she became a social butterfly. She joined the Bluebirds, a group for young girls similar to Girl Scouts, and routinely sold the most cookies each year due to her outgoing personality and ability to make others trust her.

After Emily's parents got divorced, her father moved almost twenty-five hundred miles away to tiny Brookshire, Texas, located smack-dab in the middle of Houston and Columbus, about thirty-seven miles west of downtown Houston and about thirty-seven miles east of Columbus.

Elizabeth, Emily, Geraldine, and Franklin junior stayed put in Washington. To make ends meet for the low-income family, Elizabeth LaQua was forced to work two jobs. As a result, a lot of the household chores and family responsibilities fell on Emily's shoulders.

Elizabeth LaQua stated that her daughter was an active participant in school, church, and at home. She described Emily as "an intelligent girl" who excelled in school. She enjoyed writing poetry, participating in ballet, and ice-skating. Emily's mother also described her youngest daughter as a polite young woman. "She had the social graces of a cultured Boston lady," her mother poignantly recalled, "with an old-fashioned name that fit her perfectly."

Emily was also an accomplished musician, who played cello in the school orchestra. She also helped out at the First Baptist Church in Bellevue, Washington, where she was a class assistant for the younger children in Sunday school. She also worked with the mentally challenged parishioners in the special-education classes.

At home, she helped out with her younger brother, Franklin, who was "retarded," or mentally challenged.

Emily's mother appreciated her daughter's help with Franklin, whom she described as a "handful."

"Emily accepted too much responsibility too young," her mother recalled, "and wanted to be eighteen years old when she was only fourteen."

Emily's need to appear more mature began two years earlier, when she was only twelve years old and in the seventh grade. She began to hang out with people her mother considered to be from the "wrong crowd." The wild group of teenagers helped lead Emily astray. She began staying out late at nights, oftentimes with older boys. She even informed her mother that "she had good judgment of men." Emily's grades began to fall. It was apparent her interests had been severely sidetracked. Her mother eventually took her out of public school and placed her in an alternative school for problem students.

Elizabeth LaQua did not believe her daughter was taking drugs. Of course, parents are usually the last to know.

Emily's best friend, Elaina Davison, was another problem child. After Emily was transferred to the alternative school, Elaina moved to Florida with her parents. Soon after, Elaina ran away from home and hitchhiked all the way back to Washington, to be with her best friend.

Elizabeth LaQua allowed Elaina to move in with the LaQua family, as well as two or three other troubled teenage girls. Elizabeth, who had aspirations of becoming involved in the ministry, believed it was her duty to care for these troubled souls.

It was tougher than she ever imagined.

"I had a terrible time," Elizabeth recalled. "I have certain rules that must be obeyed. It seemed like they would gang up on me. They all seemed to work under the same thesis—that the world owed them a living," she declared of her own daughter and her teenage friends.

Emily became even more bored with school. She informed her mother that because she appeared to look eighteen, she wanted to become an adult. She also informed her mother that she had no interest in completing her scholastic education and that she wanted to drop out of school and take her General Educational Development test (GED), which would give her the equivalent of a high-school diploma. Her mother was adamantly opposed.

Emily threatened her mother that she would leave if her mother did not let her do what she wanted. She warned her mother that she would go live with her father in Brookshire, Texas. She even sarcastically told her mother, "Don't worry about me, Mom, I'll be okay. I can take care of myself."

In mid-March 1982, Emily LaQua disappeared. At first, Elizabeth LaQua did not think much of it, since Emily had run away several times before. This time, however, it was the real deal. She hoped her daughter would find a nice group of churchgoing youth that would guide her back onto the right path.

"She had potential," Emily's mother acknowledged, "but she needed the right peer group. To her, it was more important to be accepted and loved by her peers than anything else."

Emily LaQua and Elaina Davison stuck out their thumbs and headed for Texas. The girls were stopped in Fort Worth, Texas, near Dallas, by juvenile authorities, but they were released and continued their trek to Brookshire.

Twenty-five hundred miles later, they made it. Emily knocked on her father's door and told him that she and Elaina needed a place to stay. Her father worked as a cook at the local Union 76 truck stop and gas station. He wanted to make sure she got a job as well. Within two days, Emily landed a job as a waitress.

It also did not take long for father and daughter to go after one another. During her first week in Brookshire, Emily came home late at night with two young men in tow. Her father was furious. He, in essence, grounded her and told her she could only go to work and then had to come home and stay home every night.

The following day, March 20, 1982, one day after Coral Watts moved into his new apartment in Houston, Emily was stewing in her juices. She was furious with her father for grounding her. She stormed out of the house and headed off for work at 5:00 A.M. She had been in Brookshire for one week.

Frank LaQua never saw his daughter again.

Emily was last seen hitchhiking alongside Interstate 10.

Coral Watts just so happened to be driving on Interstate 10 the same day.

According to Frank LaQua's supervisor, Hattie Bonner, Frank was despondent when his daughter did not show up the next morning. He immediately filed missing persons reports with the Brookshire Police Department and the Waller County Sheriff's Department.

"He was really worried about her [disappearing]," Bonner lamented. "He put her picture up on the cash register out front [of the Union 76] in case anybody knew where she was, but he didn't hear anything." Frank LaQua believed, at first, that his daughter probably just ran away again. Maybe even back to her mother in Washington State. But he never heard anything in regard to her whereabouts.

After several months with no word on Emily, Frank LaQua moved out of Brookshire to Wenatchee, Washington. He could not take it in Texas any longer.

CHAPTER 16

Edith Anna Stokes was born to parents Ray and Laura, but Ray Stokes passed away and Laura Stokes then married James Allen, who subsequently adopted Edith. "Anna," as she would most commonly be called, was the oldest of the Allen children.

Anna's father was one of the top prosecuting attorneys in Dallas County. Allen, a first assistant district attorney, was considered one of the fiercest opponents against criminals in a Texas courtroom.

His specialty?

Death penalty prosecutions.

Allen was considered "hard-core" when it came to the death penalty. Indeed, he oversaw twenty cases in which the jury returned death verdicts.

District Attorney (DA) Allen was known for his impassioned speeches in the courtroom, practically demanding that juries find each and every defendant to be guilty and to consider them evil. At times he cried during his own closing arguments because he was so filled with fervor and disgust for the criminals on trial.

Allen was eventually elected to the state criminal district judgeship. Judge Allen continued his fervent opposition to defendants and was known to make defense attorneys' lives a living hell. He had little patience for petulant lawyers and even less patience for their "scumbag" clients.

Allen parlayed a successful tenure as a criminal judge to a position on the state appellate court in the Fifth District Court of Appeals.

Justice Allen and Laura Allen raised their wonderful children, but were especially proud of their oldest daughter, Anna, who excelled in education.

Laura Allen recalled the perspicacious manner of her then two-year-old daughter. As Laura watched Anna's one-year-old brother, she heard what she described as a "gleeful chortle," which came from the kitchen. Laura went in to investigate and found her oldest child perched on top of the refrigerator. It was even more unusual, since there was no countertop next to the appliance. Anna simply smiled and laughed as her mother pondered how in the world she got up there.

Laura Allen described her daughter as a "smart girl" who always did "good in school." She stated that Anna was the type of person that "anything she attempted, she learned to do."

A shy and timid girl, Anna was sometimes too smart for her own good. Her mother stated that she was known to "foment trouble" amongst her brothers and sisters. Anna was good at getting everyone else in trouble, but somehow managed to avoid it herself.

As Anna matured, she started to come out of her shell. At Edward H. Carey Junior High School, Anna joined the drill team. Her mischievousness never quite left her. She convinced her mother to hold a slumber party at their house for the entire drill team. Her mother remembered that everything was proceeding smoothly—until the boys showed up. Surprisingly, Anna's father let the boys stay, but under one condition. They could only stay for a half hour. Amazingly, the boys agreed and complied with her father's wishes.

By the time Anna entered high school, she had moved out of her geeky phase and had turned into a beautiful young lady. She also kept her focus on her education. When she received her scores for the Scholastic Aptitude Test (SAT), the college entrance exam, Anna was ecstatic.

She informed her mother that she had scored a 1540.

Her mother, even though she was a teacher, had no idea what the SATs were about or what a good score was. She asked, "Is that good?"

"Mo-ther," the exasperated daughter sighed, "a perfect score is sixteen hundred."

Anna parlayed her excellent SAT score and high-school education into an easy entry into college at the University of Texas in Austin. Anna succeeded at University of Texas from the very beginning. Her freshman year, she received Alpha Lambda Delta honors for her grades. By the time she completed her college degree in 1970, she was awarded Phi Beta Kappa honors for Latin and the classics.

After graduation Anna moved back to Dallas to be near her family and became a teacher. She was not satisfied with the work, so she decided to turn to business. Anna got a job with the financial firm Goldman Sachs, became a trader, and transferred to Houston to work in their corporate offices.

Anna, however, knew she needed to do more than just crunch numbers. She had always expressed an interest in medicine. She constantly bemoaned to her mother the fact that she hadn't gone to medical school. Finally her mother said, "Why don't you?"

Anna applied to the University of Texas Medical Branch (UTMB) in Galveston, Texas. Despite her stellar academic and business accomplishments, she was turned down because of her age. She was all of thirty and the school did not believe she would last or, much less, become a physician. On her second go-round, she interviewed with a professor who took one look at her, rolled his eyes, and began to berate her.

"Wouldn't you know it, I get an old girl who is going to take up a space in the medical school and is not going to be able to finish, is not going to be able to practice medicine. Let's get on with it."

Anna looked up at the professor and said, "Wouldn't you know it, I'd get some son of a bitch like you interviewing me."

She was accepted.

Anna excelled in medical school. She also found time to enjoy her family. Her mother recalled that she spent hours baking the "most exquisite cookies" for her nieces and nephews. She took the time out to write letters to friends and family and would never forget an anniversary, birthday, or holiday with either a letter, a phone call, or a visit in person.

Anna also fell in love while she was in medical school. She began to date one of her classmates, John C. Ledet. The couple's courtship was quick and they married right away. Unfortunately, their relationship struggled and the couple soon divorced. Anna returned her focus to her studies and tried to look out for herself.

One week after Emily LaQua went missing, thirty-four-year-old Anna Ledet went for her early-morning ritual: a jog around the UTMB campus. She liked to take off in the dark, when it was peaceful, quiet, and no one would bother her.

She left, as usual, at 4:30 A.M., on March 27, 1982.

Anna was thrilled that she would be officially graduating

in less than two months. All of the hard work, all of the pain from her failed relationship with John, all of it would finally come to an end. She had already been accepted to conduct her residency in nephrology, which is the study of kidneys, especially their functions and diseases, at the University of Iowa in Iowa City. She was especially excited on this particular day because the day before she had completed all of her medical school coursework.

A positive end.

She had a bright future awaiting her.

The man in the brown Grand Prix, however, would snuff out that bright light.

Anna Ledet's best friend and UTMB classmate, Linda Ray, said that Anna usually ran with some friends. She assumed Anna ran alone that particular day because the campus had let out for spring break. Most of her friends took vacations or went home to visit their families.

Anna Ledet's body was discovered at sunrise near the 200 block of East Postoffice Road and Ferry Road. Her jogging suit–clad body was drenched in blood as she lay sprawled across the concrete walkway. She had been stabbed repeatedly in the chest.

Seventeen times.

Ledet's attacker's appetite was not satiated. Covered in the coed's blood, he slid back into his Grand Prix and drove away.

He wanted more.

The man spotted another UTMB medical student, Glenda Kirby, walking down a sidewalk just two blocks away from Ledet's death scene. The man pulled up to the curb behind the woman as she walked, oblivious to any danger. The man got out of his car, stepped onto the side-walk, and headed toward Kirby.

Anna Ledet's blood literally dripped from his hands.

The man approached Glenda Kirby. He began to sprint toward her. He flew through the air and tackled her to the concrete. The man grasped at his latest victim with his hands—his already bloody hands. They were too slick. Glenda Kirby slipped out of his grasp and fled for safety. She had no idea who had attacked her.

CHAPTER 17

Toward the end of March 1982, Acting Police Chief John Bales fired thirteen police officers for "questionable activities." Bales, who would soon be replaced by incoming police chief Lee Brown, stated he was merely "cleaning house." The effect on the rank and file was not positive, to say the least.

By the beginning of April 1982, Mayor Whitmire was quoted in the *Houston Chronicle* as stating that the police were suffering from severe corruption. The morale within the Houston Police Department hit an all-time low.

While the police and the politicians continued to bicker, a killer remained loose on the streets of Houston.

Yolanda "Yollie" Gracia was always the "cool aunt." Her niece, Maricela Gracia, who lived across the street from her on the 5600 block of Tucker Street, on the east side of town, remembered a sweet aunt who always included her in more adult endeavors. Yollie would take Maricela driving around in her yellow Maverick. The young ladies would listen to blaring disco music while they went shopping at the nearby Edgewood Shopping Mall.

Despite being the cool aunt, twenty-two-year-old Yollie was also a good mother. She and her husband, Hector Gracia, gave birth to their only child, Myra Lynn Gracia, on September 28, 1981. Gracia maintained a clean, cozy home, worked a full-time job at Gordon's Jewelers, located on the 1100 block of Main Street, and doted on her newborn baby. Despite all of her numerous responsibilities, Yollie maintained a healthy, happy demeanor.

On April 15, 1982, Yollie went to work at Gordon's Jewelers. That night she wore a white dress with flowery design and a beige jacket and shoes. Usually after she finished her shift, her husband would pick her up and drive her home. Some nights he was unable to get her, so she would take the bus home instead. On this particular evening, Hector informed her that he had to work overtime and that she would need to catch the bus. Gracia's coworkers believed she left work at 6:00 P.M. and took the bus home.

She never made it there.

Gracia's bus stopped at the corner of Midvale Street and Moline Street. She stepped off the bus and headed toward her home. As the bus sputtered off, Coral Watts scooted out of his trusty Grand Prix. He had been watching the bus when he noticed the young woman step off. She was only four blocks and one-half mile from home.

Yolanda Gracia's lifeless body was discovered the following day at 6:00 A.M., in between the yards of two residences on the 7200 block of Moline Street. A neighbor had stepped outside to retrieve his morning paper when he spotted Gracia's body facedown in the yard. Her purse lay next to her body. It had not been opened and nothing had been taken from it.

It was later discovered that Gracia had been stabbed four times, twice in the chest. The other two were considered superficial defense-type wounds. Apparently, Yolanda Gracia attempted to put up a fight for her life.

Dr. Vladimir Parungao, the coroner, placed her time of death at somewhere between 10:00 P.M. and midnight. An analysis of Gracia's stomach contents showed she had digested peas that evening. Dr. Parungao estimated that the victim had eaten approximately two to three hours before her death. Toxicology tests showed that she had not drunk any alcohol or taken any drugs.

According to police reports, some of Gracia's family members did not believe that she had taken the bus home. The reason they gave for their doubt was that Yollie was found wearing her high-heeled shoes. They believed that she always took a pair of sandals with her when she had to ride the bus home because her high heels were too uncomfortable. They also indicated that when Yollie took the bus home, she always got off on Moline Street and Telephone Road. She would then walk west on Moline Street to her home.

Interviews with Gracia's coworkers indicated something entirely different. Her fellow employees informed police officers that Yolanda Gracia may have been having an affair. Allegedly, Gracia had told her friends at work that she and her husband had been having marital difficulties. She never did elaborate. Also, around March 1982, Gracia began receiving telephone calls at work from a young Hispanic male. The man had called her at least twenty times in the previous month. Houston police officers speculated that Gracia may have dined with her unknown male friend prior to her death.

Another young man became a suspect. The man had been arrested previously in nearby Pasadena for a burglary. He also happened to live on the 7900 block of Moline Street, very near to where Gracia's body was discovered. The man was eventually disregarded as a suspect.

CHAPTER 18

Carrie Mae Jefferson met her husband, James Jefferson, in Rayville, Louisiana, when she was a teenager. The two started off as just friends and remained that way for several years. In 1963, Jefferson signed up to join the air force. He did not return until four years later, in 1967.

When James returned, he headed for Houston, Texas. The following year, Carrie joined him. The couple eventually fell in love with one another and soon got married. Carrie was all of nineteen. Marie O'Bryant, James's sister, said of Carrie, "I didn't gain a sister-in-law because she was already my sister."

James landed a job as a postal carrier delivering the mail to his fellow Houstonians.

In January 1969, they had the first of two daughters, Tawanda. In August 1975, they had their second daughter, Jakisha. Carrie loved her daughters more than she could imagine. She loved to give them gifts, especially around Christmastime. But the greatest gift she bestowed, not only on her daughters, but on all she encountered, was her infectious laughter, her strong will, and her intense love.

In 1978, Carrie decided to join her husband at the

main post office downtown at 401 Franklin Street. She signed on to work the night shift with her normal working hours between 5:00 P.M. and 1:30 A.M. James was not happy about her late-night hours, mainly because of safety issues. Carrie alleviated his fears by having one of her coworkers follow her home every night to make sure she got home okay. Her coworker Delores McAfee would usually follow her all the way to Cullen Boulevard and East Orem Drive, about ten blocks from her house.

On April 16, 1982, one day after Coral Watts murdered Yolanda Gracia, he spotted Carrie Mae Jefferson. She looked like an easy target. She only stood five feet tall and weighed 112 pounds. She had a light complexion and a short, tight, curly black afro. She wore maroon pants and a pink blouse.

Carrie Mae Jefferson parked her car in the family driveway of their cozy home, located on the 12600 block of South Spring Drive. Her girls were sleeping soundly in their feminine bedrooms. Her husband was snoring away, waiting for her to come to bed.

As Carrie reached for her keys, Coral Watts grabbed her and dragged her through the front yard. A patch of dirt in the front yard was disturbed with her dragging shoes. Watts grabbed her keys and heaved her toward her small blue car. He unlocked the trunk and tossed the struggling mother and wife inside. She kicked and screamed, but James could not hear her. He was all the way in the back of the house.

Watts fired up Jefferson's car, with its owner entrapped.

James Jefferson woke the following day at 5:00 A.M., just like he always did. Only, this time, his wife was not lying next to him. Less than thirty minutes later, James called the police after his neighbor Robert Francis informed him that he had discovered Carrie's purse in the middle of their street. James Jefferson and Francis then noticed something shiny up against the concrete curb. Upon closer inspection, Jefferson realized that it was Carrie's gold wedding ring. Her watch lay right next to the ring.

James Jefferson went to his friends across the street and told them about his wife. They dressed in a hurry and went out looking for her. It did not take long for them to find her car. It was parked about five blocks away from their house at the corners of Rubin Street and Marchant Road. The trunk had "protrusions" from the inside out and the driver's side seat was pushed all the way back. Carrie was only five feet tall and would never have her car seat so far back. Furthermore, there were blood smears on the inside of the trunk.

James Jefferson mentioned that his wife chewed tobacco and used a spit cup for the excess tobacco juice. The cup was at the front door, which led James to believe that she must have been abducted as she approached the front door.

As is often the case when a spouse goes missing, the police first looked at James Jefferson as a possible suspect. Marie O'Bryant joked about Carrie years later. She said, "There was talk going around that Carrie may have left her husband and children. Her husband, maybe"—she paused—"her children, only through death."

According to James Jefferson, the couple did have some marital problems six years earlier. Apparently, Carrie was stepping out on her husband with another man. James claimed that he confronted Carrie about her illicit affair, to which she admitted. The couple, however, reconciled, and everything was supposedly just fine with their relationship.

CHAPTER 19

Suzanne Searles was born in Iowa on April 19, 1957, to parents Beverly and Harry. Her mother called her "Suzi."

Suzi was the only child of the Searleses. Oftentimes she would have to entertain herself, so she became fascinated with the make-believe world of fantasy. She loved to immerse herself in stories of dragons, fairies, and goblins.

Suzi also loved animals. She would often adopt animals that she discovered while on nature hikes. "We always had a shoe box ready for any animal she might bring home," recalled her mother.

Suzi also became a talented artist at a very young age. She started off with designing clothes. When she was fourteen, Suzi's parents divorced. After her husband left, Suzi's mother had to return to work. Suzi pitched in by making clothes for her and her mother.

Beverly Searles was amazed at her daughter's abilities. "She came out very artistic and I can't draw a straight line with a ruler."

By the time she was sixteen, Suzi was seriously beginning to mature. The tomboyish, bright red-haired, freckle-faced kid was turning into a beautiful young woman. She even politely asked her mother to stop referring to her as Suzi, and instead call her "Sue."

Sue graduated from Roosevelt High School in Des Moines, Iowa, in 1975. After graduation she attended college at the University of Iowa in Iowa City.

After she graduated from college, she applied for and was accepted to graduate school at Drake University, a private school in Iowa, where she received her master's degree. There she met her best friend, Lorraine "Lori" Tafoya. According to Lori, Drake was mostly comprised of spoiled rich kids from back east who were from law schools or medical schools. Lori, in her usual outfit of jeans and boots, did not fit the usual Drake prepster mold. So, when Sue walked into class wearing vintage clothes that came off the Salvation Army rack, Lori knew she had found a kindred spirit. The two young women became fast friends and shared everything. They spoke of their dreams and aspirations they had for themselves. They spoke of lives filled with husbands and children and what their lives would be like once their parents passed away or when their own children grew up and went off to college.

Lori cherished her friendship with Sue. "She was an open book," Lori recollected. "She was the most spiritual and magical person. She didn't get it from church. No one taught that to her. She just had it inside of her." Lori believed Sue had a profound effect on her life just by being her friend.

"She had so much charisma. People just let down their walls when they were around her. She could get right through them."

After Sue completed her graduate degree and obtained her master's, she went to work in the public information office of the Iowa Legislature.

At the end of 1981, Sue decided she wanted to be near her good friend Lori. The two young women dreamed of collaborating on a children's book. Lori would write the text and Sue would illustrate the work. Lori had moved to Houston and Sue soon followed. She moved in with Lori at the Memorial Village Apartments on the 700 block of International Boulevard, located next to Interstate 10, or the Katy Freeway. The young women shared an apartment in the S section until December 28, 1981, then moved into the T section and a nice two-story town house.

Sue landed work as a layout artist for a small design firm called Professional Typographers Printing, located on the 2500 block of North Boulevard. She enjoyed the work and her coworkers; unfortunately, the job did not pay enough. After just a few months, she could no longer afford to pay her $600-a-month rent. Furthermore, Lori had found a new job as a police reporter, but it was all the way in Pueblo, Colorado. Lori moved out on April 5, 1982.

Sue decided she wanted to tag along with her best friend, so she decided to join her in Colorado about a month later. In the meantime she had planned to move in with another friend, Theresa Albury, at the end of the month.

Sue spoke with her mother on the telephone at least once a week. Though her mother knew Sue could handle herself, she still worried. "She's an only daughter and things have changed so much since I was young," her mother warned. "I've always reminded her to be careful." Sue always heeded her mother's warnings.

On April 24, 1982, Sue went to a birthday party for one of her coworkers, Liz, from Professional Typographers. The party was thrown at the 16000 block of Cairnway

Drive, just northwest of Bear Creek Park, located in northwestern Harris County, off Highway 6 and Clay Road. Approximately forty to fifty people were entertained by a live band at the house of James Berendt. Sue partook in the free-flowing alcohol and smoked a couple of joints. One of the men at the party, Stephen "Mark" Jahn, tried to hook up with the five-feet-six-inch, 120-pound, red-haired, blue-eyed beauty. Apparently, Sue did not warm up to Jahn's advances.

James Berendt recalled that he saw Searles sitting on the couch in his house talking to a different man than Jahn around 5:00 A.M.

After the late-night celebration, Sue drove back to her apartment, approximately fourteen miles away. She parked her 1974 gold Volvo station wagon, with its distinctive blue hood, in her designated parking spot in the apartment complex's parking lot.

She never made it inside.

Instead, she ran into one of the monsters.

Later that Sunday evening, Sue Searles was supposed to go to a concert with a group of friends, including Greg Irving, who played in the band that performed at the party the night before. He had called her during the afternoon at her apartment but got no answer. By 7:30 P.M., when Irving still had not heard from his friend, he drove over to her apartment and saw the lights on inside. He knocked on her door, but nothing. Irving left a note for Sue and told her to try and make it to the concert if she got home in time.

She never made it.

The following day, Monday, Sue Searles did not show up for work at her scheduled 7:00 A.M. clock-in time. One of her coworkers, Joseph Powell, arrived at work at 7:30 A.M. He noticed that Searles had not come in for work. He reported to his supervisor that Searles did not make it to the concert the night before either. Powell tried to call Searles at home but only received a busy signal. Powell hung up the phone and told his boss that he could not reach her. His boss told Powell to drive to her apartment and check up on her.

Sue never missed a day of work.

When he pulled up to the complex, he spotted her Volvo. When he looked inside the car, he could see that her purse had been upended and its contents dumped out on the passenger seat. Sue's eyeglasses, which were broken, her shoes, credit cards, checkbook, and driver's license were among the items located in the front seat.

After Powell saw this, he became alarmed. He located the apartment manager, Dorothy Blackwood, and asked her to open up Sue's apartment to make sure she was okay. Blackwood used her passkey to open the locked door. Inside, the lights were still on, the telephone had been knocked off its hook, a plant had been knocked over, and dirt was sprayed across the carpet. Unfortunately, there was no sign of her anywhere.

Powell thanked Blackwood and called the police department. At 9:55 A.M., he filed a missing persons report on behalf of Suzanne Searles.

On May 1, 1982, the lock on Suzanne Searles's apartment door was changed. A "Notice to Vacate" letter was stuck in between the door and the wooden frame.

CHAPTER 20

Harriett Semander kept tracking brutal murders in Houston. She could not help but find a pattern emerging that reminded her of the murder of her daughter Elena. Young, single women, usually white, alone, late at night, and almost always on a Saturday night or early Sunday morning. Harriett, however, did not just sit on this information. She gathered together with other parents of the Houston Chapter of Parents of Murdered Children organization. The objective was to compare notes on the numerous types of murders that occurred in their city to see if they could establish a pattern.

Harriett took extensive notes on all of her research. She read through both city papers every day and clipped numerous articles about young women who were being murdered. Her obsession may have simply seemed like an escape of a mourning mother; however, true patterns began to emerge. In one entry Semander wrote, "By now, I'm beginning to notice too many similarities in the women's murders and disappearances. Maybe the actual death weapon wasn't all that important," she continued. "I'm looking for 'strangled with clothing' victims." The junior gumshoe already far surpassed the supposed "profilers" of the FBI when she theorized, "If I were a murderer, I certainly wouldn't kill the same way all the time. I would change the m.o. to fool the police."

Semander became frustrated that the city of Houston could not see the obvious right in front of their very noses. The women of Houston were being slaughtered by a madman—by a single, deranged individual.

Harriett decided she would do something about what she noticed. She started off by first contacting Police Chief Lee Brown's office on May 14, 1982. She wanted the chief to make a public announcement that a killer was on the loose. She called the police department and spoke with a sergeant who assured her he would pass along her concerns to Chief Brown. Semander seriously doubted he told his boss.

Semander spent the next three days continuing her pursuit of police assistance. She tried to get ahold of a captain, any captain, who would listen to her and, more important, take her seriously. Instead of help, however, all she got was the runaround. One captain told her that they often have "policemen just sitting around because there aren't enough patrol cars." Blame was being assigned elsewhere. "The city council just won't give us the money we need," the captain continued to complain.

Semander was told to contact the police department's public relations department. She called and spoke with Larry Troutt, who informed her that any public warnings must come from the police chief's department.

Semander called the original sergeant and informed him that she was getting the runaround. The sergeant informed her that any one of the officers she spoke with had the authority to invoke a public warning. Semander believed they were simply "passing the buck." Semander also claimed that he told her that he believed most of the officers were unwilling to help because they were still waiting to see how the new chief would shake out.

Semander then tried to contact Mayor Whitmire; however, she was once again stonewalled. The mayor's aide described the grieving mother as "overwrought." Semander described the scenario as a "fear like never before; something was terribly wrong."

Semander would not give up. Once she realized she would receive no help from Chief Brown or Mayor Whitmire, Semander turned to the media. On May 17, 1982, Harriett called news reporter Steve Petrou, of Channel 11 News, the local CBS affiliate. She described her research to Petrou and expressed her concerns that a killer or killers were in their midst. Petrou eagerly agreed to interview her. The interview with Harriett Semander aired that same night. She finally was able to get her warning out.

One of the target audience members that Semander was trying to reach was Michelle Maday. Michelle was born on May 22, 1962, to Michael and Florence "Flo" Maday, in Milwaukee, Wisconsin. She moved to Houston, Texas, with her mother and father at the end of 1980.

Michelle's parents split up, but she maintained a good relationship with both of them. She even moved in with her mother into a cozy apartment on the central west side of the city.

Michelle was an amazingly attractive blond woman, who looked like a young Farrah Fawcett. She was employed as a waitress at a nightclub on West Alabama. Despite working in the club environment, Michelle stayed away from drugs. She was known to throw back a few with her girlfriends; however, she usually stayed on top of her game.

Michelle lived with her mother at a town home apartment complex at the 6400 block of Ella Lee Lane, near Hillcroft Street and Westheimer Boulevard. Michelle recently had switched jobs and went to work as a cocktail waitress at the Bull Whip Club, on the Southwest Freeway. On Saturday, May 22, 1982, she asked for the night off so she could celebrate her twentieth birthday with her good friends Linda Rogers and Terry Clark. The three amigas planned to start the night out eating at Judge's, the same club where Elena Semander had spent her last hours the previous February.

Before Michelle and the girls were to hit the town, she planned on spending the evening with her father. Michelle's mother left their apartment at 3:30 P.M. Three hours later, her father showed up and took her to eat at the Great Caruso on Westheimer Boulevard. Michael Maday and his daughter had a wonderful time at dinner. They talked about her job, her friends, and her mother. Michael Maday also talked about the string of murders of young women in Houston. He was concerned for his daughter's safety. She told him not to worry and that she would be careful.

After dinner Michael and Michelle Maday returned to her apartment at 8:45 P.M. Her father stayed and chatted for another fifteen to twenty minutes. He could tell she was eager to go out and celebrate her big night with her girlfriends. He kissed her good night, wished her a happy birthday, and saw her for the last time.

Soon after her father left, Michelle piled into her black Camaro and drove over to Linda Rogers's apartment. The two girls were ecstatic because they were heading out to Le Bare, the hugely popular male strip club, on San Felipe Street. The girls arrived at the club at 10:00 P.M., armed with fistfuls of dollar bills and the desire to party. Their friend Terry Clark had been out of town and met the girls at the club thirty minutes later.

Michelle, Linda, and Terry had a blast. They drank mass quantities of alcohol, danced their butts off, and closed the joint down. Even though it was two in the morning, the girls were not yet ready to call it a night. Michelle and Linda hopped back into her Camaro and headed to Linda's apartment at the 6000 block of Gulfton Drive. Terry drove over to a nearby grocery store to grab some late-night munchies. The girls did not arrive at Linda's apartment until almost 3:30 A.M. Michelle, however, felt she was too worn out and opted out of the late-night dining experience. She stuck around until almost 4:00 A.M. and decided to head home.

Michelle had no idea that Coral Eugene Watts had spotted her while she was driving and had begun to follow her home. When she arrived at her apartment complex, she parked her car in the street. She did not immediately get out of her car. Watts parked his Grand Prix on the same street and watched her momentarily. He then exited his vehicle and kept his eye on the beautiful, tall, slim young woman.

Watts began to walk toward Michelle's car when he noticed two young men walking toward him. Watts slowed down his pace and noticed that the girl stayed put in her car. Watts stopped and glanced over at the two men. One man went to the car in front of Michelle, got inside, and drove off. The second man got into a separate car and also drove off. Michelle then got out of her car, which she stood next to as she collected herself. She then stumbled past Watts and toward her apartment, which was close to the street.

Michelle already had her keys poised as she approached the front door of her downstairs apartment. As she went to insert the key, Watts silently shuffled up behind her. Feeling his presence, she turned around and began to say something to him as he lunged for her neck with his strong hands. He began to squeeze them around her lithe throat. He was too strong for her to struggle.

Watts clutched Michelle's limp body, unlocked and opened the door, and heaved her inside. He placed her body on the floor of the living room and began to disrobe Michelle. He first removed her dress, then a necklace, then a ring. Allegedly, she did not wear a bra or panties.

Watts then carried Michelle to her bathroom, where he delicately placed her into the bathtub. He placed her feet under the faucet and her head toward the back of the tub. Watts plugged up the drain with a stopper and reached for the water handles. He began to fill the tub up with water. He let the water run until it engulfed her body. Her wide open eyes stared back at her killer.

Coral Watts would later claim he submerged Michelle Maday in the bathtub water "so that the spirit would not get out."

After the evil baptism, Watts ventured into his victim's bedroom. There, he began to unleash his rage. He pulled dresser drawers out and tossed everything inside all across her room. He thrashed around and made a huge mess in the normally well-kept bedroom.

Watts took off with Michelle's dress, two rings, and a necklace. He later tossed the rings and necklace into a sewer and tossed her dress on the ground.

* * *

Michelle Maday's body was not discovered until almost 6:00 P.M. later that day. Her mother, Florence, pulled into their apartment complex's parking lot as it was raining. She noticed that Michelle's black Camaro was parked out in the street with the window rolled down. Florence parked her own car and walked to their apartment. She unlocked the front door, slipped inside, and wiped off the raindrops.

"Michelle? Michelle, honey?" she called out. "You need to go and roll up the window to your car."

No response.

Florence looked around the living room of the apartment. Everything seemed in order. Michelle was always a neat girl. Today was no different. She then walked down the hall and peered into her daughter's bedroom. It looked like a disaster area, with clothes tossed about carelessly, the closet door was wide open, several drawers were pulled out and rifled through, with most of their contents strewn across the floor.

Florence turned her attention from Michelle's bedroom back to the hallway, where she noticed a gleam from the corner of her vision. She looked down and saw a pair of scissors lying in the carpet. It was definitely not like her daughter to leave such a mess. She started to worry and picked up her pace as she bolted toward the bathroom.

Florence's heart skipped several beats as she spotted her daughter in the bathtub. Michelle was completely nude except for a bracelet around her wrist and a gold ring on her finger. Her hair was completely wet. She was not breathing. Her mother screamed and rushed to her daughter's side. She noticed that there was no water in the bathtub; however, there were two soaked towels in the tub with her daughter.

It was unmistakable. Michelle Maday, Florence Maday's daughter and best friend, was dead.

The coroner confirmed that Michelle Maday had been either partially strangled or drowned. Coral Watts had knocked her unconscious by choking her with his hands, filled up her bathtub with water, and then proceeded to hold her underwater until she was dead. Dr. Aurelio Espinola, the medical examiner, determined that her killer either had worn gloves or had some type of cloth covering his hands.

Several hours before Florence Maday arrived at home to discover her dead daughter, Coral Eugene Watts had not finished. Less than two hours after he strangled Michelle Maday, Watts's blood lust had not been satisfied. He returned to his Grand Prix and continued to prowl the northwestern side of Houston. He drove until almost 6:00 A.M., until he came to a midsized apartment complex on Hammerly Boulevard.

CHAPTER 21

Later that Sunday night, May 23, 1982, after Watts had attacked Lori Lister and Melinda Aguilar, and was subsequently captured, Houston police paid Sheila Williams a visit on Sunnyside Street.

Williams, who had been attending a paralegal course, had a basic understanding of the law. Instead of acquiescing and allowing the search, she demanded that the officers provide her with a warrant. They did not have one.

According to prosecutor Ira L. Jones II, a warrant was secured the following morning. "We got a search warrant and the next day she'd cleared the place out." He added that there was only "trash and some twisted coat hangers on the floor."

Jones stated of Williams that she was "extremely uncooperative with police at the time of [Watts's] arrest. If she had let us in the apartment then, there's no telling what we might have found—possibly something that belonged to one of the victims."

Jones gave no explanation as to why the Houston police officers did not have a search warrant on their first attempt to search the apartment.

On May 26, 1982, attorneys Don Caggins and Zinetta

Burney met Coral Watts in Harris County Jail. Watts's fiancée, Sheila Williams, hired Caggins after taking the
paralegal course with him. Caggins, thirty-one, was born
and raised in Mississippi. After college he applied for law
school and was accepted at the Thurgood Marshall
School of Law at Texas Southern University (TSU), a predominately black school located just south of downtown
Houston. It has the unique distinction of being the first
Historically Black College and University to house a law
school. It is also the home of such distinguished graduates as the late United States congresswoman Barbara
Jordan and former congressman George "Mickey"
Leland. Caggins joined his distinguished alumni when
he graduated from Thurgood Marshall in May 1975.

Caggins focused on civil matters in his practice, so he
informed Williams that he would ask his law partner,
Zinetta Burney, who handled all of the criminal matters
in their office, to take the lead on Watts's case.

Burney, forty-one, a 1974 graduate of the Thurgood
Marshall School of Law at TSU, had no problem taking
on Watts. "When I heard about the case, he sounded like
a churchgoing working man with a nice fiancée. He
seemed like a stable person to me."

Burney's opinion would change soon enough.

Burney was informed that Watts was a suspect in multiple murders. Watts himself had been convinced by the
police that they had a rock-solid case against him. As a
result, he admitted to Burney that he had, indeed, murdered several women.

Burney was scared to death. Watts confessed to her and
wanted her to strike a deal with the prosecution. She
could not believe the tales of horror that spilled from
Watts's lips. Despite the heinous nature of his crimes,
however, Burney and Caggins knew Watts needed their

support and representation. "Everybody has a right to have their rights protected and Coral Watts is no exception," Burney later told reporters.

As Burney spent more time with Watts, she would come to fear him. She began to wear a crucifix around her neck every time she met with him. "He never threatened me. He was always quiet and polite to me, but he scared me more than anyone I've ever dealt with."

She added, "There's something evil in the man."

Despite her fears of her own client, Burney represented his interests to the best of her ability. She and Watts decided their best avenue was to request a plea bargain in exchange for information and confessions to numerous murders, as well as locations to some of the missing bodies.

Negotiations between Burney and the prosecuting attorneys lasted several months.

CHAPTER 22

In June 1982, Judge Douglas Shaver presided over Watts's hearings. Judge Shaver had a successful career as a Harris County prosecutor prior to his judgeship. He worked on many high-profile cases out of Houston, the most notorious being the prosecution of Elmer Wayne Henley, the young charge who aided Dean Corll in the sexual killings of at least twenty-seven boys and young men in and around the Houston and Pasadena areas.

On the request of prosecutor Jack Frels, one of Judge Shaver's first orders of business was to compel Watts to receive a psychiatric evaluation. The reason for this was to establish whether Watts was mentally sound to understand the nature of the charges against him. Frels cited "the grotesque nature of the crime" as reason for the evaluation request.

Watts was admitted to Rusk State Hospital, located in Rusk, Texas, 130 miles east of Waco, Texas, by court order. Rusk State Hospital was a hospital for the mentally ill. It was opened in 1919 as a care facility for the "Negro insane," according to *The Handbook of Texas*. Watts was admitted to the Skyview Maximum Security Unit of the hospital on June 15, 1982. At the time he was one of 952 patients.

Watts received physical and neurological examinations. Doctors took blood and urine samples from him and his chest was X-rayed. He also received a sickle-cell anemia test to screen for a blood disorder that adversely affects the hemoglobin, usually found in African descendants. Watts also undertook a psychometric examination and a psychiatric examination.

Watts's physical exams all came up negative, as did the X-ray and sickle-cell test. His blood and urine tests also came back fine.

Watts's psychological examination consisted of several parts. They included the following:

- Clinical interview
- Staff observations
- Wechsler Adult Intelligence Scale–Revised
- Projective Human Figure Drawing Test
- Bender Visual-Motor Gestalt Test
- Sentence Completion Blank
- "Competency to Stand Trial" Questionnaire

Dr. James A. Hunter, the clinical director of the security unit, conducted the battery of tests on Watts. The first thing that jumped out to Dr. Hunter was the fact that Watts performed poorly on the Wechsler Adult Intelligence Scale, or IQ test. Watts's scores were 69 verbal, 71 performance, and 68 full scale. In other words, Coral Watts's IQ was measured at only 68. Under Texas law at that time, he would be considered to be mentally retarded. Dr. Hunter attributed a portion of Watts's poor performance on anxiety and apprehension.

Dr. Hunter considered Watts's intelligence level actually to be in the normal range.

The doctor described Watts's drawings for the Bender test as "expansive in arrangement with perseveration" on two drawings, which meant that he was prone to repeated gestures or responses without appropriate stimuli, and "flattening of curves" for two different sketches. The doctor interpreted Watts's drawings to show "emotional constriction and transient anxiety."

Watts's human figures were "large in size and undetailed with no significant elements."

Dr. Hunter noted that Watts tended to respond to the sentence-completion questions with one word responses. As a result, Watts was marked as resistant to the test-taking conditions.

Watts also was rather uncooperative when it came to answering the competency questionnaire. He mainly responded with "I don't know" answers.

Finally Dr. Hunter denoted that Watts's results from the pencil-and-paper tests suggested "limitations in reading and writing skills which may be embarrassing to the patient."

Dr. Hunter observed that Watts was "guarded and evasive in his answers to questions. He has good eye contact, but also appears sullen and unconcerned during the interview. He is alert and appears to be controlling his hostility." Dr. Hunter's report added that Watts was "oriented as to time, person and place. His memory is intact. Mood is guarded and his affect is controlled but he smiles appropriately at times." Dr. Hunter added that "his grasp of general information is good. Insight and judgment are impaired. His psychiatric diagnosis is: Without Psychosis."

Dr. Hunter concluded his findings on Coral Watts:

"Based on the above findings, it is my opinion that there is no justification for a finding of incompetence to stand trial in that he has sufficient ability to consult with his lawyer with a reasonable degree of rational understanding. He also has a rational, as well as a factual, understanding of the proceedings against him."

Less than one month later, Watts's attorneys scheduled a psychiatric evaluation from one of their experts, Dr. Jerome N. Sherman, of the Sherman Clinic in Houston, Texas.

Dr. Sherman examined Coral Watts in the Harris County Jail on July 12, 1982, along with psychiatrist Nicky Edd. Dr. Sherman's analysis, unsurprisingly, was different from Dr. Hunter's.

Watts discussed his family background. He spoke of the poor relationship his mother and father had and how his father left the family. He spoke of attending several different schools in Michigan and West Virginia. He also spoke of his stepfather and how he became the oldest child of ten siblings. Watts also claimed that his stepfather, Norman Ceaser, physically abused him and his mother. He also spoke of his criminal history that included aggravated assault, assault, larceny, theft, kidnapping, and attempted murder.

Dr. Sherman described his impressions of Watts's behavioral mannerisms during the interview as "quiet, restrained, reticent." Watts was also "alert, coherent, and oriented." As the conversation progressed, Dr. Sherman noted that Watts began to show a bit more spontaneity.

Watts appeared to be "mainly flat and depressed." Interestingly enough, Watts also appeared to be "reacting at times to apparent hallucinations." This observation was based on inappropriate responses by Watts, which was measured by "sudden and unexpected motor activity and expressions (facial and gestural) not relevant or in reaction to the present proceedings."

Even more surprising was that Watts actually broke down and started to cry. Sherman wrote that he "broke down and wept while discussing the demise and subsequent elusive search for an uncle who was supposedly killed by his wife when the client was much younger." This was in reference to Watts's uncle Smitty, who was killed, he claimed, by Watts's aunt, Smitty's wife. Sharon Watts, Coral's sister, later disputed this claim. She detailed that their uncle Smitty was actually killed by a male police officer and not his wife.

Dr. Sherman admitted many of the same tests that were performed by Dr. Hunter, in addition to a Rorschach Psychodiagnostic Technique, a Thematic Apperception Test, and the Minnesota Multiphasic Personality Inventory.

Watts's score improved slightly on the IQ test, with a 75, which was considered borderline as far as intellectual functionality is concerned.

Watts also displayed a "concrete orientation" based on his responses to what he believed certain proverbs meant. One example was the proverb "Strike while the iron is hot." Watts's response was "Be the first to strike." Another proverb, "Shallow brooks are noisy," was interpreted with "They make a lot of noise."

Dr. Sherman interpreted Watts's concreteness to mean that Watts was mentally impaired. The doctor also believed that Watts was not able to cope with incoming stimuli or situations. He also commented on Watts's lack of concentration.

From an emotional perspective, Dr. Sherman believed Watts to be disorganized, alienated, and somewhat paranoid and suspicious of those around him. Watts described his world as unfriendly and that others were out to harm him. As a result he felt the need to defend himself.

Dr. Sherman wrote about Watts's inability to function with others: "He appears only marginally attuned to the practical realities of the world around him. Instead, he is absorbed in his own fantasies which revolve, to a large extent, around the struggle against 'evil,' which he sees lurking everywhere."

Watts's anger also caught the good doctor's attention. "The client harbors a great deal of internalized anger," the psychiatrist examined. "Much of this hostility is directed at female figures, whom he tends to perceive as deceitful, unfaithful, and parasitic. It is primarily to the female that he attaches the 'evil' quality." Sherman believed that Watts felt that all women have "ulterior motives" and that it would be dangerous to have a relationship with a woman.

Dr. Sherman noted that Watts was not prone to over-the-top self-expression or even the most basic of interpersonal skills: "It is not characteristic of the client to freely display his emotions or to express himself spontaneously, as he is a guarded individual. He is capable of maintaining a marginal façade of outward intactness. However, rational controls are weak and his actions are likely to be determined strongly by irrational, emotional forces."

Dr. Sherman concluded that Coral Eugene Watts suffered from "Schizophrenia, Paranoid Type." The results indicated that Watts suffered from "psychotic thought disorder" and that "he is especially sensitive to the existence of 'evil.'"

According to Sherman, Watts also "harbors a great deal of internalized hostility, which is directed primarily at females. He is defensively reactive to the perceived threats around him, which intensifies the dangerousness of the situation."

Dr. Sherman added that Watts's condition "is chronic and of long standing and is likely to persist. This client is in need of attention and close supervision. Psychiatric help is essential."

The conclusions reached by Dr. Hunter and Dr. Sherman could not have been more diametrically opposed.

In between Watts's psychiatric evaluations, Harriett Semander continued to demand answers. She, along with three parents from the Parents of Murdered Children group, including Michael Maday, father of Michelle Maday, contacted Harris County district attorney John B. Holmes Jr. and requested a meeting. Representatives from Holmes's office agreed and scheduled a visit to Semander's home for June 29, 1982.

While dining over a traditional Greek meal, Holmes, ADA Jack Frels, Semander, and Maday gathered to discuss the Watts situation. Semander felt nothing but hostility from Holmes and Frels. Semander believed that neither man was there to help her and were only there hopefully to get her off their backs.

They had no idea whom they were messing with.

Harriett Semander wanted to know a few things: how was Watts allowed to roam the streets of Houston if there was evidence provided to the Houston Police Department that he was a murder suspect in Michigan, and why did HPD drop surveillance on Watts despite knowing what they knew about him?

DA Holmes, known as one of the toughest law enforcers in the nation, seemed to cower before the small Greek mother. His response let Semander know he was not going to be any help whatsoever.

"No way! I wouldn't touch HPD with a ten-foot pole."

CHAPTER 23

Harriett Semander was not about to give up. On July 9, 1982, she received a surprise in her mailbox. Assistant District Attorney Ira Jones had sent her detailed information on forty unsolved murders in Houston: it included victims' names, addresses, dates of death, and methods of murder. She was grateful to receive the information, since she had tried to receive the material from her city council member Jim Westmoreland. Jones informed Semander that Westmoreland was "just passing the buck" and that Jones would take care of it for her.

The bonus surprise, however, came in the form of confidential police records that Jones included in the package. Upon discovering these documents, Semander called Jones to tell him about their inclusion. Jones, however, was not in and Semander chose not to leave a message. Instead, she decided she would make copies of the material before she gave it back to Jones.

According to Semander, Jones called her at approximately 2:00 P.M. and told her that he needed the material so he could "study" it over the weekend. Semander stated she knew Jones was lying, so she rushed to finish making copies. When Jones arrived, she recalled, he told her that the detectives in Homicide were "in an uproar" that she had gotten her hands on the material, albeit inadvertently.

Semander added that Jones asked for the documents, which she readily handed over. He then allegedly said, "And any copies you made." She handed over the copies as well.

Semander noted that Jones thanked her and told her, "The buck stops with me."

By the end of the month, Harriett Semander still had not received word from the police chief or the mayor. She decided some surveillance tactics of her own were needed. Chief Brown was scheduled to speak at the Neartown Civic Association meeting. Semander contacted the organization and informed them that she and her husband, along with Michael Maday and others, were interested in participating in the Q&A session with the police chief.

At the conclusion of the meeting, Harriett Semander approached the seemingly untouchable Lee Brown. She introduced herself. He recognized her and shook her hand. She asked to speak with him and he smiled and handed her a business card.

On July 28, 1982, Semander called Chief Brown's office and set up a meeting over coffee for August 4, 1982. She would finally have the ears she wanted all along.

On the day of the meeting, Harriett Semander informed her group that she was "tired of all this running around and I'm going to just go ahead and ask for an internal investigation on police procedures in the handling of all the unsolved murders." The group agreed and headed over to the police department's coffee shop. They waited for thirty minutes.

Finally Chief Brown, flanked by Lieutenant Guy A. Mason and Detective Kenny Williamson, decided to join them. Semander was surprised Brown showed up. She was not, however, surprised by Brown's response. He informed her that he, as well as the Houston Police Department, believed the murders were not the work of one person and that he backed his police officers.

Harriett Semander began to cry. "I broke down and cried because I realized that I had come to a brick wall and a dead end." She was worn out from having gotten this far and to, once again, have been stonewalled. She asked, one more time, why Watts was not watched.

Brown ignored her last question.

Five days later, Coral Eugene Watts turned Chief Lee Brown into a liar. Watts agreed to plead guilty to "aggravated burglary" and "attempted murder" in the cases against Lori Lister and Melinda Aguilar in exchange for information that would lead to the discovery of some of his murder victims. For this information Watts would receive immunity for thirteen murders and six assaults.

The district attorney's office claimed that they struck the deal because there was no physical evidence to link Watts to any of the murders. They also claimed that they had spoken with the families of the victims and agreed that the plea bargain would help ease their minds about the deaths of their daughters—especially, the women whose bodies had not yet been discovered.

Most of the families denied ever being informed of the plea bargain. Many of the surviving family members, such as Harriettt Semander and Jane Montgomery, were livid when they heard the news. They could not believe that the state would negotiate with a serial killer. Especially without conferring with them first.

CHAPTER 24

On August 9, 1982, Watts began to confess to police and prosecutors from Austin, Texas, Galveston, Texas, and Grosse Pointe Farms, Michigan. His confessions lasted more than twenty-eight hours.

The following text is the actual interrogation and confession by Coral Eugene Watts in regard to the murder of Elizabeth Montgomery:

Tom Ladd (TL): The first case we'd like to bring up we talked about yesterday, about the female over on the southwest end of town who was walking the dog. Do you remember that one?
Coral Watts (CW): Yes.
TL: Alright, now start it out. You just go ahead in your own words and tell us what happened. About what time of night was it?
CW: I don't remember what time it was.
TL: Was it after dark?
CW: Yes.
TL: Well, do you believe it was before or after midnight?
CW: It was before midnight.
TL: On the night did you drive over to that area of town in your own car?

CW: Yes.

TL: Alright, when did you first see her?

CW: Ah, walking the dog down the street.

TL: Alright, do you remember what was on the street? Houses, businesses, apartments?

CW: Apartments.

TL: Apartments. Alright, and she was walking her dog?

CW: Yeah.

TL: How many dogs was she walking?

CW: Two.

TL: Alright, do you remember what kind of dogs they were or what color?

CW: They was two white dogs.

TL: Two white dogs. Were they on a leash, or were they running loose?

CW: I think one was on a leash. I don't know about the other one.

TL: Alright, do you want to tell us what happened here? How did you approach her?

CW: Ah, from the side.

TL: Did she see you approach?

CW: No.

TL: Alright, when did she realize that you were by her?

CW: Ah, after I grabbed her.

TL: Alright, now you grabbed her by what? The shoulder?

CW: Ah, by the neck.

TL: By the neck. Then what happened?

CW: Then I stabbed her one time.

TL: All right, what type of knife did you have?

CW: Kitchen knife. A pretty long one.

TL: Are you talking about a knife that you would use in the kitchen to cut meat and vegetables? Something with a sharp point?

CW: Yes.

TL: *Alright, what did she do after you stabbed her?*

CW: *Ah, turned around and looked at me.*

TL: *Then what?*

CW: *Ran off.*

TL: *Did you run off?*

CW: *No, she did.*

TL: *Alright, do you know where she went?*

CW: *No.*

TL: *Where was she the last time you saw her?*

CW: *Ah, running across the grass.*

TL: *Alright, what were the dogs doing?*

CW: *I don't remember.*

TL: *Alright, describe the person as you can remember, what does she look like?*

CW: *I don't know.*

TL: *Remember the color of her hair?*

CW: *Blonde.*

TL: *Blonde hair. Was it long or short?*

CW: *Long.*

TL: *About how old was she?*

CW: *I don't know.*

TL: *Alright, do you know what she was wearing?*

CW: *I believe a white shirt with a blue jean jumpsuit or something like that.*

TL: *Did you take any property from her?*

CW: *No.*

Unknown (U/K): *What direction was she running? Was she running . . . where would you say she was running to?*

CW: *Towards the apartments.*

TL: *Notice if she had on any shoes?*

CW: *I don't remember.*

TL: *Did you see anybody out there immediately after the stabbing?*

CW: *No.*

TL: *Alright, how did you come to spot this woman? Were you driving around or walking?*

CW: *Driving.*

TL: *Alright, do you remember what street you were driving on?*

CW: *No.*

TL: *Alright, when you saw her, was she just walking her dogs?*

CW: *Yes.*

U/K: *Is this a major street or a side street?*

CW: *It may have been. I'm not sure. It was a wide street, but I don't think it was a major street.*

Ted Thomas (TT): Did you hear her say anything at all?

CW: *No.*

TT: *No scream, nothing?*

CW: *No.*

TL: *Where did you park your car?*

CW: *Ah, across the street.*

TL: *And immediately after the stabbing you got in your car and drove away?*

CW: *Yeah.*

Jim Ladd (JL): Earlier, I think you told someone that . . . right after it happened you got mixed up [and] run the wrong way or something and . . .

CW: *Well, I went through some . . . I went across, through some apartments or something and it was the wrong way so I came back around and went out.*

JL: *So, you actually ended up then, [back at the apartments] is this correct? Tell me if I'm wrong. You actually ran back in through the apartments?*

CW: *No, I'm at the apartments there and I went this way, then they went up back around . . . one side come back and go out and down about thirty feet to get to my car.*

JL:　Could you find this location again? Where this happened at if you were in the vicinity?

CW:　If I was there, yeah.

U/K:　You could show us where all this did take place at?

CW:　Uh huh.

TL:　Had you ever been there before?

CW:　No.

TL:　Okay.

U/K:　Do you remember what you were wearing that night?

CW:　Blue coat and blue pants I believe.

U/K:　Did you have a hat on or anything?

CW:　No.

U/K:　Gloves?

CW:　No.

TL:　Okay, what did you do with the knife?

CW:　I don't remember. I threw it away I believe.

TL:　Alright, did the knife come from your apartment?

CW:　Uh huh.

TL:　Is it one of a set?

CW:　No, it was just a knife I used.

JL:　On this occasion here though, did you not wear gloves, is that correct?

CW:　No.

JL:　Let me ask you this, in the majority of the cases or in most of these did you in fact wear gloves, in some of them and not in some of them or what was the usual for you in such as that?

CW:　Sometimes I did and sometimes I didn't.

JL:　Was there any particular reason you didn't wear gloves this particular night?

CW:　No.

* * *

After Watts killed Elizabeth Montgomery, he drove about one mile away and came upon Suzi Wolf. One body was not enough.

The following text is the actual interrogation and confession by Coral Eugene Watts in regard to the murder of Suzi Wolf:

Unknown (U/K): Okay, we were talking yesterday, I believe, in the relationship to this one here where the girl was walking a dog, that happened a short time before a second one happened that same night, is that correct?

Coral Watts (CW): Uh huh.

Jim Ladd (JL): On this same night, where the girl was walking her dog, was there another one that happened the same night?

CW: Yes.

JL: Okay, was it nearby or, where in relationship to the first one was the second one that night?

CW: I don't know exactly where, but I believe it was nearby.

U/K: Okay, tell us what you remember about that one.

CW: Well, there was a woman, I think she was driving out of a shopping center. I think it was a white car or something.

U/K: (unintelligible)

CW: Yes. She drove down about two or three blocks and made a right and then I don't exactly remember too much where she parked at or whatever. She got out and went up through a walkway and I got out and I went up behind her and grabbed and stabbed her.

TL: Remember what store she came out of?

CW: I think it was a Safeway store.

TL: Alright, was she carrying anything when she came out of the store?

CW: One bag.

TL: One bag?

CW: Yeah, I believe it was one bag.

TL: Alright, how many times did you stab her?

CW: I'm not sure. About three or four times probably.

TL: What area of the body?

CW: I think in the chest and stomach.

TL: Did you use the same knife that you had previously used on that other girl we just talked about?

CW: Yes.

TL: Alright, during this stabbing did you encounter anybody or did anybody see you?

CW: I think there may have been a man somewhere.

TL: Do you know where the man came from?

CW: No.

TL: Did you hear him say anything to you?

CW: I just remember somebody saying, "Hey!" I don't exactly remember what was said.

TL: Do you remember what this girl looked like?

CW: No.

TL: About how old she was?

CW: No.

TL: Color of hair or how she wore her hair?

CW: I think it was brown, light brown, brownish kind of hair. I'm not sure.

TL: Alright, remember what she was wearing?

CW: I think she had a white coat or white or beige jacket on.

TL: Remember what she was wearing below?

CW: No.

TL: Blue jeans, a dress?

CW: I think it was a dress.

TL: You can't remember?

CW: No.

U/K: When she got out of the car was she carrying anything?

CW: A bag of groceries.

TL: Did she drop the groceries when you approached her or when you grabbed her?

CW: I think when I grabbed her.

TL: And was she carrying anything else in her hands?

CW: Not that I can remember.

TL: Alright, now where did this take place? Was this in an apartment complex?

CW: Yeah, it was an apartment complex.

TL: Do you remember how the apartments were situated or what they looked like?

CW: No, I remember like walking between two apartments then there was set in front of it.

TL: Alright, when you stabbed her, was she standing or what?

CW: On the ground.

TL: On the ground, was she lying on the ground?

CW: Uh huh.

TL: Alright.

U/K: If she was lying on the ground, where were you?

CW: Over her.

U/K: What do you mean by "over her"?

CW: Just over the top of her. I had her down on the ground.

TL: You were straddling her?

U/K: Or were you standing?

CW: I'm not sure.

U/K: You don't remember if you were on the ground with her or if you were . . . ?

CW: I was on the ground with her, I don't know how I was on the ground with her. I was on the ground with her.

TL: What were you wearing that night?

CW: *Blue coat and blue pants.*

TL: *Blue coat and blue pants?*

CW: *Or brown, it was a dark color.*

TT: *Is this a uniform, these blue coat and blue pants? Is that your uniform?*

CW: *No.*

JL: *This night, were you driving your Grand Prix or were you in some other vehicle?*

CW: *I was driving my Grand Prix.*

JL: *Same one that you had when . . .*

CW: *Yeah.*

JL: *. . . you got arrested over there off Hammerly?*

CW: *Uh huh.*

JL: *Do you remember when she pulled into the lot, did she pull into a regular space or did she pull in like, uh, did she illegally park or anything like that exactly where she parked?*

CW: *No, I don't.*

JL: *And this man, do you remember where he came from?*

CW: *No, I never seen him. I just heard him.*

JL: *Is this what stopped you from stabbing her, when this man appeared or had you finished and were leaving, or when, when did he come into the picture?*

CW: *Ah, before I stabbed her.*

TL: *Was she fighting or struggling?*

CW: *Yeah.*

TL: *You remember her saying anything at all?*

CW: *No.*

JL: *What did you do then after you ran off?*

CW: *I got in my car and left. Went home.*

U/K: *Went home, where were you living at this time, do you remember?*

CW: *I think I was staying in Eagle Lake.*

TL: *Talking about the town of Eagle Lake?*

CW: *Yeah.*

JL: *It's kinda curious that these were on the same night
and close together and that you were still in the area. After
the first one happened, is there a particular reason that you
stayed in that same area, did you, or why was it that you're
still in that area of town? Is that normal? Is that normal
for you to stay around a scene or something like that to be
able to go back and look to see what's going on later or . . .*

CW: *No.*

JL: *Was there any particular reason you were still in this
same area of town so near the first one?*

CW: *No.*

TL: *Just for the record, how long was it from the first girl
you stabbed 'til you stabbed this second girl? In a time span,
you talking about what, an hour, thirty minutes, an hour-
and-a-half, the best you can recollect?*

CW: *I don't know. Maybe fifteen minutes.*

TL: *Fifteen minutes? Alright, is this, we've talked yesterday, now this one incident where there is two girls killed the
same night, are there any other nights when you killed more
than one girl? On the same night?*

CW: *No.*

TL: *This would be the only time?*

CW: *Yeah.*

CHAPTER 25

The following text is the actual interrogation and confession by Coral Eugene Watts in regard to the murder of Phyllis Ellen Tamm:

Tom Ladd (TL): You said you remember another case?
Coral Watts (CW): Yeah.
TL: Alright, which one is that?
CW: The lady out joggin'.
TL: Lady out jogging. Alright, where was this?
CW: It was over off Main.
TL: Off of Main?
CW: I think it was off . . . I don't know.
TL: Alright, tell me about it.
CW: I was driving down the street and I seen her.
TL: What time of day or night was this?
CW: Um, think it was in the morning.
Jim Ladd (JL): Early in the morning?
CW: Uh huh.
TL: Alright, what is she wearing?
CW: Some shorts and a thing around her neck and . . .
TL: What kind of thing around her neck?
CW: Uh . . .

TL: *Speak up Coral.*

CW: *I don't know what it is. It was a little cloth thing.*

TL: *Like an elastic deal?*

CW: *Yeah.*

TL: *Alright, so she was jogging down Main Street and she had this around her neck, and it was early in the morning?*

CW: *Uh huh.*

TL: *Alright. Was this a white female?*

CW: *Yeah.*

TL: *How old do you estimate her to be?*

CW: *Um, about twenty-seven, twenty-eight.*

TL: *Do you remember what color hair she had?*

CW: *Blonde, I believe.*

TL: *Dark blonde? Is that what you said? I'm sorry, I didn't hear.*

CW: *Yeah. Blonde, dark blonde it was. Yeah.*

TL: *Alright, do you remember which way she was running?*

CW: *Away from Main.*

TL: *Okay. What happened? Were you driving when you saw her?*

CW: *Yeah.*

TL: *Alright, was it daylight?*

CW: *Yeah.*

TL: *Alright, she's jogging and you're in your car?*

CW: *Yeah.*

TL: *What car are you driving?*

CW: *The Grand Prix.*

TL: *And you see her jogging and what happens? You pass her or tell me about it from the time you see her jogging.*

CW: *She was jogging and I went by and she had went down a street or something or other, that I couldn't go down, so I went around and I couldn't find her for a while. Then I see her going down a street. I don't know what the name of the street was.*

TL: *Would you know it if you heard it?*

CW: *No. I didn't even look at the . . .*

TL: *Okay.*

Unknown (U/K): *What kind of street was it that you couldn't go down? Why couldn't you go down it?*

CW: *It was a one way street.*

U/K: *Did it have any bars or chain across so that you couldn't turn in?*

CW: *I don't think so.*

U/K: *Who do you know over there? What was down there that made you go by?*

CW: *Nothing. I was just driving.*

TL: *Alright, so you're behind, you see her and you can't go down the street, so you go down another street?*

CW: *Yeah.*

TL: *Then you come, do you circle around and come up behind her?*

CW: *Yeah.*

TL: *Alright, then what happened?*

CW: *I drive down the street and parked the car. And she was running down the side of the street and I ran up and grabbed her. And choked her.*

TL: *Okay, then what happened?*

CW: *Ah, then I choked her and I took a branch and broke it off. I took the thing and hung it up.*

TL: *Alright, now for the purpose of this tape, what's her first name?*

JL: *Phyllis.*

TL: *Okay, for the purpose of this tape, Coral Watts has just told us about the murder of Phyllis Tamm. That was*

T-A-M-M. Okay, you broke the branch and you hung her on the branch?

CW: Yeah.

TL: Alright, how did you choke her? With your hands?

CW: No, with the thing she had around her neck.

TL: Was it a . . . a slow choke or exactly how did you manipulate that elastic device around her neck?

CW: Just took it and pulled it back.

TL: Fast?

CW: Yeah.

TL: Did the young lady struggle at all?

CW: Yeah.

TL: She did?

CW: Uh huh.

TL: Did she say anything?

CW: No.

TL: Alright, and you, when you hung her on the broken branch what position was she in when you left?

CW: Facing out towards the street.

TL: Alright and where were her legs?

CW: They were in front of her.

TL: Alright, were they under her or straight out?

CW: Straight out, I think.

TL: Straight out. Alright, was . . . did she appear to be hung like in a standing position or in a sitting position?

CW: Sitting.

TL: Alright, when you broke this branch . . . let's see, why did you decide to hang her?

CW: No reason. I just hung her up there.

JL: How big was the branch that you broke?

CW: I don't know. About like that.

JL: Indicating, what, about an inch in diameter?

CW: Yeah.

TL: Was this . . . the branch that you broke, was it

from a tree or a bush, among many bushes or a single bush or a single tree or what?

CW: Bush.

TL: *Among many or by itself?*

CW: *I think it was with a whole lot of other ones.*

JL: *You say there was a whole lot of bushes?*

CW: Yeah.

TL: *Do you feel like she was dead before you hung her?*

CW: No.

TL: *Do you think that it was the actual hanging that caused her to die?*

CW: Yeah.

TL: *Did you have to support her weight while you hung her?*

CW: Yeah.

TL: *Was she . . . was she struggling at this time?*

CW: No.

TL: *Was she moving at all?*

CW: *A little.*

TL: *Like a twitch, jerking, was she trying to free herself from a . . . ?*

CW: Yeah.

TL: *Did she actually try to free herself from the thing around her neck?*

CW: No.

TL: *How did she act? Describe her actions.*

CW: *She just moved a little, lift her hand up to her neck and dropped it back down.*

U/K: *How big of a woman was this?*

CW: *She was pretty big.*

U/K: *How tall was she?*

CW: *About right here on me."*

Ted Thomas (TT): Okay, to your nose?

CW: Yeah.

JL: How much do you think she weighed?

CW: I don't know.

TT: Was she slim?

CW: No.

U/K: How would you describe her weight-wise? Slim, medium, heavy?

CW: A little heavy.

TL: Remember how she wore her hair?

CW: No.

JL: You say she came up to your nose. Shows you to be about 5' 10" so you imagine that she would probably be somewhere around 5' 6" or so?

CW: Uh huh.

JL: That would be a fair estimate?

CW: I guess so.

JL: Think back real carefully now. Kind of visualize when you first see her out jogging and try to think as hard as you can and tell me exactly what you remember she was wearing.

CW: I think it was some shorts and a jogging suit.

JL: By "jogging suit," what do you mean exactly?

CW: Jogging suit, you know, one of them cotton jogging suit(s).

JL: What color?

CW: White, I think, or gray.

JL: Did it have a hood or not?

CW: I don't know.

TL: Are you referring to a sweatshirt?

CW: Yeah.

TL: What about the pants?

CW: I'm not sure about the pants. All I know she had on some shorts and some pants, I think.

TL: What color shoes did she have on?

CW: I don't know.

TL: *Did she have on shoes?*

CW: *Yeah.*

TT: *Did you take anything from her?*

CW: *Yeah.*

TT: *What did you take?*

CW: *Um, she had some socks on her hands.*

TT: *Socks on her hands?*

CW: *Yeah.*

TT: *What, for gloves? For warmth?*

CW: *Yeah.*

TT: *And you took those socks?*

TL: *What color socks were they?*

CW: *I'm not . . . I don't know. I thought they were . . .*

TL: *How did you . . . ?*

JL: *Why did she have the socks on her? What was the weather like?*

CW: *Kinda cold.*

JL: *So we're still talking about what [would] be in the winter or early spring or something?*

CW: *Uh huh.*

TL: *What did you do with the socks?*

CW: *I don't . . . I believe I burned 'em. I'm not sure.*

TL: *Why?*

CW: *Huh?*

TL: *Why?*

CW: *Why what?*

TL: *Did you burn the socks?*

CW: *To kill the spirit.*

TL: *You didn't think that hanging her would accomplish that?*

CW: *No.*

TL: *Why did you hang her?*

CW: *It was easy to hang her, I guess.*

TL: *It was easier?*

CW: Yeah.

TL: *Do you think she was still alive when you hung her?*

CW: Yeah.

JL: *Why did you kill this woman?*

CW: *Cause she was evil.*

JL: *You see it in her eyes?*

CW: Yeah.

TL: *Speak up!*

CW: *Yes.*

CHAPTER 26

The following text is the actual interrogation and confession by Coral Eugene Watts in regard to the murder of Meg Fossi:

Jim Ladd (JL): We were talking about the girl in the vehicle that you followed while driving out Main Street, remember that one?

Coral Watts (CW): Yes.

Unknown (U/K): Can you talk about it?

JL: When, about how long ago was that?

CW: About four or five months.

JL: Do you remember exactly when it happened or is that just sort of an estimate?

CW: About an estimate.

JL: There's nothing that you can relate to it that would pin it down closer or anything?

CW: No.

Tom Ladd (TL): Alright, on that night do you remember what time of night it was? Was it before midnight or after midnight?

CW: Um, I think it was after midnight.

TL: What were you doing that night? Just driving around?

CW: Yes.

TL: Alright, this particular girl, where did you first see her?

CW: Um, I'm not sure. I think I was on the street.

TL: Was she driving the vehicle?

CW: Yes.

TL: Alright, what kind of vehicle was she driving?

CW: A small blue car.

TL: Alright, what direction was she driving?

CW: I don't know.

TL: Was it towards . . . the freeway by the Astrodome, is that right?

CW: Okay, a . . . now what you talking about now?

TL: The direction the girl was driving when you saw her?

JL: First saw her.

CW: Oh, okay. I think we was mixed up a little. You was talking about one thing, I was talking about something else. Uh, she was driving down Main Street, the one you talking about.

TL: When you first saw her, she was already in her car driving?

CW: Yes.

TL: Alright, was she in a blue car?

CW: Yes.

TL: Alright, she was driving down Main Street going in what direction?

CW: Towards the Astrodome.

TL: Alright, did she cross over that, cross underneath that freeway and continue going down Main?

CW: Yeah.

TL: Okay, how far do you think you followed her?

CW: About a half, about a mile, half mile.

TL: Alright, then what happened?

CW: Uh, she turned off on the little street and went down that a way.

U/K: Which way would she have turned?

CW: Right.

TL: This way?

CW: Right.

TL: Did she turn right off Main?

CW: Uh huh.

TL: Alright, where she turned, was this a subdivision, a bunch of houses, or what?

CW: There was some houses.

TL: Okay, and you turned in behind her?

CW: Yeah.

TL: Do you think she was aware you were following her?

CW: Mmmmm, I don't know. I don't think so.

TL: Alright, then what happened?

CW: Uh, then she drove around the corner and went down about a half a block and I drove around the corner and parked at the corner. And when I got out the car another guy came around the corner and asked me if I knew how to get to some street or something or another. Then he drove off, cause I told him I didn't know how to get there. And he stopped where she was and asked her something and I don't know what it was, then he drove on off.

TL: Alright, was she out of her car?

CW: Yeah.

TL: Alright, did she have anything in her hands when she got out of the car?

CW: I don't know. Some papers and stuff.

TL: Alright, what type of papers?

CW: Drawing papers, blueprints, or something like that.

JL: Where would she have been stopped at? Was this in a neighborhood or was it on a main street or . . . ?

CW: In a neighborhood.

JL: It's in a neighborhood. Was it well-lit or was it, how was the lighting?

CW: Pretty lit.

JL: So she, correct then that she stopped on the street?

CW: Yes.

JL: Did she stop on the right hand side of the street or the left hand side of the street?

CW: On the right.

JL: The right. Was it in the middle of a block or was it on a corner or was it in a driveway or where?

CW: About the middle of the block, I think.

JL: Was it in a driveway?

CW: No.

JL: It was on a curb?

CW: Uh huh.

TL: Alright, she got out of the car and she had some papers in her hands, then what did you do? Just approach her from behind?

CW: Yeah, I was already walking up.

TL: Walking fast, slow, running?

CW: Running.

TL: When did she see you? How far were you from her when she saw you?

CW: Um, about five feet.

TL: She turn around and looked at you?

CW: Yeah.

TL: Then what happened?

Ted Thomas (TT): Did you have the knife in your hand?

CW: No.

TL: When she turned and looked at you, what happened?

CW: That's when I grabbed her.

TL: *Alright, how did you grab her?*

CW: *From the side.*

TL: *Alright, where did you grab her?*

CW: *Around the arm and by the neck.*

TL: *Around the arms and around the neck? Speak up Coral!*

CW: *Okay.*

TL: *Then what happened?*

CW: *Ah, then I choked her.*

TL: *Alright, how long did you choke her?*

CW: *Um, I don't know. About a minute, two.*

TL: *Did she struggle?*

CW: *Yeah.*

TL: *Did you hit her?*

CW: *No.*

TL: *You just choked her?*

CW: *Uh huh.*

TL: *You choked her to the ground?*

CW: *Uh huh.*

TL: *Alright, did she say anything?*

CW: *No.*

TL: *Did she fight?*

CW: *Yes.*

TL: *Alright, describe her as best you can remember.*

CW: *I think she was about 5' 4", blonde hair, and she wore glasses and stuff. And might have had a brown coat or something. I think it was a blue coat. Either blue or brown. One of the two.*

TL: *What type of pants, or did she have pants on or a dress or . . . ?*

CW: *I think it was a dress.*

TL: *Alright, after you killed her what did you do with her body?*

CW: *Put it in the trunk of the car.*

TL: Alright, were her keys in her hands or how did you open the trunk?

CW: Had the keys in her hands.

TL: Alright, when you opened the trunk, how did you put her in the trunk?

CW: I think it was face down.

TL: Alright, standing at the rear of the vehicle, looking towards it where the left tires would be on your left, the right tires would be on your right, did you put her head out the left side or the right side?

CW: The left side.

TL: Alright, did you have any trouble fitting her in the trunk?

CW: I don't think so.

TL: Alright, how did you position her legs?

CW: I think I might have folded one back.

TL: Folded one back?

CW: Uh huh.

TL: What about the other leg?

CW: I don't remember.

TL: Alright, did you, what about her shoes?

CW: I took them.

TL: You took them. Do you remember what kind of shoes they were?

CW: Uh, some kind of plastic shoes.

TL: Alright, and what about her socks?

CW: No, I don't remember.

TL: Alright, what else did you take from her?

CW: Some papers, a coat, and a purse, I think.

TL: Alright, and her shoes?

CW: Yeah.

TL: Did you take any other jewelry off her?

CW: I don't think so.

TL:　Alright, what else did you take? You said you took her purse?

CW:　Yes.

TL:　Describe the purse if you can remember it.

CW:　I don't remember what it looked like.

TL:　Was it a handheld purse or . . . ?

CW:　Like a bag or something.

TL:　Like a bag?

CW:　Yeah.

TL:　Alright, did you take anything else?

CW:　I don't think so.

TL:　Alright, what did you do with the drawings?

CW:　I think I burned them.

TL:　Alright, what about the purse?

CW:　That too.

TL:　Alright, the shoes?

CW:　I threw those away.

TL:　Where did you throw it?

CW:　In the trashbin.

TL:　Alright, what about her coat?

CW:　I threw that away.

TL:　Alright, why did you burn the drawings.

CW:　I figured it would kill the spirit.

JL:　The property you burned, you burned the drawings and what else was it you burned?

CW:　I think it was the bag, whatever it was.

JL:　Where did this burning take place at?

CW:　I don't remember. I just stopped and burned them.

JL:　How did you go about burning something like that?

CW:　Just take a match and burn it up.

JL:　Well, like the bag, obviously wouldn't, you know, just automatically burn up if you put a match under it.

Did you use any type of a something that accelerates flame or . . . ?

CW: No.

TL: *You burned the drawings and the bag at the same time?*

CW: Uh huh.

TT: *While we're on the drawings here, what did they look like?*

CW: Uh, looked like just drawings like a building or something.

TL: *Do you know if there was any damage to that car, which the girl was driving?*

CW: No.

TL: *Okay, what did you do with the keys? To the car?*

CW: I don't know.

U/K: *Remember a watch or anything like that?*

CW: No.

U/K: *There's a lot of areas you're sorta unsure on. We ask questions like this, talking about rings and watches and stuff and you seem to be unsure. Is that that you're unsure in your own mind on these cases if those things were taken or . . . ?*

CW: Yeah, I be sure. I'm not sure of what if I took it or not. I don't think I did.

U/K: *You don't think you did? Is it possible you could have though?*

CW: Yeah.

TL: *Did you take anything from inside the car?*

CW: No.

TL: *Did you go inside the car at all?*

CW: No.

TL: *Let me ask you something. Why did you put the body in the trunk?*

CW: No reason. I just put it there.

TL: *Why didn't you stab her?*

CW: *Just didn't, that wasn't, I didn't stab her.*

TT: *Had you already thrown the knife away? The kitchen knife you used on the other two?*

CW: *Yeah, I throwed that away.*

TL: *Alright, just for the records, that's gonna be the Margaret Fossi case we talked about.*

JL: *Do you remember reading anything about that case or anything after it happened?*

CW: *No.*

JL: *Do you read the newspapers?*

CW: *No.*

TL: *When was the last time you read a newspaper?*

CW: *In jail.*

TL: *Alright, before you were arrested, when was the last time you read a newspaper?*

CW: *Um, I'm not sure.*

TL: *A long time?*

CW: *Yeah.*

TL: *Alright, do you watch the news on television?*

CW: *Not too much.*

TL: *Did you hear, remember hearing anything at all about that particular case either on television, the radio, or read it in the newspaper?*

CW: *No.*

TL: *Did you know that she was a student at Rice?*

CW: *No.*

TL: *When did you first find out she was a student?*

CW: *Just now.*

TL: *First time you've known about it?*

CW: *Uh huh.*

JL: *You described her shoes, plastic shoes. Do you know what happened to them?*

CW: *I think I threw them away or something. I'm not really sure.*

TL: Any particular reason why you took her shoes?
CW: No.

Later that same morning, Coral Watts attacked Julie Sanchez as she repaired a flat tire on her automobile on the Southwest Freeway. Watts walked up behind her, grabbed her head, pulled it back, and slit her throat twice. Sanchez managed to escape, ran into traffic, and nearly caused a multicar pileup. She was rescued by her husband and taken to a nearby hospital. Sanchez barely survived the attack.

The following text is the actual interrogation and confession by Coral Eugene Watts in regard to the attack on Julie Sanchez:

Coral Watts (CW): Okay, well a girl was off by the Astrodome. Right off, was right off the freeway. It was on the freeway out by the Astrodome. There was a girl standing by a car and I walked up to her and grabbed her and cut her across the throat. Think they were changing a tire or something or other.

Jim Ladd (JL): You said "they"?

CW: Yeah, it was just one there when I got there but someone else may have been there and went off somewhere.

JL: How long ago was this?

CW: Um, I don't know. About a few months ago. About six months ago maybe.

JL: What time of day was it?

CW: It was at night."

Tom Ladd (TL): Was it on the freeway itself?

CW: Yeah. On the side of the freeway.

Ted Thomas (TT): On the service road or what?

CW: No, on the freeway, on the side where you pull over to the shoulder.

TT: Okay.

TL: Describe the person.

CW: Huh?

TL: Describe the person.

CW: Ah, I don't know. All I seen was her back. I think it was a short woman, kinda skinny.

TL: White or black?

CW: Wasn't black. Was either white or Mexican, either one.

TL: You say you cut her across the throat?

CW: Yeah.

TL: Deep?

CW: I don't know.

TL: What scared you off?

CW: She managed to get away and run into the freeway where the cars were coming.

TL: Did she get hit?

CW: I don't know. I turned around and walked away. She had on like a, well, she had on a shirt and some pants.

TL: Was she an older woman or a younger woman?

CW: I don't know.

TT: What kind of car was she changing a flat or what?

CW: Hmmm, I don't know that. Yeah, I think it was a Caprice maybe.

TL: New or older model?

CW: An older car.

TT: What color?

CW: Huh?

TT: What color was it?

CW: I'm not sure but I think it was green.

TT: Was the car jacked up?

CW: I think so.

TL: Was she there alone?

CW: Yeah.

TL: Did you see anybody come up?

CW: Yeah, that, somebody else came up and stopped right after she had ran into the freeway.

TL: Did she get in their car?

CW: Yeah.

TL: How bad did she bleed?

CW: I don't know.

TL: Was it just one slice across the throat?

CW: Yeah.

TL: Did she try to fight you or anything?

CW: Yeah.

TL: What did she do? Claw you or scratch you or kick you or what?

CW: She was scratching and kicking and somehow she got around and slipped under and ran out.

TL: Slipped under what?

CW: My arm.

TT: Did you cut her for sure?

CW: Yeah.

TT: Could you see the Astrodome from where you were at?

CW: It was just off Main, as you would turn off going down Main and making a right. Going towards the freeway, it was maybe a block or two blocks down past there.

TL: Going back away from the Astrodome?

CW: Yeah.

CHAPTER 27

The following text is the actual interrogation and confession by Coral Eugene Watts in regard to the attack on Alice Martell:

Tom Ladd (TL): Are you sure she was driving a solid white car?

Coral Watts (CW): Uh huh.

TL: Alright, you saw her . . . Is this about January, February? For the purpose of the tape, we're talking about a possible victim, at the time this occurrence was in the winter months believed to be in January or February. Coral Watts had driven to the Kemah-Seabrook area after following a female in a vehicle. During the course of his following this female she lost him, and at this time, he saw another female pulled over off the street past NASA. This female turned onto NASA Road 1 and drove in the direction of Highway 136. Alright, this is where we are right now. Alright, so how far did you follow her? All the way down that curvy road over the railroad tracks?

CW: Yeah.

TL: Alright, so she crossed over the railroad tracks and then across 136 then went back in those little . . .

CW: Uh huh.

TL: Little streets back there. Okay, then what happened?

CW: Ah, she stopped and got out.

TL: What did she stop in front of?

CW: Some kind of white apartments or something like that.

TL: Were there many apartments or just a few of them or what?

CW: There was . . . I'm not sure. I know they were white.

TL: She park her car?

CW: White apartment building.

TL: What?

CW: White apartment building.

TL: Did she park her car?

CW: Yeah.

TL: Alright, then what happened?

CW: She got out and walked into the apartment.

TL: Alright, did you come up behind her? Or to the side of her car or . . . ?

CW: Behind her.

TL: Directly behind her?

CW: Behind her.

TL: Okay, did she see you at this time when you pulled up behind her?

CW: Ah, she seen the car, I believe. Yeah.

TL: Alright, did she do anything?

CW: No.

TL: Did she appear to be alarmed in any way?

CW: No.

TL: Alright, so she's walking towards the apartments?

CW: Uh huh.

TL: Alright, then what happened?

CW: She had walked in and a . . .

TL: . . . Walked in where?

CW: *Into the apartment. By that time, I had got . . .
parked my car and got out and I was running up there and,
uh, then she turned around and looked and I just kept running up there and I grabbed her.*

TL: *What, had she already opened her door? To the
apartment?*

CW: *. . . stopped walking and turned around.*

TL: *How close was she to the building when you grabbed
her?*

CW: *What you mean "to the building"?*

TL: *Was she within like the front porch or . . . ?*

CW: *She was just like downstairs on the sidewalk.*

TL: *Alright, you grabbed her, then what happened?*

CW: *I choked her.*

TL: *How did you choke her?*

CW: *I'm not sure. Front maybe, I guess.*

TL: *Was she originally fighting and struggling?*

CW: *Yeah.*

TL: *Did she quit?*

CW: *Yeah.*

TL: *Alright, then what did you do?*

CW: *Then I stabbed her.*

TL: *Alright, how many times did you stab her?*

CW: *Ummm, about five times, I think.*

TL: *Alright, what area of the body did you stab her?*

CW: *In the chest.*

TL: *Did she fight or make any sound while you stabbed
her?*

CW: *No.*

TL: *What kind of knife were you using?*

CW: *It was an ice pick.*

TL: *An ice pick? Did you stab her hard to the point
where the ice pick went entirely into the body cavity? To the
hilt?*

CW: *I'm not sure.*

TL: *Alright, what made you stop?*

CW: *Nothing. I just thought that she was dead and I got up and walked away.*

TL: *Alright, what made you think she was dead?*

CW: *I had stabbed her.*

TL: *Were all the stab wounds approximately the same area or were they . . . how were they?*

CW: *I'm not sure.*

TL: *You said when you were stabbing her, you were stabbing her hard or were you with a lot of thrust to the ice pick?*

CW: *I believe so.*

TL: *Alright, what happened to the ice pick?*

CW: *I don't know what I did with that.*

TL: *Okay. Do you remember what she was wearing?*

CW: *No.*

TL: *Alright, was she white or black?*

CW: *White.*

TL: *Alright, how old was she?*

CW: *I don't know.*

TL: *Alright, you seem to be a little vague on this particular description. Could you tell if she was your age or younger or was she the general age of all the other girls that you've described or was there anything different from her appearance than the others?*

CW: *No. She was about the same age, I guess. Yeah, about the same age.*

TL: *What age?*

CW: *About twenty-five, I guess.*

TL: *Alright, was she tall or short?*

CW: *Tall, I think.*

TL: *Alright, what hair color?*

CW: *Dark brown.*

TL: *How did she wear it?*

CW: Long, to the back.

TL: Way to back, past her shoulders?

CW: I'm not sure about that.

TL: Alright, you remember if she had any shoes on?

CW: High heels.

TL: Alright, what did you take from her?

CW: I'm not sure. I think I took her purse.

TL: Alright, what kind of purse did she have?

CW: I think it was burgundy. I'm not really sure about that. I think it was.

TL: Was there anything in the purse?

CW: I don't remember.

TL: What did you do with it?

CW: Burned it.

TL: To kill her spirit?

CW: Yeah.

TL: Remember where you burned it?

CW: No.

TL: The girl say anything at all during the attack?

CW: No.

TL: Was she screaming?

CW: Maybe once or twice.

TL: Did anybody come to her rescue or aid?

CW: No.

TL: What time of day or night was this?

CW: It was about 4:00 I guess.

TL: In the afternoon? Or in the morning?

CW: At night.

TL: Alright, the car was a small white car. Was there anything else about the car that you can remember?

CW: No. No, I don't. No, it was just small white.

TL: Bucket seats? Or did you ever look in the car?

CW: No.

TL: Alright, when you left her was she laying motionless?

CW: Yeah.

TL: Alright, did you have her, when you stabbed her was she on the ground when you stabbed her? Or was she standing up?

CW: On the ground.

TL: Alright, where were you? Were you straddled over her or to her si . . . to her right or to her left?

CW: To the left. From the right to the left.

TL: To her left?

CW: Yeah. To her right, to my left.

TL: To your left. All right, so you were on her right?

CW: Yeah.

TL: Alright, and when you left her she was laying motionless? Was she laying on her back or on her stomach?

CW: On her back.

TL: On her back. Was her arms, do you know if her arms were outstretched or to her side?

CW: No.

TL: Did she have any jewelry that you can recall?

CW: No.

TL: The only thing you took off of her was her purse?

CW: Uh huh.

TL: Did she have her keys in her hand?

CW: No, I don't remember that.

TL: Alright, what about her purse? Was she carrying her purse in her hand or did she have it hooked over her shoulders?

CW: In her hand, I believe.

TL: Did she try to defend herself in any way?

CW: Yeah.

TL: How?

CW: To get loose.

TL: Did she try to scratch or kick or claw or anything like that?

CW: No, she just tried to get loose.

TL: And the only thing you took from her was her purse? You didn't remove any articles of clothing?

CW: No.

TL: Do you remember if she was wearing a jacket or some kind of coat?

CW: She had a coat on, I know.

TL: Do you remember what color it was?

CW: It was a dark color. I don't know exactly what color.

TL: Was it a full-length coat down to her knees or like a jacket to her waist?

CW: Somewhere in between.

TL: Alright, what car were you driving?

CW: Grand Prix.

TL: And to your knowledge, no one saw you?

CW: No.

TL: Did you dispose of the purse the same day that you stabbed her?

CW: Uh huh.

TL: Did you have an opportunity to look through it?

CW: Yeah, I did go through it. Yeah.

TL: Did you dump the contents out before you burned the purse?

CW: No.

TL: Was there a lot of different items in the purse or . . . ?

CW: I don't remember that.

TL: Alright, so the victim was laying on her back, you had choked her, with your hands or did you use any kind of clothing or . . . ?

CW: With my hands.

TL: Were you wearing gloves?

CW: No.

TL: Okay, and after you choked her into unconscious-

*ness she was on the ground and you were to her right. That's
when you stabbed her with an ice pick?*

CW: Uh huh.

TL: *And you think you stabbed her five times? In what
area of the body?*

CW: The chest.

TL: *Are you talking about the left side of the chest or the
right side of the chest?*

CW: Left side.

TL: *Alright, when you stabbed her, was she moving at
any time then, or . . . ?*

CW: I don't think so.

TL: *She was motionless when you stabbed her with the
ice pick? Ah, did you feel like it was necessary to stab her?
Did you think you had already killed her by choking her or
did you think it was necessary to stab her to finish the job?*

CW: I just stabbed her.

TL: *No particular reason? Why did you stab her?*

CW: That's what I had to do to her. Stab her.

TL: *What purpose? Why did you pick this girl?*

CW: I had seen her.

TL: *And the first time you had seen her, she was in her
car driving?*

CW: Yeah, she was coming across the light.

TL: *All right, so in other words, you were going in one direction, came to the intersection. Were you stopped at a red
light?*

CW: Uh huh.

TL: *Do you have any idea how long in time you followed
her?*

CW: No, I don't.

TL: *Was she driving erratic or anything like that, that
made you think she was trying to get away from you?*

CW: Not that I remember.

TL: In your mind do you feel like she even knew you were present? Prior to you grabbing her?

CW: No.

TL: Did you see her bleed? From the stabbing?

CW: It was a little. Not much.

Jim Ladd (JL): Through her clothes?

CW: Uh huh.

TL: You stabbed her through her clothes?

CW: Yeah.

TL: You saw a small amount of blood on her clothes?

CW: I believe so, yeah.

TL: This took place somewhere down in . . . have you ever been in NASA before? Where the missiles are?

CW: Uh uh.

TL: Alright, now I'm gonna give you a rough description of that facility and see if it matches what you're talking about when you say the missiles. Driving in the direction you were driving, away from the Gulf Freeway, this facility would be on your left. This facility houses several buildings, large buildings. And in front of these buildings there's probably a 100 [to] 150 square yards area there's numerous rockets that are on display representing different projectiles that were sent into space. Proceeding past these missiles or rockets, whatever you want to call them, you would encounter a bridge which kinda goes over a small bayou or a small stream and immediately to your right you could see a body of water. Does this sound familiar to you? As you cross the bridge, when you cross the bridge and look to your right you see a large body of water.

CW: Okay.

TL: Alright, and as you drive down this road this body of water continues to run parallel to the road. Alright, that would probably be NASA, then shortly afterwards, after crossing the bridge you would come to a red light and *then from that red light would be a series of what you describe as hooks or turns in the road. Where the road is actually winding but still continuing in the direction of Highway 146. Does that sound familiar?*

CW: Uh, yeah.

TL: Alright, and you definitely remember going over some railroad tracks?

CW: I'm not sure about the tracks.

TL: Alright, but you came to a junction in the road and you had to either go left or right and there was a light? Or you could go straight ahead and go about in a bunch of small streets that kinda curved around?

CW: Yeah.

TL: Alright, this is where the attack took place?

CW: Yeah.

TL: She was wearing high heel shoes, a coat, probably down to her waist or longer, dark coat. Do you know if she was wearing a skirt or pants?

CW: A dress, I believe.

TL: Okay, do you know what color the dress was or anything about the dress?

CW: Dark color.

TL: Dark colored dress. Did she have makeup on like she looked like she just came from work, from a party, or from her boyfriend's house? She have any . . . ?

CW: I'm not sure about that.

TL: What about her shoes? Were they high heels?

CW: Yeah.

TL: What color were they?

CW: Brown or burgundy, I guess.

Ted Thomas (TT): What finally happened to the shoes?

CW: Nothing.

TT: You still got them?

CW: I don't think I took the shoes.

CHAPTER 28

The following text is the actual interrogation and confession by Coral Eugene Watts in regard to the murder of Elena Semander:

Jim Ladd (JL): Yesterday when we were talking we were discussing if you had ever placed any women actually inside a Dumpster. Was it, am I correct in assuming you told us yesterday that you had?

Coral Watts (CW): Yeah.

Tom Ladd (TL): Alright, what time of the day or the night did this one occur where you placed the female in the Dumpster? Was it before midnight or after midnight?

CW: I'm not sure.

JL: Do you know what day of the week this might have been?

CW: No.

JL: Was there any particular day of the week or anything that most of these things have happened on?

CW: The weekend.

JL: You say that most of them would be weekends or would all of them be on weekends? Would it be unusual for you to do something on Tuesday or Wednesday?

CW: No.

JL: So, you did do some of them during the middle of the week? But most of them on weekends, is that correct?

CW: Uh huh.

TL: Alright, where did you first see this girl?

CW: On the street somewhere.

TL: Alright, first of all, were you driving around in your car when you saw her? Or were you walking?

CW: Driving.

TL: You were driving, the same Grand Prix?

CW: Yeah.

TL: Alright, do you remember where she was when you first saw her? What area of town?

CW: No.

TL: Whether it was in the North side of town? South side of town?

CW: I don't know.

TL: Was she driving, was her car one of among many cars in traffic or was it real late at night where just a few cars were out?

CW: There were quite a few cars out there.

TL: Alright, how did you spot her? What brought your attention to this one particular girl?

CW: It was at a light or something or other.

TL: She was stopped at a light.

CW: Yeah.

TL: Alright, did you pull up aside her or behind her?

CW: I was going the other way.

TL: And you turned around?

CW: Yeah.

TL: Alright, what kind of car was she driving?

CW: A brown station wagon, I believe.

TL: Large or small?

CW: Small.

TL: *Alright, how far did you follow her?*

CW: *I don't know.*

TL: *A long distance or . . . ?*

CW: *I'm not sure, it may have been a long distance.*

TL: *Alright, was she by herself?*

CW: *Yes.*

TL: *Alright, where did she go?*

CW: *To her apartment.*

TL: *Know what apartments they were?*

CW: *No.*

JL: *What did she look like?*

CW: *Had dark hair with a furry coat?*

Unknown (U/K): How old of a woman was she?

CW: *I don't remember.*

*U/K: What would you say? What would you give [as] a
reasonable guess? Young or old or in between?*

CW: *Guess about twenty-two or twenty-three.*

TL: *About how tall was she?*

CW: *About 5'5", 5'4".*

TL: *Remember anything else about her?*

U/K: Thin or heavy? What would you say?

CW: *In between I guess.*

TL: *You said she had a coat. What kind of coat did she
have?*

CW: *A furry coat, kinda like . . .*

TL: *Fur coat?*

CW: *Yeah.*

TL: *Remember what color?*

CW: *Dark brown.*

TL: *Solid dark brown?*

CW: *Yeah.*

TL: *She was wearing it?*

CW: *Yeah.*

TL: *Alright, she drove up into some apartments?*

CW: Uh huh.

TL: Where did she park her car?

CW: On the, on the curb.

TL: In front of the apartments or behind the apartments? Or inside the apartments?

CW: On the side.

TL: On the side of the apartments? Alright, then you parked in behind her?

CW: No, down the street.

TL: Down the street, huh? Could you still see her from where you parked and where she parked?

CW: Yeah.

TL: Alright, she got out of her car?

CW: Uh huh.

TL: Alright, then what happened? Do you remember what direction she walked? Did she walk towards the apartments or away from the apartments?

CW: Towards the apartments.

TL: Alright, you followed behind her?

JL: And where was it, where was it that you grabbed hold of her?

CW: Um, I forgot. I lost her, she went somewhere and then she came back out from the apartments to get in her car.

JL: How long was she gone?

CW: I don't know. About two or three minutes.

TL: The next time you saw her she was coming back to her car?

CW: Yeah.

TL: All right, then you approached her. Were you running towards her?

CW: Walking.

TL: Alright, when did she, did she realize that you were present?

CW: Yeah.

TL: When? How far away were you from her?

CW: About a good little ways.

TL: Fifteen, twenty feet? More?

CW: About twenty, about fifteen feet.

TL: Alright, then what happened?

CW: She walked over and got in her car.

U/K: Did she get in, actually get into the car?

CW: Yeah.

TL: Then what happened?

CW: Then I walked over to the car and she said something. Open up, getting out of the car.

TL: She said what?

CW: Something, I don't know what she said. She got up to get out the car.

TL: She got back out of the car?

CW: Yeah.

TL: Did she know you were standing there, right close to her?

CW: Yeah.

TL: Did you tell her to get out?

CW: No.

TL: Do you know why she got out of the car?

CW: She was trying to flag somebody down.

TL: Did she see somebody?

CW: Yeah.

TL: Alright, who did she flag down or who was she trying to flag down?

CW: It was some people going by.

TL: They were walking or driving?

CW: Driving.

TL: Alright, so she stepped out of the car to flag these people down?

CW: Yeah, she blew her horn at them or something, then got out of the car.

TL: *Do you think she realized you were there?*

CW: *Yeah.*

TL: *Do you think she was blowing the horn trying to get some help?*

CW: *Yeah.*

TL: *Or did you say anything to her at all?*

CW: *No.*

TL: *You didn't say anything at all?*

CW: *No.*

TL: *Alright, then what happened?*

CW: *I grabbed her and choked her.*

JL: *Where did all this take place after you grabbed her?*

CW: *On the other side of the car.*

JL: *Was she already out on the other side of the car?*

CW: *No.*

JL: *So, you grabbed her, she was by her driver's door?*

CW: *Yeah.*

JL: *Okay, and then where did you take her?*

CW: *On the other side of the car.*

TL: *On the passenger side?*

CW: *Yeah, on the grass, on the other side of the car. Across the sidewalk. Or whatever.*

TL: *Was there anything near the car?*

CW: *No.*

TL: *Did she fight?*

CW: *Yeah.*

TL: *Was she still wearing that coat?*

CW: *Yeah.*

TL: *Remember what she said during her struggle?*

CW: *No.*

TL: *Then what happened?*

JL: *What was this that you choked her with?*

CW: *My hands.*

JL: *Okay, then what happened?*

CW: Then I took, took her coat and her pants and shirt off.

JL: You took her coat, pants and shirt all the way off?

CW: Yes.

JL: Then what happened?

CW: I tied the shirt around her neck and one end around her leg.

TL: You tied the shirt around her neck?

CW: Uh huh.

JL: What did you do this for?

CW: I don't know.

TL: So you tied the shirt around her neck, then you tied her legs?

CW: Uh huh.

TL: With what?

CW: The other end of the shirt.

TL: Did you have her bent?

CW: Yeah.

TL: Were her legs behind her back?

CW: Uh huh.

TL: Alright, then what did you do?

CW: Picked her up and put her in the Dumpster.

TL: Remember what the Dumpster looked like? What color it was?

CW: Gray, I believe.

TL: Was it a tall Dumpster or . . . ?

CW: A short one.

TL: Was she heavy to lift?

CW: Yeah.

JL: Was the Dumpster, was it full or was it empty or how would you say the volume of the Dumpster [was] at the time that you put here in there?

CW: Full. Well, almost full.

Ted Thomas (TT): Did she go in the top or the side door?

CW: Over the top.

TL: Alright, what property did you keep? That belonged to her?

CW: I think a coat, a watch. May have been a ring.

JL: How many rings?

CW: Two, I think. And the pants.

TL: Did you take her shoes?

CW: I don't know. I don't think so. I don't know.

JL: You remember what kind of watch it was?

CW: Uh huh.

JL: Would it have been silver?

CW: I don't remember.

TL: What did you do with the watch and ring?

CW: Threw them away.

TL: Know where you threw them?

CW: In the garbage.

TL: Why did you take the watch and rings if you were going to throw them away later on?

CW: I don't know. I just took them.

JL: Where would this Dumpster be that you threw the stuff?

CW: I don't remember.

JL: Was it the same one that you placed the body in?

CW: No.

U/K: Was it on the same street?

CW: No.

U/K: About how far away was it? Do you think?

CW: Oh, about two miles I guess.

TL: You threw it away the same day you killed the girl?

CW: Yeah.

TL: Anybody see you or did anybody come out or were present prior to you throwing the girl in the Dumpster?

CW: Yeah.

TL: *Remember who it was? Was it a male or female or how many?*

CW: *About three or four people.*

TL: *Males, females?*

CW: *I'm not sure. I think it was two males and a female.*

TL: *They say anything or look in your direction . . . ?*

CW: *Yeah.*

TL: *What did they say?*

CW: *Nothing, they just looked and drove on off. Drove up into their apartment.*

TL: *Alright, had you already thrown the girl in the Dumpster when these people come out?*

CW: *No.*

TL: *Had you already strangled her?*

CW: *No.*

TL: *Were you fighting with her then?*

CW: *Yeah.*

JL: *Do you remember what color her blouse was?*

CW: *It might have been black, I think.*

U/K: *What about her purse?*

CW: *I don't remember.*

JL: *Do you remember seeing her purse?*

CW: *No.*

JL: *You don't remember taking her purse or anything you know about the purse? What might have happened to it or where it might have been placed or anything?*

CW: *No.*

TL: *Why didn't you put her in the car? What made you decide to put her in the Dumpster?*

CW: *I don't know. I just put her in the Dumpster.*

TL: *It was right there close?*

CW: *I guess.*

TL: *Was the Dumpster close to where you strangled her?*

CW: *Yeah.*

TL: *How close?*

CW: *Right there. Right next to where I was.*

JL: *Ever placed anybody else in a Dumpster? In Harris County?*

CW: *No.*

U/K: *Ever place anybody by a Dumpster?*

CW: *I don't think so.*

JL: *This same night. What were you driving that night?*

CW: *I think I was driving my van.*

TT: *Did you notice if she had been drinking or anything?*

CW: *No.*

TT: *Smell any alcohol on her? Or when you saw her in traffic was she weaving or anything when you pulled up?*

CW: *No.*

JL: *Did you have any sexual contact with this woman?*

CW: *No.*

JL: *Or anything sexual at all to do with any part of her?*

CW: *No.*

CHAPTER 29

The following text is the actual interrogation and confession by Coral Eugene Watts in regard to the murder of Yolanda Gracia:

Jim Ladd (JL): The next case we're talking about is one you were telling us about yesterday when you were talking about driving around Hobby Airport. And watching the girl walking down the street. The Spanish girl. Remember that one?

Coral Watts (CW): Uh huh.

Tom Ladd (TL): Speak up now, Coral.

JL: To start with what time of day or night was this?

CW: I think it was in the evening.

JL: How late in the evening?

CW: Uh, I'm not sure. In between light and dark, getting, just starting to get dark.

JL: Where did you first see her?

CW: Walking. At a corner by a light. To an intersection. Uh, two lights, traffic lights.

JL: Is it a big intersection?

CW: Yeah.

JL: Do you remember what else was on that intersection?

CW: A motel, I think, and a gas station.

TL: Was she walking by herself?

CW: Uh huh.

JL: This was a Spanish female? Is that correct? Was she Mexican?

CW: I think so.

JL: About how old of a woman was she?

CW: I don't know. About twenty-five, twenty-eight. Something like that.

TL: Did she come out of a store or anything or . . . ?

CW: No.

TL: First time you spotted her she was just walking down the street?

CW: Yeah.

JL: Do you know that area of town very well?

CW: No.

TL: What were you doing out there?

CW: Driving.

JL: Do you even know the names of any of the streets that you were near?

CW: No.

JL: Would you recognize it if you saw it again?

CW: Yeah.

JL: This area. What was this? You say this was, this one was twenty-five, twenty-eight years old. Do you remember what she was wearing?

CW: I think it was a white dress. It might have flowers in it or something or other and glasses.

JL: What else did she have on?

CW: That's all that I can remember.

TL: Was she carrying anything?

CW: She might have had a purse, I think.

JL: You say it was almost dark?

CW: Uh huh.

TL: *What, did you follow behind her in your car?*

CW: *No, I parked the car and got out.*

TL: *Was this behind her, then walked up behind her or did you pass her and park the car, get out, and let her walk towards you?*

CW: *I passed her and parked the car.*

TL: *Let her come towards you?*

CW: *Uh huh.*

TL: *By the time she reached the point where you were, was she in some kind of neighborhood or what?*

CW: *Yeah.*

TL: *Houses on both sides of the street?*

CW: *Uh huh.*

Unknown (U/K):   *What about any other businesses, do you remember?*

CW: *No.*

Ted Thomas (TT):   *All residential?*

CW: *Yeah.*

JL: *At this time, was it, how was the lighting? Was it to where you could see a good distance or a . . . ?*

CW: *Yeah.*

JL: *So it was still, people could probably still see you if anybody was watching?*

CW: *Yeah.*

JL: *Isn't this kind of unusual? For you? Like in that light in the neighborhood where people could see you for distances and such as that?*

CW: *It didn't seem unusual to me.*

JL: *Did you see anybody around before this happened?*

CW: *Yeah, there was some people. There was some people in a car, ah, white car. I think it was an old Plymouth or something.*

JL: *Why'd you kill her Coral?*

CW: *Evil eyes. She had evil in her eyes.*

CHAPTER 30

The following text is the actual interrogation and confession by Coral Eugene Watts in regard to the murder of Michelle Maday:

Jim Ladd (JL): Okay, the two men were talking to each other. They went their own way. She got out of the car. Then what did she do?

Coral Watts (CW): Oh, then she walked across the street and passed where I was.

JL: Then what did she do?

CW: She walked over to a door and pulled out some keys to go in.

Unknown (U/K): When she walked in, are we talking about walking into an apartment complex? Or where did she go into?

CW: To apartment complex.

JL: So then she came in from her car and I assume there's a sidewalk there?

CW: Uh huh.

JL: When she came into this set of apartments would she have went to her left or to her right?

CW: To the left.

JL: Would she have been near the street or would she have been going back deep into the apartments?

CW: Near the . . .

JL: So, she walked into the apartment project itself, to that set of apartments, not too far when she went to the left?

CW: Uh huh.

Ted Thomas (TT): How far would you say?

CW: Ummm, probably the first turnoff.

Tom Ladd (TL): Apartment upstairs or downstairs?

CW: Downstairs.

TL: She got the keys in her hands, then what happened?

CW: Ah, she went to open the door. And I walked up and then she turned around and looked at me I think. I think she said something or mumbled something or something like that and turned back around. Then I grabbed her.

JL: When she opened the door?

CW: No.

TL: You grabbed her how?

CW: By the neck.

TL: Alright, then what happened?

CW: I choked her.

TL: To what point? Did you kill her right there?

CW: Yeah.

TL: Before she was in her apartment?

CW: Uh huh.

TT: Well, were you ever out in the . . . out in the front yard when you did this? On the grass or what?

CW: Yeah, out, right there out in front by the sidewalk.

TL: Then what did you do?

CW: Went and opened the door, took her inside.

TL: Alright, once you got her inside what did you do then?

CW: Hummm, took her dress off.

TL: Where? In the living room?

CW: Yeah.

TL: What else did you take off of her?

CW: Umm, like her ring and her necklace.

TL: She have any other clothes on other than her dress?

CW: No.

TL: She didn't have a bra or panties?

CW: I don't think so.

TL: Alright, then what?

CW: Then I took her and put her in the bathtub.

TL: Why did you put her in the bathtub?

CW: To run . . . I just put here in there and I ran water on her.

TL: You ran water on her? Did you have her . . . was her head down by the faucet or was it at the back of the tub?

CW: At the back of the tub.

TL: You mean her feet were down by the faucet?

CW: Uh huh.

TL: And you ran water on her?

CW: Yeah.

TL: Hot or cold water?

CW: Ah, hot water, I think.

TL: How long did you run water on her?

CW: 'Til the tub was full.

TL: Alright, did you block the drains some way?

CW: Yeah.

TL: How did you do that?

CW: Think there was a stopper in there or something.

TL: With a stopper?

CW: Yeah.

TL: Alright, when the tub was full, then what?

CW: Then I let the water out.

TL: Alright, why did you do this?

CW: So that her spirit couldn't get out.

JL: How was she laying in the tub? Face up?

CW: I don't remember. On her side I think.

JL: On her side with her face pointing in which direction?

CW: I don't remember.

TL: You're sure she was dead though before you put her in the tub?

CW: Yeah.

TL: With her eyes open?

CW: Yeah.

TL: Did you have to hold her down in the water as it filled up the tub?

TT: Or did she float up?

CW: I don't remember.

TT: Did you completely cover her with water?

CW: No, not really. I think so, but it wasn't, the tub wasn't all the way full.

TT: What did you do? Cover her with water?

CW: Yeah.

TT: Is that what you're saying?

CW: Uh huh.

TL: Then what did you do? After you let the water out?

CW: Tore up the place.

TL: In what way? How did you tear it up?

CW: Threw stuff all over.

TL: In what rooms?

CW: The bedroom.

TL: Her bedroom?

CW: Yeah.

TL: What else?

CW: That's all I think.

TL: What about the living room?

CW: I don't remember.

TL: What was the purpose for tearing up the rooms?

CW: None.

TL: You had no reason in mind for doing it? Were you

*trying to make it look like a burglary or something like that?
Or were you just doing it?*

CW: I was just doing it.

TT: Where was . . . where was the bedroom located to the bathroom?

CW: Um, almost right next to it I think. There was [a] bedroom here and then a bathroom on the left side, I think.

TT: As you entered the house, which would be . . . which would be on the left and which would be on the right?

CW: Bathroom would be on the left.

TT: And the bathroom would be on the right?

CW: Yeah.

JL: Were there any pets in this apartment?

CW: I didn't see any.

TL: You do anything with her car?

CW: No.

TL: Did you ever go in it or touch it?

CW: No.

TL: What did you take out of the apartment?

CW: Um, her dress and some jewelry.

TL: Alright, the dress. The same dress she was wearing?

CW: Yeah.

TL: And what type of jewelry?

CW: Necklace and two rings she had on her.

TL: Was she wearing the necklace?

CW: Yeah.

TL: And the rings?

CW: Uh huh.

TL: How many rings did she have on?

CW: Um, I don't know.

TL: Okay, what did you do with the jewelry?

CW: Threw it away.

TL: Do you remember where?

CW: Yeah.

TL: *Where?*

CW: *In a sewer.*

JL: *Why did you take the jewelry?*

CW: *I don't know. I just took it.*

JL: *You seem to have a reason for, like, taking the clothes and stuff. I just wondered why you'd take jewelry?*

CW: *Um, no reason. I just took it off.*

TL: *Was this a regular chain necklace . . . or was there stone or . . . ?*

CW: *Uh, regular chain necklace I believe.*

TL: *What did you do with the dress?*

CW: *Threw it away.*

TL: *Remember where you threw it?*

CW: *Umm, yeah, on a . . . in her apartment place somewhere.*

TL: *Where in the apartment place?*

CW: *This . . . it was a different apartment. Some apartments somewhere else.*

TL: *Just threw it on the ground out there? Or in a Dumpster? Or what?*

CW: *Umm, on the ground.*

TT: *Did the dress have a belt?*

CW: *Yeah.*

TT: *What color was it?*

CW: *Ah, white.*

TT: *Was it leather, material, or what?*

CW: *Material.*

JL: *Why did you not burn the dress?*

CW: *I didn't have to.*

JL: *Why didn't you have to? Why did you not have to?*

CW: *Because I had put her in the bathtub.*

* * *

Once again, Coral Eugene Watts's lust for death was not satisfied. After he murdered Maday, he then drove to the northwestern side of town, where he encountered Lori Lister and Melinda Aguilar.

The following text is the actual interrogation and confession by Coral Eugene Watts in regard to the attacks on Lori Lister and Melinda Aguilar:

Jim Ladd (JL): You know, I said that, you know, about the bathtubs. I was just checking back through here and I notice you did the rest of them outside.

Ted Thomas (TT): On the last one you did, were you wearing gloves?

Coral Watts (CW): Right.

TT: In the bathtub?

CW: Uh huh.

TT: You were wearing gloves that time?

JL: On the . . . previous one, the first one that you put in the bathtub, I think you said, correct me if I'm wrong, but I think you said that she was dead when you put her in the bathtub.

CW: Uh huh.

JL: Okay, on the case that you were caught on and which you've taken the plea for, that woman was not dead when you put her in the bathtub.

CW: No.

TT: Did you think she was dead?

CW: At first I did.

TT: When you first put her in the tub you did?

CW: No, before I put her in the tub. Before I brung her up the step.

Unknown (U/K): How did you know which apartment she lived in?

CW: She was . . .

*U/K: If you were down at the base of those steps with apart-
ments all around, how did you know which one it was in
particular that she lived in?*

CW: She stay in the one that was upstairs. Because . . .

*U/K: There were several upstairs. How did you know
which one upstairs it . . . ?*

*CW: There were two I think. I just went up the steps and
tried the lock and went in.*

*TT: What were your plans for the second girl? What were
you going to do with her?*

CW: Same thing as the first lady.

*TT: Were you planning to put her in the bathtub also?
Had your plans gone that far?*

CW: No, not at first.

*JL: It was kinda unusual, the fact that you went in the
closet and took coat hangers, flexible enough to bend to secure
their hands behind them. Ever done that before?*

CW: No.

After Watts had completed his confessions, he spoke
with Detective Tom Ladd. He told Ladd he was glad
they captured him and he hoped he never got out of
prison. The reason why, he told Ladd, was that he "would
kill again" if he was ever released.

Detective Paul Bunten eventually spoke with Watts.
Bunten tried to elicit confessions in the three Ann Arbor
murders; however, he was unsuccessful. Watts would talk
only if he received the plea deal. Bunten had no intention of bargaining with Watts. He did, however, try to find
out just how sinister Watts truly had been.

"How many people have you killed, Coral?" Bunten asked.

"There aren't enough fingers and toes in this room to match how many I killed," Watts stated without braggadocio.

There were three other people in the room in addition to Watts and Bunten.

A total of one hundred fingers and toes.

CHAPTER 31

On Tuesday, August 10, 1982, at 2:15 P.M., Coral Watts led police to a partially fenced-in vacant lot at the 700 block of Antoine Drive, just south of the Katy Freeway, on the western side of Houston. District Attorney John B. Holmes Jr. called the trip a "show of good faith" on Watts's part.

Watts was there to lead investigators to the grave of Suzanne Searles.

He was accompanied by his defense attorneys, Zinetta Burney and Don Caggins, various assistant district attorneys, and a team of six detectives, as well as the chief medical examiner.

The vacant lot was blanketed with overgrown weeds. One of the detectives on the scene went directly to where Watts pointed out where he believed the body to be. After less than an hour of digging, the detectives uncovered something unusual. They had to dig almost two feet deep in the corner of the vacant lot. What they found made some of the men sick.

It was the decomposed body of Sue Searles. Her discolored corpse had withered away to a scant sixty-seven pounds. Her body lay prone on its right side. The officers dug nearly three-and-a-half feet deep to unearth completely the once-vibrant young woman.

Watts stood next to the grave site as the detectives dug up Suzanne Searles's body. He was dressed in a beige button-down shirt, which was opened all the way to the waist, and blue jeans. His hands were bound together in front of his waist with handcuffs. Watts appeared nonplussed as the digging continued. He also answered every one of the detectives' questions.

As the trustees dug closer to Searles's body, Watts began to spill the beans about another body. Detective H. W. Kersen stated that "when we got to the point where we thought we had reached the woman, he decided to tell us about the other woman."

The other woman in question was Carrie Mae Jefferson.

Harris County chief medical examiner Cecil Wingo, who came to the grave-digging scene, gave a quick perusal of Suzanne Searles's corpse. He indicated that she had been dead for several months, as noted by the decomposition of her body. He could not determine her age or cause of death, due to the advanced stage of decomposition. She had no distinctive identification marks on her body, such as a tattoo or birthmark. She still wore a "necklace and a ring with a large flat stone setting," in addition to a bra and a pair of socks.

Watts never seemed upset or remorseful about the uncovering of Suzanne Searles's body. Prosecutor Ira Jones recalled, "We were there digging up a woman and it didn't seem to bother him. He wanted a hamburger; so when we were done, we took him out and bought him a hamburger."

* * *

The following day, Wednesday, August 11, 1982, Coral Watts went before Judge Douglas Shaver to plead guilty to charges of burglary. The judge informed Watts that his sentencing would take place the following week.

Later that same day, Watts informed authorities of the location of the body of Carrie Mae Jefferson, who had been missing since April 15, 1982. This time, at least a dozen detectives packed along some Harris City Jail trustees to help search for the body. The group, which again included Watts, Burney, and Caggins, headed toward the Astrodome. Their destination, according to Watts, was the 1900 block of White Oak Drive and Taylor Street, next to the White Oak Bayou.

After scouring the tall weeds that encompassed the north bank of the bayou, the trustees began the difficult job of digging. At approximately 5:00 P.M., in a relatively short period of time, the trustees were able to unearth Jefferson's body from a grave forty inches deep. Jefferson's body was less than one mile away from where detectives had uncovered Sue Searles's body.

Jefferson's body, like Searles's, was partly decomposed but intact. She was wearing a bra, panties, and a blouse. Medical Examiner Wingo was unable to determine cause of death from the initial observation. Dental records would have to be used eventually to confirm the identification of the body.

The following day, Thursday, August 12, 1982, Watts directed authorities to a third body. This time it was fourteen-year-old Emily LaQua.

Lieutenant Guy A. Mason and Detective Mike Kardatzke were informed by Watts's attorney Don Caggins that Emily LaQua's body was located in a drainage ditch in Brookshire,

Texas, located approximately thirty-seven miles west of downtown Houston. It also happened to be located in Waller County—not Harris County, per Watts's plea bargain.

Watts's directions were spot-on.

At approximately 7:00 P.M., a body was located in a field about 150 yards off Interstate 10, at Bains Street. Crammed inside a two-foot-wide metal drainage pipe, which was used as a culvert, covered in dirt, lay the mangled body of Emily LaQua, the fourteen-year-old runaway from Washington State.

As the three men removed the young girl's badly decomposed corpse, it broke apart in their hands. They were unable to determine at first whose body it was. They could not even tell what sex or what race it was. But they assumed it was Emily LaQua's.

The clothes on the body had deteriorated. Also, a locket that contained a photo of Emily, her brother, her sister, and her mother, which was taken for the family's 1981 Christmas card, was found near her body.

For the third day in a row, Coral Watts promised to lead detectives to the unmarked graves of three of his victims, and did as promised. Ira Jones commented that he "led us to three graves and he hits them bull's-eyes."

Later that night, Watts took a trip to the beach. He, along with Tom Ladd, who drove, Zinetta Burney, Detective Felix Bergara, and Galveston County investigator Felix Mares headed out in a car to the eastern end of Galveston Island, near the Bolivar Point Ferry. Other key figures out for the tour included Jack Frels, Harris County investigator Ken Rogers, Galveston County district attorney

James Hury, and Houston police officers Ted Thomas and Jim Ladd.

Watts led Tom Ladd to the spot on Postoffice Road where he believed he killed Anna Ledet. He was allowed out of the car and pointed to the sidewalk where he believed the attack occurred.

He was right on.

Watts got back into the car and directed Ladd to another apartment complex just around the corner. Again he got out of the car and pointed to the spot where he believed he attacked Glenda Kirby.

Again he nailed it.

Watts then led the group to the general area where he believed he killed Patty Johnson.

CHAPTER 32

By Thursday, August 12, 1982, officials from Michigan had hopped on a plane to Texas to speak with Coral Watts. The intuitive Sergeant Paul Bunten, who had tailed Watts after three suspicious murders in Ann Arbor and sent HPD officials a dossier that suspected Watts of being a serial killer, led the charge. He was joined by Ann Arbor Major Crimes lieutenant Dale Heath and Washtenaw County district attorney William Delhey.

Bunten was ecstatic. The time had finally come. He was going to catch his killer. The Sunday Morning Slasher would have to answer for his murderous deeds. The inevitable confessions for the murders of Shirley Small, Glenda Richmond, and Rebecca Huff, as well as several other Michigan murder victims, were just around the corner.

"It was our understanding Watts was willing to talk," declared Ann Arbor Executive Major police officer Walter Hawkins to the *Houston Post.* "We're certainly willing to listen."

Unfortunately, for the two detectives and the district attorney, the city of Houston was not ready to listen to them. When the three Michigan officials landed, they were told, in no uncertain terms, to buzz off. As the men departed their airplane at Hobby Airport, they were greeted by Harris County ADA Jack Frels, who was flanked by several Houston police officers. After the initial greetings, Frels came right out with the terms of their opportunity to sit and talk with Coral Watts: immunity in exchange for information.

The Michigan officials, however, had been clearly instructed, in no uncertain terms, not to bargain with Coral Watts. DA Delhey was adamant that Watts would not receive any preferential treatment.

"I agree with what the Houston authorities have done," Delhey diplomatically stated, "because they obtained two bodies that were unknown and solved nine cases." That was where Ann Arbor drew the line. "But if I gave him immunity for killing three people, it would serve no purpose. Something could develop to prove the cases. At this time I am not ready to make an agreement."

Detective Bunten was much blunter: "We told them there was no way we'd offer him immunity. . . . We don't give immunity in our cases. I don't think you can justify it."

The Michigan authorities' firm stance kept them from their potential nemesis. "That was it," Bunten lamented. "We spent two days in a hotel in Houston and we never got to see Watts. We finally gave up and [Houston police] wouldn't even give us a ride back to the airport."

Officer Hawkins reiterated the point. "I keep reading about the sixty-year sentence they talk about Watts getting down there. Well, when you count time off for good behavior, and then parole, he's not getting anywhere near sixty years." Hawkins added, "We're not going to grant immunity and have him come back here in a short period of time. Now, if the sentence was sixty years straight out, we'd take a look at it because he'd be eighty-eight years old when he got out."

The Ann Arbor officials were not the only Michigan authorities to refuse to grant absolute immunity to Coral Watts in exchange for testimony of any murders. Kalamazoo County assistant prosecuting attorney James Gregart was also unwilling to make a deal with Watts in exchange for testimony of the murder of Gloria Steele. After conferring with Steele's family, Gregart and Western Michigan University police chief John Cease decided not to negotiate with Watts.

"I don't make deals with murderers," the tough, nononsense district attorney declared. "I'm not going to sell my community a murder."

According to Gregart, the opinion of the Steele family played a large part in his decision not to offer immunity. He added, "In essence, what Coral Watts wants is a free murder in Kalamazoo County and I won't give it to him. There's nothing to be gained by us giving him immunity from prosecution."

Wayne County (Detroit), Michigan's chief assistant prosecutor Dominick Carnovale, however, believed there was something to gain from a Coral Watts confession. Carnovale offered Watts immunity in return for his testimony of the murder of forty-four-year-old Grosse Pointe Farms resident Jeanne Clyne, who was killed on Halloween in 1979.

"There were sufficient details (given by Watts about the killing) that only someone who was involved in that would know," Carnovale explained. Watts was considered a suspect in at least nineteen more Wayne County murders. Carnovale was unwilling to offer immunity in any of those cases.

One person who was relieved that a deal was struck with Watts was Michael Clyne, Jeanne Clyne's husband.

"In my own mind, I never thought the case would be solved," Clyne stated. The remarried widower had been a prime suspect in the murder of his wife from the beginning. "I had just dropped off my wife at her psychiatrist's and gone to do some errands. Jeanne was going to walk home, but she never made it. The next thing I knew, the police were at my door telling me she had been killed."

Michael Clyne recalled being a suspect in what police called "a killing of passion." He also mentioned that Jeanne Clyne's psychiatrist was also a suspect in the murder. "The police questioned me, all my friends. They didn't harass us, but they were looking at someone with a motive."

The questioning made it difficult for Michael Clyne in Grosse Pointe Farms. "This is a small town; there was a lot of publicity with my name in the papers all the time. It made my life very complicated for a while."

Needless to say, Watts's admission took Michael Clyne off the hook. "This is all just sinking in, but I am relieved, that's for sure. The police told me five days ago they thought Watts was their man, but I never thought he would confess."

Clyne did not complain about the immunity deal either. "At least he's in [prison] for a maximum sixty years." Clyne was, however, concerned that Watts may get paroled before serving his entire sentence. "If the situation were different and immunity would have allowed him to be back out on the streets, it would be a different case. But I feel the citizens of Houston won't forget him"—Clyne hoped—"and with what the parole board knows about him, he would not be let out on the street. Public sentiment wouldn't allow it."

Grosse Pointe Farms police officer Timothy Morrison stated that the immunity offer was imperative. "He was a suspect, but we had nothing hard to go on. Frankly, we're trying to clear the case, if he did it."

Once the confessions poured out of Watts's mouth, other cities that suspected Watts in other killings stepped forward. They wanted to see if the Houston police had their killer in their midst and if they could clear their own unsolved cases. In addition to Gloria Steele and the three Ann Arbor victims—Shirley Small, Glenda Richmond, and Rebecca Huff—officials from Toledo, Ohio; Windsor, Ontario, Canada; College Station, Texas; and Indiana all had Watts on their radar for possible murders. Some of the victims included were Hazel Conniff, Peggy Pochmara, Denise Dunmore, Linda Monteiro, Connie Sue Thompson, Kristy Kozak, and even a Catholic nun from Detroit.

Houston police detective Tom Ladd foresaw the rush to clear cases, so he made certain that there was no misperceptions of wrongdoing on their behalf. He made sure that all the cases tied to Coral Watts were legit and thoroughly documented. Watts's confessions occurred months before alleged serial killer Henry Lee Lucas "confessed" to nearly three hundred murders. It was later proved that Lucas did not commit hundreds of murders. There was also an outcry against Texas authorities for encouraging Lucas to confess falsely so they could write off large portions of their caseload.

Ladd, along with brother Jim, drove Watts out to the crime scene locations and had Watts point out everything he could remember about a murder. "We didn't want some dickhead saying we were trying to dump cases on this poor little black boy."

Ladd was amazed at Watts's ability to recollect. "He

came across as articulate and very smart. He'd never get the details of one murder mixed up with another."

Two unsolved cases near Detroit also seemed to be tied to Coral Watts. The murder of sixty-three-year-old Lena J. Bennett, whose nude body had been discovered hanging in her garage in Harper Woods, and Helen Mae Dutcher, the thirty-six-year-old waitress who had been stabbed multiple times in a back alley near Eight Mile Road.

Ferndale police chief R. Russell Rey stated that his office had "reactivated the [Dutcher murder] investigation. Actually, the case was never closed." Rey stressed that he would not offer an immunity deal for Watts. "We're going to develop this case further and see where it leads. We have some evidence and we're working on it to see if it will connect Watts to the slaying."

CHAPTER 33

Once word of the immunity deal offered to Coral Eugene Watts got out through the media, the Houston citizenry went into an uproar. Judge Doug Shaver received numerous phone calls from outraged Houstonians who could not believe that Watts would not receive the death penalty. Some of the callers wished death on Judge Shaver for the decision.

In addition, several letters were sent to the editors of the *Houston Chronicle* that expressed total disbelief in the decision. Here is a sample of some of the letters:

- *A guy with an IQ of 68 getting hired as a Metro bus mechanic may give some insight to their problem. But how was he able to kill 10 women while under surveillance by the HPD?*
- *Coral Eugene Watts kills . . . women because he "thought they were evil." A typical example of a confused, deluded, irrational Christian mind. "Put women in their place."*
- *Reasons why Coral Eugene Watts should be executed: Because he admitted to have killed 10 women and possibly more. Because you should do unto others as you*

would have them do unto you. To set an example. Be-
cause 60 years is too short, expensive and useless in his
case. Because everything short of death is an insult to
the victims' families. Because if the authorities do not,
someone else will (Watts will not die a natural death in
prison).

Some of the victims' surviving family members also had something to say about the plea bargain offered to Watts. The same plea bargain that DA John B. Holmes Jr. claimed that he spoke with all of the families about and that they agreed was a worthy deal.

Harriett Semander, mother of Elena Semander, wrote a letter to the editors of the *Houston Chronicle:* "Watts deserves the death sentence. His oral confession should be allowed to stand up in court. At what point did his rights violate Elena's right to life, liberty and the pursuit of happiness?

"If I were Jack Frels, I would tell Watts: 'Fooled you! I had my fingers crossed the whole time' when he finally confesses.

"Then give him the death penalty."

Marta Ryals, a good friend of victim Elizabeth Montgomery, had mixed emotions on Watts's plea bargain. "On a personal level, I want to see him suffer as much as possible. I don't think any human can get revenge from him. But I'd like to see it tried."

Montgomery's fiancé, Bill Daigle, stated, "I don't know if he's going to be crazy when he gets out, but he'll be back. It seems a little much that you would kill nine people at least and then walk away with a burglary and attempted murder charge."

Garry Montgomery, Elizabeth's brother from North Reading, Massachusetts, concurred. "I have a brother who occasionally does things wrong and goes to jail. But if he went off killing innocent people, I'd say, 'An eye for an eye and a tooth for a tooth.'"

Flo Maday summed up the families' discontent when she responded to Watts's accusations that the women he killed had "evil eyes." She blasted Watts. "Khomeini is evil," referring to the former ayatollah of Iran who oversaw the hostage situation in the American embassy in Tehran, Iran, from 1979 to 1981. Originally ninety people, including sixty-three Americans, were held captive, with fifty-two Americans that were held for 444 days. Maday continued her justified tirade: "The Mafia is evil. He (Watts) didn't let these girls live long enough to find out if they were evil. The man does not know what the word evil means."

Maday concluded with very succinct feelings: "I hate him. I hate his mother. I resent the fact that he has a three-year-old daughter who is alive and I don't."

The victims' family members were not only frustrated with the plea bargain but with the Houston Police Department.

"I only wanted to know if she was wearing her contacts at the time of her death," Harriett Semader exasperatedly recalled. She believed the families received almost no help and no guidance from the detectives working the various cases. The official "blue tape" was thick and impenetrable.

"I tried going to Chief (Lee P.) Brown, the Beechnut substation, to (public information officer) Larry Troutt and wound up back at the chief's office speaking to one of his assistants," Semander detailed her frustrations.

"I wanted them to issue a public warning" (about the murders of young girls before Watts had confessed). "I was told that would start a panic, people would be frightened.

Meanwhile, another girl was killed." Harriett referred to Michelle Maday.

Semander mentioned how her meeting with the police chief Brown went earlier that month, where he stated that the murders were not the work of one person. "He said the media was just blowing the whole thing out of proportion." When Semander asked Brown why Watts was not under constant surveillance, despite having been warned by Detective Paul Bunten, Brown responded, "If we were prophets, there's a lot more we could have done. I'm sorry we're not prophetic."

Prophetic, no.

Pathetic, absolutely yes, as far as the victims' families were concerned.

Michael Maday, Michelle's father, was also disgusted with the Houston Police Department. "I really have seen nothing from the police from the beginning. No police report, no autopsy, nothing."

Flo Maday spoke of directing her anger toward the Houston Police Department. In a letter to the *Houston Chronicle*, Flo wrote: "The tired tale of not enough police grows more tired when the Police Department chooses easy marks such as prostitutes, drunks and marijuana offenders." She then slammed the officers themselves as looking for the easy bust as opposed to trying to stop a murderer. The grieving mother did not believe in quantity over quality. She concluded that having more cops would "only perpetuate the mediocrity that now thrives."

Harriett Semander was furious when she found out that Houston police officers had been forewarned about Watts. "To think, my daughter was killed because a harassment charge might be filed against the police department. I was told (recently) there are other suspected killers walking the streets [because police are] afraid of

A battered and bruised Lori Lister lay in a hospital bed after surviving an attack by Coral Eugene Watts. *(Houston Police Department)*

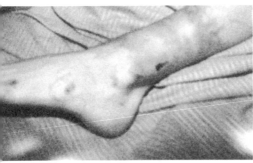

Lister's injured foot. *(Houston Police Department)*

Lister's scraped calf and bruised ankle. *(Houston Police Department)*

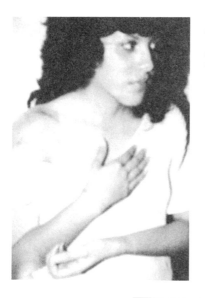

Tiny Melinda Aguilar shows cuts and scrapes inflicted by Watts. *(Houston Police Department)*

Aguilar's wrists were bruised from being bound with wire hangers. *(Houston Police Department)*

The wire hangers Watts used to tie up Lister and Aguilar. *(Houston Police Department)*

Watts dragged Lister upstairs into her Hammerly Apartment residence. *(Corey Mitchell)*

The entrance to Lister's bathroom where Watts attempted to drown her. *(Houston Police Department)*

Watts's Grand Prix, parked outside of Lister's apartment.
(Houston Police Department)

Coral Eugene Watts
was arrested for
assaulting Lori Lister
and Melinda Aguilar.
*(Harris County District
Attorney)*

Watts confessed to the murders of thirteen women to Houston Police detectives Tom and Jim Ladd and his attorneys Don Caggins and Zinetta Burney. *(Houston Police Department)*

Watts was led away in handcuffs after receiving a plea bargain for thirteen murders. *(Harris County District Attorney)*

Watts's home in Inkster, Michigan. *(Michelle N. Hartmann)*

One of Watts's many residences in Houston, Texas. *(Corey Mitchell)*

Linda Tilley fought with Watts before he drowned her in an apartment swimming pool.

Elizabeth Montgomery's apartment complex, where she walked her dogs before she was stabbed to death. (Corey Mitchell)

Free-spirited Suzi Wolf lived in Michigan while Watts was there and moved to Texas soon after Watts did.

Wolf was murdered less than two hours after Montgomery outside of her apartment complex. *(Corey Mitchell)*

Ellen Tamm was found hanging from a tree with her own tube top near the Rice University campus. *(Corey Mitchell)*

Home where Margaret Fossi stayed with her sister-in-law while attending graduate school at the University of Houston. *(Corey Mitchell)*

Julie Sanchez's throat was slit by Watts on the side of the Southwest Freeway. *(Corey Mitchell)*

The Seabrook, Texas apartment where Watts stabbed Alice Martell. *(Corey Mitchell)*

Elena Semander excelled in athletics, including soccer and field hockey.

Elena's siblings, Maria, John, and JoAnna, dearly loved their oldest sister. *(Harriett Semander)*

Watts murdered Semander behind the West Hollow apartment complex and tossed her body into a Dumpster. *(Corey Mitchell)*

Fourteen-year-old Emily LaQua ran away from home in Washington and moved to Brookshire, Texas. She was murdered one week later.

The culvert where LaQua's body was found after she had been missing for several months. *(Corey Mitchell)*

Edith "Anna" Ledet completed her medical school studies the day before Watts murdered her in Galveston, Texas.

The residence where Watts attacked and kidnapped Carrie Jefferson after she returned home from work. (Corey Mitchell)

Watts abducted Jefferson and buried her near White Oak Bayou in north Houston. (Corey Mitchell)

Suzanne Searles planned on moving to Colorado less than one month before she was murdered by Watts.

Searles's apartment complex, where she was abducted by Watts.
(Corey Mitchell)

Coral Eugene Watts—America's most prolific serial killer? *(Harris County District Attorney)*

Houston crime victims advocate Andy Kahan fought to keep Watts behind bars. *(Corey Mitchell)*

Helen Dutcher's bloody body was found in a back alley behind H&M Cleaners. *(Oakland County District Court)*

Dutcher's blood was found splattered on the snow. *(Oakland County District Court)*

A composite sketch of Watts was drawn, based on witness Joseph Foy's description of Dutcher's murderer. *(Oakland County District Court)*

Harriett Semander received the Crime Stoppers citizen award from Kim Ogg in 2005. *(Corey Mitchell)*

Andy Kahan and Harriett Semander—the two main forces behind keeping Watts behind bars. *(Corey Mitchell)*

harassment charges." It was a miracle he was caught. That man could be walking the streets right now." She added, "He was caught, not because we have an efficient police department. How can a man with an IQ of sixty-eight outwit our police?"

CHAPTER 34

Coral Watts's sentencing date was originally scheduled for Monday, August 16, 1982, before state district judge Shaver. The original date, however, was postponed so more investigators could question him. Assistant District Attorney Jack Frels noted that Watts had been cooperative. "We believe he's obviously fulfilled his part of the plea bargain." As a result, Judge Shaver rescheduled Watts's sentencing hearing to Friday, August 27, 1982.

On August 27, authorities from Michigan, Indiana, and Canada continued to question Watts. Once again, at the request of Harris County DA John B. Holmes Jr., Judge Shaver postponed the sentencing hearing. The new date was September 3, 1982.

Before the new sentencing hearing date, discussions arose as to when Watts might be paroled. Ruben M. Torres, chairman of the Texas Board of Pardons and Paroles, explored the frightening possibilities. "If he's never paroled, I would say [he could serve] somewhere in the neighborhood of thirty years."

Under the state of Texas's "good time" provision, located in the Texas Government Code §508.142 (b)—

PERIOD OF PAROLE—"Good conduct time is computed for an inmate as if the inmate were confined in the institutional division during the entire time the inmate was actually confined"; in other words, inmates are allowed to leave prison early without having to serve their entire sentence. This allows for crowded prisons to empty their bunk beds and bring in fresh new recruits on an ongoing basis. If prisoners behave behind bars, they will receive good-time days that will count toward their early release.

According to Rick Hartley, former spokesman for the Texas Department of Corrections, as well as an assistant director, the majority of inmates enter the Texas prison system with the title of "Class I" prisoner. Class I's receive twenty days' extra credit for each thirty days served. In other words, thirty gets you fifty.

"From that point," Hartley said, "they can go up or down—up to thirty days extra for every thirty days they serve, or down to ten extra days for every thirty days." Hartley added, "I'd say a large number of inmates are getting thirty for thirty. You're getting sixty days' credit, although you're only serving thirty days."

Hartley also stated that Watts could actually be restricted to the actual time served—if he misbehaved. "There's a small percentage of inmates in the system that actually serve day-for-day time."

In Texas, if a criminal is convicted of a violent crime, he or she is ineligible for good-time early-release credit. That could have posed a problem in the upcoming sentencing hearing for Coral Watts. The charge levied against Watts—burglary with intent to commit murder—did not necessarily fall under the purview of a violent crime. (To prove that a violent crime has been committed, the state has to prove that a deadly weapon was used in the commission of the act.) Watts did not use a traditional weapon, such as a gun or a knife, when he attacked Lori Lister and Melinda Aguilar.

Judge Doug Shaver said, in regard to the deadly-weapon inclusion, "We're still looking into that. I will do everything possible to write the judgment to show Watts's violent nature," but he did not know if the Texas Department of Corrections would be bound to disallowing good-time credits.

The judge had one week to make it stick.

The following week, on September 3, 1982, at 11:15 A.M., Watts stood before Judge Shaver. The atmosphere had taken on a more serious tone. Prosecuting attorney Ira Jones wore a bulletproof vest inside the courtroom. Apparently, the public dissatisfaction rose to an unacceptable level with threats made against the judge, all of the attorneys, and Watts.

"All the people in the courtroom were advised to wear them," Harris County ADA Ira Jones informed the media in regard to the bulletproof vest. Watts included.

Judge Shaver had also relocated the proceedings to a more easily securable courtroom. He ordered a metal detector to be set up at the front entrance of the courtroom. Thirty minutes before the hearing began, the judge had the courtroom completely cleared out and swept through with a bomb-sniffing German shepherd. He was not taking any chances.

Kathy Gregory, Meg Fossi's sister-in-law, sat in the gallery, as did Harriett Semander. Watts's girlfriend, Sheila Williams, also sat in the crowd. Surprisingly, two very conspicuous people did not appear in court: Lori Lister and Melinda Aguilar. Lister begged out, claiming she could not take time off from work. It was unknown why Aguilar did not appear.

Before the hearing Jones talked about Watts. "Our indication is he already is shutting up," referring to any additional murders Watts may have committed. "He's realized he might have talked too much." The general consensus among all parties involved was that Watts would clam up once behind bars. Judge Shaver added that there was "some suspicion that Watts might shut up" after he received his sentence.

The time had come for the sentencing of Coral Eugene Watts.

The twenty-eight-year-old confessor of multiple murders slowly rambled into the courtroom dressed in a brown velour sport coat with thick grooves, brown shirt, and grayish brown dress slacks. He looked like a second-tier Billy Dee Williams, minus the Lando Calrissian cool.

Watts took his place behind the defense table. He was flanked by Zinetta Burney to his left and Don Caggins to his right. Soon after Watts's arrival, Judge Shaver entered the courtroom and took his place behind the bench. The judge wore a large white neck brace, due to a pinched nerve. The encumbrance would not hinder the judge in any way.

Zinetta Burney, Watts's defense lawyer, hoped the proceedings would zip along quickly. She objected immediately to the presence of cameras in the courtroom. Judge Shaver let it be known that there would be no cameras during any testimony during the hearing; however, cameras would be allowed during the sentencing of Watts. A very unusual move in the pre–Court TV days of 1982.

Furthermore, Burney also objected to any testimony by witnesses in the hearing as "immaterial and irrelevant." Her argument was that her client already had accepted the plea bargain and the hearing was merely a formality. Judge Shaver overruled her objections.

Prosecutor Ira Jones, uncomfortable in his bullet-proof vest, stepped forward. He declared that the first witness would be Patricia Kay McDonald, Lori Lister's upstairs neighbor and guardian angel.

McDonald recalled when Officers Schmidt and Domain knocked on her door in May 1982. She described the black man in a hooded sweatshirt. She described how she bolted up the stairs and into Lister's apartment. She then described how she found Lori Lister.

"The first thing, the door was partially open," she recalled. "I pushed my way in and heard the bathroom water running."

"Did you proceed to where the water was running?" inquired Jones.

"Yes. I was in the area of the hall and looked into the bathroom and at that time I saw Lori. At that time I didn't know who it was in the tub." The twenty-three-year-old geophysical technician looked calm, cool, and collected on the stand—even with the gaze of Coral Watts drilling metaphorical holes through her like an offshore oil well.

"Is this Lori Lister?" prodded Jones.

"Yes, sir," McDonald replied.

"Was there any water in that tub?"

"Yes, there was."

"How did the girl appear to you?"

"Deathly." The crowd of more than one hundred spectators drew its collective breath in like an asthma victim. "Her head was underwater. There was a blue coloring."

"Of whom?"

"In her face. It was a very pale blue tint."

"Did she have any type of thing around her head?" asked Jones.

"There was some sort of gag twisted and tied around the back of her head through her mouth," McDonald testified in regard to the restraints used on Lister.

"Did she appear to be breathing, to you?"

"Not at the time." Neither was the gallery in Judge Shaver's temporary courtroom.

"Upon seeing the girl underwater, what did you do, if anything?"

"First thing I did," McDonald remembered, "I immediately lifted her out of the water, grabbed the bandanna, or whatever it was wrapped around her head, pulled it out of her mouth and noticed her tongue was swollen. I then reached around under her arms and pulled her out of the tub, laying her on her stomach in the bathroom."

"After laying her on the floor, could you observe whether or not anything was on her hands?" Jones asked, slowly getting comfortable with the environment of the court.

"I was amazed I could pull her out of the water just by grabbing her," McDonald said with a look of bemusement. "Her hands had been tied around the back quite well with a coat hanger. I tried to take it off, but I couldn't."

The crowd in the courtroom scooted forward in their seats.

"What did you do with her then?"

"I pounded her lower back." What seemed like the entire courtroom finally exhaled as McDonald continued her tale of heroics. "I couldn't remember any of the CPR or lifesaving measures. That's the only thing I did. After a few seconds of that, she started coughing up water and a little bit of blood."

"After doing this, what did you see Lori do?"

"She started thrashing around, moaning, and groaning like she was still struggling with someone."

Once McDonald completed her testimony, Jones passed the witness to the defense. Burney had no questions for the witness. McDonald stepped down from the witness stand.

Next up was medical examiner Dr. Joseph Jachimczyk. Again Burney objected to the testimony of the doctor as "immaterial and irrelevant"; again Judge Shaver overruled her objection.

Prosecutor Ira Jones questioned Dr. Jachimczyk about his educational background. The doctor received his degree in medicine from the University of Tennessee College of Medicine. He later served as the assistant medical examiner for the state of Maryland in Baltimore. He then served in the Department of Legal Medicine at Harvard University in Boston, Massachusetts, for over three years. He moved to Houston in 1957 and began work as the first forensic pathologist to the medical examiner. Three years later, he was promoted to chief medical examiner.

Prosecutor Jones asked, "During your course of duties as medical examiner for Harris County, have you come to examine few or many bodies with the purpose of determining the cause of death?"

"Approximately one hundred twelve thousand, as of the end of last year," the doctor noted.

Jones directed the questioning toward the attack on Lori Lister. "Have you come to examine few or many bodies during the course of your profession to determine whether or not they were drowned?"

"Yes, sir, many."

Jones showed the doctor a photograph of Lori Lister's bathtub and also one of Lister.

"If you will hypothetically assume that on May 23, 1982, an individual seized a young woman and choked her into unconsciousness . . . dragged her up ten concrete steps into an apartment and bound her hands behind her back with a coat hanger . . . then placed her on her back in a bathtub full of water. . . . Assume further, if you will, Doctor, that the depth of the water is such that it covers the woman's face . . . that she has stopped breathing. Based upon those facts and your education and your experience, do you have an opinion as to whether or not that particular bathtub, with that particular amount of water, and those coat hangers were used in such a manner as to be considered, in your opinion, as a deadly weapon?"

Zinetta Burney piped in with an immediate objection. She claimed that the doctor was not qualified to answer the question and that, again, it was "immaterial and irrelevant" to the agreed-upon proceedings at hand.

Again Judge Shaver overruled her objection.

Dr. Jachimczyk replied, "My opinion is the water used in that fashion would certainly constitute a deadly weapon."

Jones followed up with a photograph of Lister's swollen tongue. "Do you have a medical opinion as to why the woman's tongue could be in that condition if she were placed in a bathtub underwater?"

"In my opinion, that is a result of the lack of oxygen. The individual's attempt to breathe causes the tongue to protrude and then get caught between the teeth."

"Is the condition of that tongue on that particular woman consistent with strangulation?"

"Yes, sir."

"And is it consistent, also, with drowning?"

"Yes, sir," came the doctor's affirmative reply.

"Pass the witness." Jones was done with Dr. Jachimczyk.

Again Burney chose not to question the witness.

Next up on the docket for the state was Houston police detective Jim Ladd.

Ladd was sworn in. He stated that he had worked in the Homicide Division for six years. When asked if he had come to know Coral Eugene Watts, he stated, "Yes, sir, I have."

"For the record," Ira Jones stated, "would you please point to him?"

The husky, blond-haired detective looked up to see Watts smiling at him. Nonplussed, the detective pointed a finger at the defendant and said, "The man in the brown coat sitting next to the attorney."

Jones declared, "May the record reflect this witness identifies the defendant, Coral Eugene Watts."

The prosecutor continued: "After a hearing with Mr. Watts in which he pled guilty and agreed to a plea bargaining, particularly that he would assist the homicide division with the clearing of certain murders here and around Harris County and other places, were you then assigned to work with Mr. Watts in determining the cause of certain homicides in and around Harris County and other jurisdictions?"

"Yes, sir, I was."

Detective Ladd began the methodical listing and descriptive retelling of the women Watts confessed to murdering, beginning with Jeanne Clyne.

Zinetta Burney, once again, renewed her objection to the questioning. She believed that the hearing "should be for the limited purposes of whether or not he (Watts) has complied with the plea-bargaining agreement."

Judge Shaver responded, "This is a sentencing hearing and your objection will be overruled."

Detective Ladd continued the gruesome murderous

litany of Coral Eugene Watts: Jeanne Clyne, Linda Tilley, Elizabeth Montgomery, Phyllis Ellen Tamm, Margaret Fossi, the attempted murder of Julie Sanchez, the attempted murder of Alice Martell, the attempted murder of Patty Johnson, the murder of Elena Semander, Emily LaQua, Anna Ledet, the assault on Glenda Kirby, the murders of Yolanda Gracia, Carrie Jefferson, Suzanne Searles, Michelle Maday, as well as the attempted murders of Lori Lister and Melinda Aguilar.

Assistant District Attorney Jones asked the detective, "During your investigation, how many murders did Coral Watts admit doing, to you?"

Ladd replied, "Thirteen."

"This is in Texas?"

"Thirteen murders, yes." The number of murders Watts confessed to committing in Texas was actually twelve.

"How many attempted murders?"

"I believe there was five."

"How many assaults?"

"One."

"Did he rob any of these victims?"

"Not per se of robbing for monetary value. There were times he would take articles, but not to convert to cash."

"What type of articles would he take?" questioned Jones.

"Mostly clothing articles. Every now and then, small articles of jewelry."

"What would he do with them?"

"Burn them or throw them away."

"Did he tell you why he would take the articles and burn them?"

"Yes, sir. He said he burned the articles, as he would call it, to kill the spirit."

"Did he ever sexually assault any of the victims, to your knowledge?"

"Not that we know of," the detective methodically stated in a hushed tone.

"Had he previously met or had he known any of those victims?"

"No."

"Totally random strangers?"

"Yes, sir."

"Prior to questioning Mr. Watts," Jones began to wrap up, "under a plea-bargaining agreement, had you exhausted every avenue of investigation to solve each of these cases in Harris County that you have described here today?"

"Yes, sir. These cases and many more."

"Did you have any lead whatsoever that it would have led you to Coral Eugene Watts?"

"No, sir," Ladd concluded.

Jones passed the witness to Burney. This time she actually had a cross-examination question. "Officer Ladd, has Coral Watts cooperated with you and the Houston Police Department and the other agencies in every aspect?"

"Yes, ma'am."

Burney excused herself. The state rested. Burney requested that Watts take the stand so as to determine whether or not he understood the parameters of his plea bargain. As Watts walked to the witness stand, the eyes of the gallery ripped through his being. Once Watts took his seat, he merely answered Burney's questions about whether or not he knew what he was doing in regard to the deal he struck. He sat in the witness chair for less than three minutes. He did not speak specifically of the crimes he was charged with or the murders he confessed to committing.

Once Watts stepped down and returned to his place behind the defense table, Judge Shaver took over. The judge formally found Watts guilty of the felony offense of burglary of a habitation and that the burglary was committed with the intent to commit murder. The judge also added an additional factor to the charges. He stated, "The court now makes an affirmative finding based upon the evidence produced in that case today that the water in the bathtub and the manner and means of its use in the commission of this offense is and was a deadly weapon." This addition would have major ramifications on Watts's good-time provisions.

Judge Shaver directly addressed Watts. "Mr. Watts, do you understand what that means, sir?" Watts looked directly at the judge. "When the court makes an affirmative finding that a deadly weapon was used, that means that the first time you can ever be considered for parole would be after you have done twenty calendar years. Do you understand that, sir?"

Watts simply nodded. "Yes, sir," he politely responded.

Judge Shaver then took the time to clearly state how he felt about the plea bargain for Coral Watts.

"I'm accepting the recommendation of the DAs office and I want you to understand, Mr. Watts, for the following reasons. The sixty-year sentence that has been recommended by the DAs office is the exact equivalent of the maximum sentence allowed under the law and the only crime—and for the only crime that you are charged with in this court and the only crime that this court has any control over and, sad to say, the only crime the state of Texas has any evidence against you on prior to the immunization agreements."

Judge Shaver looked up at Watts and addressed him directly. The annoyance on his face, painfully obvious.

"The only greater sentence that could have been imposed would have been the death penalty, if you had been successful in your attempt in this offense, and I am thankful for the victims, and, but for the grace of God, that you were not. I want you to understand that the sentence I am imposing is not what I believe is an appropriate sentence for you, but it is simply the equivalent maximum sentence under the evidence the state has to use against you."

The judge also wanted the record to reflect what he felt about the good-time provision. "I also know of no law that mandates that the Texas Department of Corrections gives good time, and I call now, using you as an example, upon the legislature of the state of Texas and the Texas Department of Corrections to make any necessary changes that they deem appropriate to fit a case such as you in order to see that in certain cases, specifically a case such as yours, that you receive no 'good time' credit and that will be the strongest suggestion of this court, and it is my fervent hope."

Judge Shaver attempted to explain his position. "I understand their reason for having 'good time' in the Texas Department of Corrections. The criminologists tell us if it were not for 'good time' credit, they could not control their prisoners; that they would have nothing to gain by trying to stay in good standing. As far as I'm concerned, I could care less if you act good or not good."

Judge Shaver's verbal spotlight burned brightly as it focused on Watts. "I don't care if the slightest thing you do is spit on the wall. If you do not act well, it is my suggestion to the Texas Department of Corrections that they put you so deep in the penitentiary, they have to pipe some light into you. And that you serve each and every minute of the sixty years that this court is going to assess against you."

Watts rocked back and forth in his chair as he received the tongue-lashing. He simply shook his head as the judge continued his harangue.

Judge Shaver ordered that a transcript of the sentencing hearing be sent to the Texas Department of Corrections and the Board of Pardons and Paroles. His reason was to make sure that the charges against Watts and his confessions were made a part of his permanent record in case someone got a wild hair and had an inkling of paroling the murderer: "If anyone is ever so foolish, in this court's opinion, to allow you to walk upon the streets again until you have completed the entire sixty years in the Texas Department of Corrections."

Judge Shaver concluded, "Therefore, since the death penalty is not available for the only offense before me, I now sentence you to confinement in the Texas Department of Corrections for a term of sixty years.

"Do you have anything else to say, sir, before the sentence of law is pronounced against you?"

Burney interjected, "For the record, Judge, we would like to object to the affirmative finding of a deadly weapon being used. We would like to add that the finding is inconsistent with the pleadings upon which he is charged."

Judge Shaver retorted, "That will be denied."

The judge signaled to his bailiff to allow the press to enter the courtroom. In an unprecedented move, Judge Shaver allowed newspaper photographers and television cameramen to shoot the sentencing phase of the Watts trial.

A gentleman by the name of Joseph Foy would be watching nearly fifteen hundred miles away in the state of Michigan as the judge turned his attention to the defendant, who was standing with his hands in his pants pockets. "Coral Eugene Watts, after having been adjudged guilty of the felony offense of burglary of a habitation with the intent to commit murder or attempted murder, and after your punishment having been assessed as confinement in the Texas Department of Corrections for not less than five years, nor more than sixty years, you are now ordered to be delivered to the Texas Department of Corrections . . . with the fervent hope of this court and the strongest possible suggestions of this court that every minute of that sixty years for you, sir, is spent behind the walls of the Texas Department of Corrections.

"Mr. Bailiff, you may remove the convict."

District Attorney John B. Holmes Jr., along with ADA Ira Jones and ADA Jack Frels, held a courthouse-step press conference after the hearing. Holmes took the heat for the plea bargain. He stated that he believed Judge Shaver had taken unfair criticism for the plea bargain. He reiterated that it was his idea to make the deal.

"I think it is a comfort to know we did have a mass killer on our streets, but we don't anymore," declared the mustachioed DA.

Holmes also mentioned that no plea bargain was made in the Emily LaQua case. This information was important in the rare event that Watts actually would ever be released from prison before his sentence ended.

Holmes also expressed his personal belief as to what should have happened to the defendant. "I think Coral Eugene Watts ought to be taken out behind the courthouse and shot in the head. But we don't do that in a free society."

CHAPTER 35

When Coral Eugene Watts's name hit the press, it was a seemingly unusual scenario. Even today, the concept of an African American, or black, serial killer does not seep immediately into the public consciousness. There are several reasons for this. At the top of the list is the glamorization of profilers, such as John Douglas and Robert Ressler.

Profilers are members of the Federal Bureau of Investigation's Behavioral Science Unit (BSU) who claim to be able to pinpoint who a serial killer is. Through interviews of a select group of captured serial killers, Douglas, Ressler (who coined the phrase "serial killer" in the 1970s), and other BSers have tried to narrow down what they believe to be the common traits among serial killers.

The most common theories were distilled down to their piquant essence in a September 1984 paper delivered at the tenth triennial gathering of the International Association of Forensic Sciences in Oxford, England. The paper, coauthored by Douglas, Ressler, Ann Burgess, and Ralph D'Agostino, detailed the top ten characteristics of serial killers. At the top of the list was the fact that most serial killers were white males.

In the United States this fact is true, and obvious, based solely on the fact that the vast majority of males in the country are Caucasian. If you dig in a little deeper, the number of black serial killers is severely underexposed.

According to a recent study by California State University, Fresno, professor Eric W. Hickey, approximately 22 percent of all serial killers in the United States are black. All blacks, men and women, make up approximately 12 percent of the United States' population. Professor Hickey stated that "blacks actually are overrepresented among serial killers."

Despite these numbers the majority of Americans do not associate serial killing with black men. It is strictly a white man's disease. The reality, however, is that the epidemic crosses racial lines.

The following is a list of some of the more notorious African American serial killers and the atrocities that they have committed:

- Carlton Gary, the "Stocking Strangler," was convicted of three strangulation murders of wealthy white elderly women in Columbus, Georgia, from 1977 to 1978. Gary was suspected of killing at least seven women. He would strangle his victims with a pair of their own panty hose.

- Alton Coleman and Debra Brown, this spree-killing couple, committed at least eight murders, seven rapes, three kidnappings, and fourteen armed robberies across the states of Illinois, Indiana, and Ohio during the early 1980s. Coleman had accumulated death sentences in Illinois, Indiana, and Ohio. Coleman was executed on April 26, 2002. Of the thirty-five hundred people on death row at the time, Coleman was the only person with death sentences in three states. Brown was also sentenced to death, but her sentence was commuted to life in prison in 1991.

- Kendall Francois, the six-foot-four-inch, three-hundred-pound, twenty-seven-year-old middle-school hall monitor, was discovered to have buried eight dead women underneath his home in Poughkeepsie, New York, in 1998. Nicknamed "Stinky," Francois killed prostitutes because "they did not give him all the sex he paid for."

- Vaughn Greenwood, aka the "Skid Row Slasher," was alleged to have killed at least eleven homeless men on the streets of Los Angeles's Skid Row. Greenwood would stab the men repeatedly and slit their throats. Sometimes he would take off the victims' shoes and point them toward the victims. He also, inexplicably, poured salt around the bodies. Greenwood received a life-in-prison sentence after he attempted to decapitate a man near the Hollywood home of actor Burt Reynolds.

- Derrick Todd Lee, aka the "Baton Rouge Killer," was responsible for the deaths of at least seven women in Baton Rouge, Louisiana, from 1998 to 2003. Lee received the death penalty in 2004.

- John Allen Muhammad, forty-one, and John Lee Malvo, seventeen, aka the "Beltway Snipers," killed nine innocent bystanders during a three-week killing spree in and around Maryland, Virginia, and Washington, DC, during October 2002. Profilers incorrectly assumed that the killers were white males and loudly promulgated the information to the media for several days.

- Gerald Parker, aka the "Bedroom Basher," terrorized women of Orange County, California, from 1978 to 1979. Parker would sneak into young women's homes and bash them over the head with a mallet or some other piece of wood. According to Corey Mitchell's *Hollywood Death Scenes*, Parker went undetected for seventeen years until DNA samples from a separate rape were used to match his semen to the victims from Orange County.

- Brandon Tholmer, a twenty-nine-year-old struggling musician from East Hollywood/Silverlake, California, stalked and murdered elderly women during the early 1980s. According to Corey Mitchell's *Hollywood Death Scenes*, Tholmer was suspected in as many as thirty-four murders, but only charged with five. He was prosecuted by a young Los Angeles County district attorney by the name of Lance Ito, who later presided over the O. J. Simpson murder trial.

- Wayne Williams, aka the "Atlanta Child Murderer," is possibly the most well-known African American serial killer. Williams was suspected of killing twenty-three of thirty young black boys in and around Atlanta, Georgia, from 1979 to 1981. Williams, however, was never convicted of murdering any children, but rather two adult convicts. The day after his conviction, the child murders task force disbanded and claimed their work was done. In 1985, an FBI confidential file was ordered unsealed. Inside was testimony from an agent of the Bureau who believed that the child killings were the work of the Ku Klux Klan. Allegedly, the Klan had wanted to instigate a race war by killing young blacks.

Additionally, lesser-known African American serial killers also include Jake Bird, Terry A. Blair, Maurice Byrd, Andre Crawford, Paul Denyer, Paul Durousseau, Lorenzo Fayne, Conz Gianni, Lorenzo Gilyard, Harrison Graham, Calvin Jackson, Devine Jones, Edward James, Richard "Babyface" Jameswhite, Henry Lee Jones, Gregory Klepper, Lamon J. McKoy, Eddie Lee Mosley, Craig Price, Cleophus Prince Jr., Robert Rozier, Troy Sampson, Maury Travis, Chester DeWayne Turner, Michael Vernon, Henry Louis Wallace, and the Zebra Killers. Their combined number of murder victims totaled more than 330.

Criminologist and assistant professor Scott Thornsley, Mansfield University in Pennsylvania, Criminal Justice Department, has spoken about the image of a serial killer. "Blacks have been ignored as serial killers in the past," said Thornsley to the *Detroit Metro Times*, speaking in regard to the "Beltway Snipers" case. "Actually it's a matter of perceived political correctness. Blacks can deal with the murder of individuals, but not this. And then you have to look at the entertainment medium," Thornsley continued. "The general public is a white audience, and blacks are less likely to appeal to a mass audience. Whites are simply not interested in black victims or black murderers."

This same mentality also has been displayed by publishing houses that release books on true crimes. Most publishers have believed that books on African American killers would not appeal to a wide-enough audience.

CHAPTER 36

Coral Watts's confession of the attack on Patty Johnson left one person very happy. Howard Mosley, who had been behind bars since before his conviction on July 15, 1982, was relieved to know that he was going to be a free man finally. Unfortunately, freedom did not come marching in immediately for Mosley.

Officials were not quite ready to believe that Mosley was *not* their man. Mosley's attorney and family friend Robert Hoskins, on the other hand, had no doubt of his client's innocence. Promptly after Watts confessed, Hoskins suggested to Galveston County district attorney James Hury that Mosley take a lie detector test. Hury acquiesced; however, the results of Mosley's test were inconclusive.

"Some people just don't react too well to polygraph exams," Hoskins tried to explain, "and we just felt he wasn't going to do well on any polygraph exam."

Hoskins also believed his client because he felt that Watts had given the authorities important holdback information, or information that only the attacker would have known. In the case of Patty Johnson, the weapon Watts claimed to have used seemed to match the type of knife used to stab the young lady. "He said it was a small knife that could have been a wood-carving knife," the attorney recalled. "The knife was never found, but his version of the weapon used seems to fit this case."

Hoskins believed Watts's confession was more than enough to release his client from guilt. "I think investigators gathered enough additional facts and this should enable them to make a determination to join with me in a motion for a new trial that would lead to dismissing the indictment against my client."

On August 16, 1982, Mosley was offered the chance for a second polygraph test. He declined. He claimed that he "doesn't have much faith in the polygraph test." He did, however, offer to undergo hypnosis. He even indicated that he would be willing to be injected with a truth serum, just to have the opportunity to prove his innocence.

On the following day, Hoskins moved for a new trial for Howard Mosley. The motion was granted but immediately rescinded by DA Hury. Instead, Hury agreed to dismiss the charge against Mosley.

Mosley's ordeal, however, was not over. Despite having the January 30, 1982, assault charge dropped, Hury informed the court that Mosley would not be released from incarceration. According to Hury, Mosley violated his parole for the aggravated robbery he committed back in 1987. The reason why Mosley did not walk was because he did commit a different misdemeanor assault on a woman in February 1982. Hury was miffed at the overly sympathetic news coverage Mosley had received for his ordeal.

"He is not a saint," the prosecutor blasted. "If he was not on parole, he could leave right now."

In fact, seven days earlier, Mosley had been allowed to

partake in a jailhouse wedding to Linda Sanchez, twenty-three. Linda, along with many of Mosley's friends, waited for Mosley to be released. They were all distraught when news came down that Mosley would not see daylight.

Furthermore, even though Hury granted Mosley a dismissal in the Patty Johnson assault, he was not so quick to dismiss Mosley completely. He speculated that Watts may not have acted alone and that Mosley was his accomplice. Assistant District Attorney Richard Crowther, the prosecutor in Mosley's case, stated that Johnson has consistently insisted that it was definitely Mosley who attacked her. Hury conceded that Watts's confession would make it near impossible to convict Mosley.

As Hury had stated, had Mosley kept his nose clean, he would have been officially paroled on August 5, 1983, from the original robbery sentence. Mosley was eventually held over by the Texas Board of Pardons and Paroles for the February 1982 attack. His revocation hearing took place on Friday, August 27, 1982.

Apparently, Hury tossed out the second assault charge while the hearing was taking place. During the hearing, the February assault victim testified that Mosley had beaten and raped her after he offered her a ride home from a party they both had attended. While the victim testified, word filtered up to Pardons and Parole Board hearing officer Alan Wilson that Hury had dropped the charges. Wilson called a halt to the proceedings and declared that the Board would reconvene at a later date to discuss Mosley's plight.

There would be a lot at stake. The Board either could let Mosley go or could force him to complete the remainder of his ten-year burglary sentence for failure to meet his parole requirements. That would mean five more years for Mosley.

District Attorney Hury claimed that he dropped the charges against Mosley after the prosecutor spoke with the alleged assault victim. He was not convinced that a jury would be completely convinced of Mosley's guilt, so he decided it would be best to drop the charges. Hury added that Mosley was not out of the woods. Just because he had dropped the charges did not mean that the Board would not revoke his parole.

Mosley waited anxiously.

He would only have to wait a few more days.

On Thursday, September 2, 1982, Mosley was called back before the Board for the final word on his parole status. Again he sat before Hearing Officer Alan Wilson. This time, Mosley's wife, Linda, and his mother, Bertha Ware, were there to support him. Not just by their presence, but by their testimony. Both women strongly affirmed that Mosley was with them at the time of the February attack.

After two hours of testimony, Wilson addressed Mosley, the skinny man, who stood six feet seven inches, was dressed in his custodial-looking jail whites. Wilson was clear cut and direct. He found that Mosley had not committed the assault and, therefore, had not violated his parole. He informed the stunned Mosley that he was a free man. After spending several months behind bars for a crime he did not commit, Howard Mosley was allowed to reenter society.

"Praise the Lord. Praise the Lord. Praise the Lord!" Mosley uttered upon the proclamation. Mosley, who led the prison choir as a director, stated that he "prayed and I prayed and I prayed. My prayers finally have paid off." Mosley squeezed his pocket-sized Bible as he rejoiced.

Mosley's mother also sang God's praises on behalf of her

son. "We came this far," the forty-two-year-old school-cafeteria cashier exclaimed. "I knew the Lord wouldn't let us down now. Let's open the doors of this church and sing."

Mosley held out hopes that divine intervention would carry him through this long ordeal. "I'm going to let the Lord direct [me] in trying to find a job. I want to get to know my wife a little better." He smiled as he clutched Linda with one hand while squeezing his Bible in the other. "I'm going to devote my life to the Lord."

Less than two years later, on March 13, 1984, Mosley was arrested for felony aggravated assault for an alleged attack on a Galveston police officer. He was no-billed on the felony charge by a grand jury. He was, however, charged with two misdemeanor charges for possession of marijuana and resisting arrest.

Mosley was unemployed at the time of the arrest.

CHAPTER 37

After being sentenced, Coral Watts was sent to a holding cell in the Harris County Jail. He stayed there until Monday, September 27, 1982, when he was sent to the Diagnostic Center of the Texas Department of Corrections at the Coffield Unit in Huntsville, Texas. There was no additional security provided for Watts to complete the transfer to the Coffield Unit.

It appeared as if the good-time credits issue quickly became a moot point. On February 20, 1983, Watts tried to escape from prison. Watts walked into the cell block recreation room just before 10:00 P.M. He was carrying a pillowcase stuffed with food, leather gloves attached to his belt, and a rolled-up blanket, also attached to his belt. In addition, he had a plastic bottle of hair lotion for his Jheri curl.

Somehow Watts had convinced several of his fellow inmates to form a human shield for him. Their main objective was to prevent the prison guards from seeing Watts as he attempted to make his getaway. Once safely hidden by the convicts, Watts scooted over to the recreation-room window and kicked out the windowpane with his foot. He then removed the activator bottle for his Jheri curl and poured it all over his body. The five-foot-eleven-inch, 165-pound Watts geared up to seek his freedom. He attempted to squeeze through the narrow opening. Despite being greased up like a 7-Eleven rotisserie hot dog, Watts was unable to propel himself through the escape route. He slithered down onto the recreation-room floor, defeated. But he was ready to try again, so desperate was he to escape. This time, however, he was spotted by one of the prison guards.

Watts spent the next fifteen days locked away in solitary confinement. In addition, he lost all 181 good-time credit days he had earned up to that point.

Watts was also added to a higher-security-risk list. As a result, he was transferred to the Texas Department of Corrections Eastham Unit in Lovelady, Texas, thirteen miles west of Trinity on FM 230. Eastham had a rougher reputation as a correctional facility that was capable of keeping its guests in line and behind bars. One way of doing that was forcing the inmates to perform difficult farm-based chores, such as working with cows, calves, and heifers, train security dogs and horses, farm maintenance, working crops and feed mills.

Watts was one of more than twenty-four hundred inmates at Eastham.

CHAPTER 38

The intervening years provided some interesting changes in the way that crime was fought in Texas and in the world. The first such situation involved the Violent Criminal Apprehension Program (VICAP). The idea for a computerized database to be used to track murders that were possibly committed by serial offenders had been kicked around for more than twenty-five years by a man named David Brooks, of Los Angeles. Brooks worked on the case of Harvey Glatman, a pseudo-photojournalist from Los Angeles who had a penchant for setting up fake photo shoots and killing his would-be models. Brooks had antagonized his superiors for decades before they finally stood up and took notice.

In August 1983, Brooks, along with Sam Houston State University criminologist Dr. Doug Moore, held a symposium at Sam Houston State, which is located in Huntsville. Dr. Moore was appointed the project director for VICAP and given a grant from the United States Justice Department for $136,000.

Moore referenced that cases such as the Coral Watts murders and the earlier Dean Corll/Elmer Wayne Henley/David Brooks (no relation to the aforementioned FBI

agent) killing spree combined with recent statistics indicated that nearly five thousand people "are murdered
each year without apparent motive by sadomasochists,
child abusers, or wholesalers of child pornography."
Moore believed that such a centralized, nationwide system
would have been useful in attempting to capture Watts
sometime during the middle of his murderous rampage.

"The fact is, there were strong suspicions about Watts,"
the professor reasoned. "A centralized information site
could have delivered more information on the patterns of
behavior he was suspected of exhibiting in other places."

Moore hoped that VICAP would be accepted by a national agency as the latest in modernized crime-fighting
technological advances. "We think we'll be able to find
more serial or mass murders, rapes, and molestations,"
Moore inferred.

Justice Department spokesman Drew McKillips lauded
the efforts by Brooks and Moore and the virtues of the
VICAP program. "The mass murders (most serial killings
were called 'mass murders' back in the day) now are turning up as if by sheer accident through a casual remark
made by two investigators on a plane." VICAP would pool
these pieces of information together and help to coor-
dinate killers' patterns for investigating authorities to use
in their attempts at capturing a killer.

Moore stated at the Sam Houston State symposium that
the formal presentation would take place the following
June before the Office of Juvenile Justice and Delin-
quency Prevention. The goal was to attain approval and
$10 million in funding.

Harriett Semander, and her husband, Zaharias, were
not going to let the pressure off Coral Watts. The couple

filed a wrongful death lawsuit against Watts for the death of their daughter Elena—despite the fact that they knew they would probably never receive a penny from the confessed killer of their beloved daughter. The lawsuit stated that they were seeking compensation for "damages to the familial unit and loss of love, advice, comfort and companionship." They also claimed to suffer from severe mental anguish over the death of their daughter.

The Semanders had no ill-conceived notion that they would ever get paid by Coral Watts. They mainly filed the suit to remind him that they were always going to be watching him, that there was someone out there who would not forget the women that he had killed and that they would always be there to remind him of their pain and loss. Watts was served with the process on September 10, 1984. It would be nearly four-and-a-half years later before a court made a decision on the case.

Less than one month later, it was discovered that the Board of Pardons and Paroles did not have any official mention of the murders Coral Watts had committed. In addition, there was no mention of the deadly-weapon charge in the attack on Lori Lister included in the file.

Harriett Semander was disgusted when she found out. "No confession? I just want to scream. I just don't want to believe it."

Harris County trial bureau chief Bert Graham, of the district attorney's office, could not believe it either. Graham was worried that there could be serious repercussions down the line when Watts would come up for parole. "There's no sense taking even a five percent chance on somebody like Watts."

Parole board chairman Ruben M. Torres did not seem fazed. He informed Graham that the file would be ready to go by the time Watts would be eligible for parole for the first time in 2002. "I can assure you," Torres attempted to comfort, "there will be adequate information in the file when the file is received." He added, "That's been my experience since 1979. You can only go by past history."

If the past history of the Coral Watts case was any indication, Graham believed the file needed to be updated immediately. "I can guarantee you they are going to have a statement of facts on Coral in a couple of days."

Another consequence to the Coral Eugene Watts murder spree involved the so-called "multiple murder" bill. Had Watts been convicted of the murders of the thirteen women he had confessed to killing, he would not have received the death penalty back then. Texas, the execution-happy capital of the United States, known for its "Texecutions," did not have legislation in place for a criminal such as Coral Watts.

Since Watts neither raped his victims nor robbed them, he would not have an additional offense tacked on to elevate his charges to a capital offense. At the time the only types of crimes that constituted capital murder in Texas were:

- Murder of an on-duty peace officer or firefighter
- Murder in the course of kidnapping, burglary, robbery, aggravated sexual assault, or arson
- Murder for hire
- Murder while escaping a penal institution
- Murder of a penal employee while incarcerated in a penal institution

On June 29, 1984, a Moroccan national named Abdelkrim Belachheb mowed down six people with a gun at a Dallas, Texas, nightclub known as Ianni's Restaurant. Belachheb was not charged with capital murder, since multiple murder was not on the books at the time.

Belachheb was convicted on November 15, 1984, and received a life-in-prison sentence. Four months later, Tony Polumbo (D-Houston), a state representative, helped pass a new measure, House Bill 8, that would include multiple murders—whether at one time, or as part of a series of ongoing murders—onto the list of crimes that would immediately constitute a capital offense. Polumbo cited not only the Dallas shooting, but also the case of Coral Eugene Watts.

The bill was passed by both the Texas House and the Senate the following month; it was later signed into law by Texas governor Mark White.

Coral Watts's time in prison from 1984 to 1987 was low-key—at least to the eye of the public. Apparently, he had been spending his time in a productive manner. He began to hit the prison library to bone up on the law. He also began to hit the weights to build up his strength, so as to protect himself. Prisoners who kill a score of females tend to be targeted by inmates looking to make a name for themselves.

As a result Watts became angrier, stronger, and smarter.

Zinetta Burney, Watts's defense attorney, spoke of an annual visit she made with Watts's mother, to visit her former client. Watts was sequestered in a prison psychiatric ward. What Burney saw scared the hell out of her.

"He's taken his evil to greater heights," Burney informed the *Houston Post*. "I feel he is more dangerous than ever before. He still thinks in terms of killing and murder, but I'm not sure that he'd only kill women anymore."

Burney also said that the prison guards basically treated Watts like an animal . . . and she felt they were right to do so. "In prison they used to treat him like anyone else. Now he comes to see his mother in handcuffs with guards on either side of him, and he looks like if they turned his hands loose, he would just attack. It's almost animal-like."

Larry Fossi, Meg Fossi's husband, still burned the torch for his late wife. The now-thirty-year-old widower stated, "I have not stopped thinking about it. I have not stopped missing Meg. I don't think I ever will." As for Watts, he simply burned: "I still get chills when I go through Huntsville."

Fossi, like Harriett Semander, wanted Watts to know that he would never quit the fight to keep him behind bars. "I will not rest in peace as long as Watts is alive. I very much regret Coral Watts is alive."

Harriett Semander spoke of an unwanted, bizarre kinship she had with her daughter's killer. "He's like a part of the family. When you think of Elena, you think about Coral Watts. He has become a part of my life."

Semander was worried that somehow Coral Watts would, yet again, slip through the cracks. He had been so lucky so many times before, she was convinced that something would happen again. "If he comes up for parole twenty years from now," the headstrong yet softspoken Greek mother insisted, "I've asked the parole board to notify me."

Finally Ken Williamson, who was part of the four-man Homicide team that interrogated Watts during the confessions, expressed his concern that Watts might be released in the future. "I know good and well he did more killings." He also said of Watts that "I don't think he's going to be cured."

Williamson added a chilling coda: "I guarantee he'll do it again if he gets out. And the exact words he told us were 'If I ever get out, I'm coming back to Houston.'"

CHAPTER 39

The thought of America's most notorious serial killer being paroled seemed impossible. And in of all places . . . Texas. The one state with a worldwide reputation as a hard-ass on all criminals—especially brutal serial murderers.

That reputation did not deter Coral Watts from seeking his freedom. The five years in prison that he had spent strengthening his body protected him from those inside. He hoped the simultaneous strengthening of his mind would protect him from those outside the prison walls.

One of his first attempts at obtaining freedom came in the form of a writ of habeas corpus that he filed on May 30, 1986. The nine-page, hand-printed petition displayed an advanced understanding of the law, usually beyond most prisoners. Watts proclaimed that he was "being unlawfully restrained of his liberty" and that his conviction for a "Bergalrey [sic] of A Habitation with Intent to commit Murder" and his subsequent sentence was "in violation of the Petitioners Constitutional Right guaranteed to him pursuant to the Fifth (5th) and Fourteenth (14th) Amendments of the Texas and United

States Constitutions thereby rendering the plea and Conviction Void and unavailable for any Purpose."

Watts reasoned that he had been tried unfairly because "Petitioner was Questioned by three (3) detectives being Tom ladd, Jim ladd, and an unknown investigator without counselor, unknown detective made threats of Physical brutality to Petitioner as well as other methods to get people to talk. . . ."

One of those methods, Watts claimed, included threatening to take his daughter, Nakisha, away. "On August 9, 1982," Watts opined, "officers made . . . threats to taking Petitioners daughter . . . and place her in a home if Petitioner would not make a confession to a series of crimes to <u>clean up the books</u>." Watts was no longer fessing up to the murders. He continued: "Whereas on August 9, 1982 Petitioner made confessions as well as Plead guilty to an offense for sixty (60) Years before of [*sic*] threats to take his daughter and placing her in a home. (Note: Defense Counsel and Prosecution were fully aware of such threats before, during and after Petitioner entered his Plead of Guilty)."

Watts attached an affidavit from former girlfriend Sheila Williams to the petition. In the affidavit Williams backed up Watts's claims in regard to his daughter. She swore that she "was living with Coral Watts prior to and during his incidental arrest for an alleged series of offenses," and that she had taken care of his daughter, Nakisha, after Watts's arrest. She added, "I was later barred from our apartment where Police confiscated the apartment whereas we had lived by changing the lock and denying me entry." Williams explicitly swore that "officers then took Coral Watts daughter <u>Nakisha Watts</u> from my custody without Coral Watts' permission or request, whereas as Coral Watts on regular intervals demanded

Houston Police to return his daughter <u>Nakisha Watts</u> back to my and my mother's custody." She concluded by saying that "this action by Houston Police was to be used as compulsion against Coral Watts."

Funny how Sheila Williams never mentioned this pertinent bit of information to the press during the intervening four years.

Watts's very well-reasoned, yet grammatically challenged petition, was dismissed without a second glance.

Watts's next petition was not so quickly dismissed.

On July 7, 1987, Watts again handwrote a petition for habeas corpus. He discovered a loophole in the Texas law, which he used to his advantage. When Judge Shaver sentenced him five years earlier, he stated that Watts had used the water from Lori Lister's bathtub as a "deadly weapon."

Had it been included, Watts would probably not have lived to see the light of day. Since it was not included, Watts had to be considered a nonviolent offender and, as a result, should have been eligible for mandatory good-time behavior credits, the prisoner argued.

The Texas Court of Criminal Appeals heard Watts's plea this time. One of the main reasons they elected to do so was because in 1987 the court had begun to enforce the deadly-weapon notification during all sentencing hearings. In 1982, when Watts was arrested and convicted, prosecutors were not required to inform defendants that they planned on including a deadly-weapon charge, thereby elevating a defendant to violent-offender status. In 1987, the courts decided in the case *Ex Parte Patterson*, 740 S.W.2d 766 (Tex. Crim. App. 1987) (en banc), that such inclusion was pertinent and necessary to the understanding of the sentencing by the defendant. All mentions of uses of deadly weapons now must be included.

On March 1, 1989, the Texas Court of Criminal Appeals handed down its opinion on Watts's petition. The court determined that "the indictment in this cause made no reference to any use of a weapon. The transcription of the plea proceedings clearly reveals that whenever the parties entered into the plea bargain agreement, it was not the intention of the prosecuting attorney to have the trial judge enter an affirmative finding in the judgment." The opinion added that Judge Shaver "found that no notice was given that the State would seek a finding of the use of a deadly weapon."

In conclusion, the court of appeals granted the relief sought by Watts. It also ordered that the following language be deleted from the original record: ". . . and the Court further found that a deadly weapon, to-wit, the water in the bathtub, was used during the commission of this offense."

The decision by the court of appeals would have incredible ramifications. Primary among them, Coral Watts's prisoner status would automatically go from a violent offender to nonviolent offender. Subsequently he no longer had to wait twenty years before his good-time behavior credit kicked in. The tolling began retroactively from the day after his prison-escape attempt back in 1983. As a result Watts would have his first parole hearing on January 15, 1990.

Miraculously, America's worst serial killer would be eligible to walk the streets again one day. He could become the first-known confessed male serial killer ever to be released from prison.

CHAPTER 40

The response to the Texas Court of Criminal Appeals decision was one of outrage. Judge Shaver, who included the bathtub-water-as-a-deadly-weapon proviso in the original sentencing, declared, "Any member of the Board of Pardons and Paroles who votes to let him out ought to be charged as a party in his next murder." District Attorney John B. Holmes Jr. had a more juvenile response: "Phooey!" Lori Lister, Watts's victim in the attack in question, stated, "I don't think he should ever be released. I wouldn't have any trouble watching him die."

Widower Larry Fossi was also outraged. He decided to fight fire with fire. Fossi, on behalf of the Texas District and County Attorneys Association, filed an amicus curiæ brief, also known as a friend-of-the-court brief, wherein a person with a strong interest in a case—but not a party to the proceedings—may request to file a brief expressing their beliefs. He urged the court to deny Watts's petition. Fossi's brief essentially attempted to dismantle the court's rendering of the *Patterson* decision.

According to William Murchison in the October 31, 1988, edition of the *Texas Lawyer,* Fossi's brief stated that "the Texas Constitution creates no right to parole, nor does it envision any role for the judiciary in parole matters." Also, there is "a century of settled law that militates against" *Patterson*. Fossi added that "the Texas legislature by no means intended to create any liberty interest or other constitutionally cognizable right in parole or good conduct time."

Fossi concluded that the court of criminal appeals decision "is a mistaken exercise of judicial power, untethered by any deference to the legislative branch. It should be expressly overruled." Almost everyone involved in the case, as well as the public opinion, was in total agreement.

Everyone, that is, except for the criminal court of appeals.

William Murchison added, "The Court of Criminal Appeals should get its act together and stop making up new constitutional protections for murderers. The court cleverly is using the Texas, rather than the federal, Constitution to avoid federal review of its decisions. The judges apparently deluded themselves that the people of Texas won't notice."

Fossi's arguments, as well as the opinion of the Texas citizenry, fell on deaf ears.

The authorities in Michigan had also kept an eye on the Texas Court of Criminal Appeals decision in regard to Coral Watts. "It's very frustrating," claimed Harper Woods police chief Gary Ford. "We know he did it," he said in reference to the murder of Lena Bennett. Ford's frustration was because "we can't extradite him even if he is paroled because we don't have any physical evidence connecting him to the crime. No prints or witnesses, but we know he did it."

Western Michigan University lieutenant Wesley

Carpenter expressed a similar frustration. "We believe he killed a coed by the name of Gloria Steele."

The only people in Texas that could be bothered to do something about keeping Coral Watts behind bars were the friends and family of the Semanders. Led by Elena's mother, Harriett, the Semanders set about distributing petitions that opposed Watts's potential release. The petition was addressed to Harry B. Keene, chairman of the Texas Board of Pardons and Paroles. It stated, "As a confessed serial killer, he (Watts) is a continued threat to women and he should be made to serve the full sixty-year sentence imposed by the court." The Semanders sought out the signatures of Houstonians who did not want a serial killer roaming their streets. The signed petitions would then be included in Watts's parole packet for any possible future parole hearings.

Family friend Gwen Pratt, a University of Houston senior, the same school that Elena attended, pitched in as well. She helped organize a petition drive at the University of Houston's University Center and the University Center Satellite to collect signatures.

On January 15, 1990, Watts had his first hearing before the parole board. Board Members John Escobedo and Kenneth Coleman heard Watts's plea for freedom. They were fully prepared with all of the necessary documentation in the Watts case, including the confessions and details of Watts's murder confessions that Ruben M. Torres showed little concern for, back in 1982.

The decision was relatively simple for Escobedo and Coleman. They denied Watts's request for parole for the following reasons: (a) parole not in the best interest of society and/or inmate at this time; (b) nature and seriousness of offense(s); (c) use of weapon in current offense; and (d) "assaultiveness" in the instant offense, or in past offenses. Apparently, the board members listened to the public's desires. Furthermore, the inclusion of the deadly weapon ran counter to the court of criminal appeals' decision.

The parole board decided that Watts's next parole hearing would take place in December 1993.

"We're so glad he won't be getting out," stated Pratt. "Not yet, anyway."

It was that sentiment, that everything was nowhere close to complete, that drove Harriett Semander. Even after Watts's parole denial, she and daughter JoAnna were still out collecting signatures. They were determined to make sure that Coral Eugene Watts would *never* be released from prison to terrorize and murder young women again.

CHAPTER 41

In 1991, Coral Watts was transferred from the psychiatric ward of the Texas Department of Corrections Ellis II Unit in Huntsville, Texas, to the Clements Unit in Amarillo, Texas. Clements is located on Spur 591, just east of Loop 335. The high-security prison houses all levels of criminals, over thirty-five hundred of them. Clements also institutes a Program for Aggressive Mentally Ill Offenders and also provides an inpatient mental-health treatment program.

On May 13, 1992, Andy Kahan was named as the head of the Crime Victims Assistance of the Mayor's Office. The prior year, according to Kahan, "crime was the number one issue in Houston." Mayoral candidate Bob Lanier met with several Houston-based victims' groups, such as Parents of Murdered Children and Mothers Against Drunk Drivers (MADD), and asked them how he could help if elected mayor. They suggested someone to work out of the mayor's office to assist victims of crime.

Lanier won the election and immediately formed a transition subcommittee. Kahan was placed on the committee, along with Harriett Semander and Vera Cronin, of MADD. They were asked to write a proposal for the position and Kahan was selected by the mayor to fill that role. Andy Kahan had worked with several people from the different advocacy groups and had developed a reputation as a straight shooter, which was quite unusual at the time for someone in the Houston criminal justice system.

Mayor Lanier had no idea what kind of monster he created.

One year later, in May 1993, Harriett Semander was notified of Watts's second parole hearing. The hearing would take place in September of that same year. Once again, the steadfast mother was prepared to put up a fight. She immediately wrote a letter in which she demanded a hearing of Watts's victims, which was her right under state law. This time around she had the backing and support of Houston mayor Bob Lanier, Judge Doug Shaver, and District Attorney John B. Holmes Jr., and Andy Kahan.

Kahan believed the Texas Legislature in Austin would also support Harriett Semander's cause: "We can go up [to Austin] anytime, not just for the hearing. They don't want to let anyone out if it's not in the best interest of society."

Holmes proclaimed, "We're not going to roll over." Holmes believed that the thirty-nine-year-old Watts would continue to be a threat if released from prison: "He is a continuing danger."

Semander wanted to make sure that the parole board members had a fully painted picture of their potential parolee. "The man is in there only for a burglary," Semander stated, exasperated. "I'm afraid he's going to look pretty good to the members. They'll think he's rehabilitated. It's important to let them know that he's not."

As Watts's parole hearing drew nearer, Semander and Kahan cranked up the media machine. They were geared up for a showdown with Watts. Semander informed the press that "when this guy is released, he will make Kenneth McDuff look like Santa Claus."

McDuff was a convicted triple murderer on death row who was released due to prison overcrowding in October 1989. Within three days McDuff went on a second killing spree, which lasted much longer. McDuff was eventually captured and convicted of murder. He was suspected of killing at least seven young women, and was, at one time, a prime suspect in the 1991 Austin yogurt shop murders of four young ladies at an I Can't Believe It's Yogurt shop.

"It is insane," Semander punctuated, "to be reviewing this case for parole.

"There is nothing we can do about him being released in fourteen years," Semander noted, regarding the fact that she learned, from Kahan, that Watts would receive a mandatory release under Texas law in 2006, "but we can stop his impending release." Semander attempted to reach out to her fellow Texans: "We want to get the public involved. Police officers, students, everyone who is concerned about a killer being released."

Semander seemed emotionally drained from yet another legal battle to keep her daughter's killer incarcerated. "It drives me batty, but, in a way, it keeps my mind off what happened, because I'm so mad at the criminal justice system." She sighed and her shoulders slumped as she said, "When this is over, maybe then I can sit down and cry."

Kahan, on behalf of the city of Houston's mayor's office, was there to lend support. "This is happening in Texas," the no-nonsense advocate pointed out, "so you never say never. We want to call everyone's attention to what is going on."

Semander and Kahan drafted another form letter that urged the Texas Board of Pardons and Paroles not to consider Watts for parole.

On September 3, 1993, Watts had his second hearing before the Texas Board of Pardons and Paroles. This time he was reviewed by board members Terri Schnorrenberg and Mae Jackson. Again, like the first time, Watts was denied parole for the following reasons: (a) nature and seriousness of offense(s); (b) involvement with a controlled substance and/or inhalants; (c) repetition of similar offenses; (d) use of weapon in current offense; (e) "assaultiveness" in the instant offense, or in past offenses; and (f) alcohol involvement in the instant offense and/or alcohol abuse history.

It would be three more years before Watts's next parole hearing. In those intervening years, Andy Kahan and Harriett Semander fought hard to try and overturn the mandatory-release laws implemented by the state of Texas in 1977. The law was enacted to relieve overcrowded prisons. Kahan and Semander were unable to rattle the Legislature awake enough to reverse the course of action.

On October 23, 1996, Coral Watts had his third hearing before the parole board. Leading up to the hearing, Andy Kahan continued to pound the bully pulpit with support from Harriett Semander.

Kahan focused his discussion on the issue of mandatory release. Kahan labeled Watts the "poster boy" for the abolishment of the mandatory-release law, implemented by the state of Texas in 1977. The victims' advocate also

believed it was ludicrous that Watts would even be considered for parole. Kahan also made a dire prediction:
"Unless we do something about the mandatory-release
laws, he will walk out [of prison] within the next decade."

Parole board members Victor Rodriguez and Bennie
Elmore made sure Coral Watts did not walk out of prison
that year. They denied Watts's third bid for parole and
gave the simple answer of "criminal record and/or nature
of offense(s)."

In 1997, it became apparent that the work of Harriett
Semander and Andy Kahan was beginning to pay off.
Texas senator Jerry Patterson (R-Pasadena) took notice
of the state's mandatory release laws. When he spoke of
Coral Watts, he used some of the exact phraseology of
both Semander and Kahan. "The poster child for ending
mandatory release is Coral Eugene Watts," Patterson
angrily informed the press. "Under mandatory release,
Coral Eugene Watts will likely be released. . . . He'll be
fifty years old, still a maniac, still a threat, and still likely
to kill more women."

Senator John Whitmire (D-Houston) echoed Patterson's sentiments. "That's nuts," the senator exclaimed
about the formula the Texas Department of Corrections used to calculate good-time behavior. "It must be
stopped this session."

Unlike many politicians who merely spout off what they
believe their electorate wants to hear, Patterson and
Whitmire actually attempted to do something about the
problem. The senators introduced a bill that would actually attempt to force prisoners to serve the full time they
were sentenced to upon conviction. Automatic release
would not be granted to a prisoner before their actual

time had been served. In other words, sixty years would mean sixty years.

The legislature had attempted to curtail this problem back in 1995, when a law was passed that gave the Board of Pardons and Paroles veto power. The problem with the Watts case, however, was that the law only covered prisoners who were convicted after September 1, 1996. Watts was convicted in 1982; therefore, the law did not apply to him.

State Representative Peggy Hamric (R-Houston) joined Patterson and Whitmire in drafting an additional bill that gave lawmakers the ability to veto any mandatory releases for prisoners convicted pre–September 1, 1996. Governor George W. Bush (R) fast-tracked the bill and declared it to be an emergency.

One of the main reasons for the expediency of the bill was the startling statistics from the previous year. In 1994, there were approximately sixteen thousand inmates released from Texas prisons due to mandatory supervision. More than nine hundred of those were convicted sex offenders.

On November 19, 1999, Coral Watts attended his fourth parole hearing. As had happened three times prior, Watts was denied parole. This time by parole board members James Bush and Rissie Owens. The reason for the rejection? "Criminal record and/or nature of offense(s)."

CHAPTER 42

One month later, something offensive surfaced surrounding the case. A personal letter written by Coral Watts appeared for sale on the Internet auction site eBay. Harriett Semander was appalled by the sale. She contacted Andy Kahan to discuss the situation.

According to the *Double-Tongued Word Wrester: A Growing Dictionary of Old and New Words from the Fringes of English,* the term "murderabilia" first publicly appeared in a January 19, 1994, *Chicago Sun-Times* article entitled "The Undersee World of Pop Culture," written by Jeff Huebner. The article focused on unique collectibles, in the Chicago area, such as posters, underground comics, and T-shirts. It also talked about a grimmer subcategory: serial killer artwork—specifically, the infamous "Pogo the Clown" paintings by notorious serial killer John Wayne Gacy, who was convicted and executed for the murders of at least thirty-three young men, several who were buried in a crawl space underneath his home. Such artwork was deemed murderabilia.

Many imprisoned serial killers have a lot of free time at their disposal. As a result they like to use their hands in a different way than they had out in the free world.

Some write; some do crafts; others draw or paint. There have been several well-known serial killers who enjoy artistic endeavors. Among them, Richard Ramirez, aka "the Night Stalker," the brutal pseudo-Satanic murderer from the early 1980s, in Los Angeles, California, who was responsible for at least thirteen deaths. Ramirez likes to illustrate pictures of the Devil, as well as pornographic renderings of his favorite sexual fantasies. Gacy was known for painting extensive watercolor paintings of "Pogo the Clown," a character he created and dressed up as to entertain little children at birthday parties. Gacy's artwork is probably the most well-known, as it has been purchased by several celebrities, including actor Johnny Depp.

Another serial killer turned "artist" was Houston's own Elmer Wayne Henley. The killer of at least twenty-seven young men and boys had parlayed his notoriety into sales of his artwork, which included everything from nude forms to placid sunflowers to interpretations of his crimes. Henley and Kahan both appear in the documentary *Collectors* about the controversy of a Houston art gallery displaying Henley's paintings.

Other forms of murderabilia include clothes from the killers, locks of hair, even the toenails of brutal serial killer Lawrence "Pliers" Bittaker, a lovely individual who, along with his buddy, Roy Norris, kidnapped and tortured at least five young women in the South Bay region of southern California during 1979.

Possibly the most common form of murderabilia, which is easily accessible, is correspondence, or handwritten letters, from serial killers. The former Hollywood Museum of Death used to display correspondence from numerous serial killers, including Henry Lee Lucas's sidekick Ottis Toole, Ramirez, Gacy, and more. The late true-crime author Dana Holliday used to correspond with several murderers, including Douglas Clark, aka "the Sunset Strip Slayer," and David Berkowitz, aka "Son of Sam."

Coral Watts claimed he used to write letters to several people outside of prison. He had no idea that a cottage industry had sprung up around serial killers and that his signature was considered a cherished find in some circles.

When Harriett Semander learned that a two-page, handwritten letter signed by her daughter's killer was up for sale, she went ballistic. She again teamed up with Andy Kahan to put a stop to the sale of murderabilia.

Ironically, Semander and Kahan had an unusual ally in their fight: Coral Watts. Watts managed to read an article in the *Houston Chronicle*, written by Mark Smith, that detailed the auction of Watts's letter and decided to contact the reporter directly.

In a neat, handwritten, page-and-a-half letter, dated December 12, 1999, Watts thanked Smith for bringing the matter to his attention. He misspelled several words in the letter: "Mr. Smith. I had no idea that this was being done. I have bee in corraspondance with several people out there in the world, but I did not know this was happening."

Watts surprisingly showed emotion for the families of his victims: "It greaves me to hear that is being done with my letters and art work. belive me when I say. I feel badly about what has happen. I would be just as up set as those familys. If it came to my attention that someone was making a profit off the death of one of my love ones in this manner."

Watts stressed that he only wrote to individuals with whom he had had an understanding that they would not turn around and sell his writings. "Anyone that has done this," he stressed, "has done this in defince of the understanding we had."

He then wrote something that should have sent shivers up the spines of the death profiteers: "What I am asking of you to give me apalogy to all those afended. And if you could please send me the address and name or names of the individuals who has done such a shameful deed."

Watts then attempted to take the high-and-mighty ground when he wrote, "This is a direct assault upon the dead and their living relatives, and a gross disrespect to my trust in that person to do what's right."

Watts then asked Smith if he would assist him in contacting eBay and putting a halt to the sale of his letters. Watts's request began to turn more dark and unusual by the second page: "Some people will do anything for a small reward that will be gone in a twinking of an eye. Such people take their oaths as a means to deceive and betray those who put their trust in them. This type of person will sale their souls for a small profit. This is one reson the world is in the chaos it is in to day."

He concluded with another plea to Smith: "Please! Get back with me on this. I must find out who this person is that has done such a hideous and dreadfull thing to my trust and to those who can longer defend for themselves."

Watts also wrote a similar, misspelled letter to Andy Kahan, dated January 15, 2000.

In the letter he spoke of "greedy fools" and "uncareing selfish people."

Midway through the letter, Watts's writing took an unusual turn, talking about death profiteers and corrupt public officials. "Mr. Kahan, I have learned from my dealing with people such as yourself. The State. That they can not be trusted. They mix truth with false hood. They lie, deieve, mislead and back stab. Some of you are more cruel and vicious then the crimals you hold in prison. And some of you belong in prison yourselves."

Watts continued his rant: "Don't get me wrong. I have nothing aganst you or the job you do. It has to do with the low down and dirty uncareing, conspireing terrorizeing and controlling ways in which the State treat those under it's supervison." He then declared his stance against Kahan: "You may say, that you are not a part of that, but you are whether you admit it or not."

But Kahan and public officials were not Watts's only targets: "The news media is no better and sometimes worse. They decive by confuseing you with words, and knowledge. They use half truths to make there point."

Watts then concluded with the chipper "Thank you for your help and concern, Coral E. Watts."

Andy Kahan's grassroots campaign to eliminate murderabilia from eBay reached a successful conclusion two weeks before the ABC news magazine *20/20* was scheduled to air a piece on the Internet auction sales of serial-killer-related merchandise. A press release was sent out by eBay that stated they would cease all sales of murderabilia. It was quite a victory for Andy Kahan and the families of murder victims.

CHAPTER 43

Andy Kahan and Harriett Semander continued their relentless media campaign to bring the Coral Eugene Watts case before the public's eye. Despite possibly murdering as many as eighty to one hundred women, Watts was relatively unknown.

Judy Wolf Krueger, Suzi Wolf's older sister, was amazed at the lack of her sister's killer's notoriety amongst the American public. "Everybody knows about Ted Bundy and Son of Sam and all of the other serial killers of the past," she declared. "And nobody knows about Coral Eugene Watts.

"It's time."

Indeed, Watts's relative obscurity was unbelievable. If he did kill at least eighty people, Watts would have slaughtered more victims than Bundy, Gacy, and Dahmer combined. Yet, in less than four years, he would be free to walk the streets.

One of the grandest and most successful attempts to draw attention to the eventual release of Coral Eugene Watts, America's most prolific serial killer, was named "A

Call to Action," conceived by Harriett Semander and Andy Kahan. It was a gathering of Watts's victims' surviving family members that took place on August 3, 2002, at the Annunciation Greek Orthodox Cathedral, the same church that Elena Semander attended, and where her personal memorial service was held after her death in 1982. It was nearly the twentieth anniversary of the beginning of Watts's confessions of murder.

Harriett Semander once again led the charge. She, along with Andy Kahan, and Dianne Clements, president of Justice for All Alliance, a victims' rights group, organized the memorial and made sure to contact as many media outlets as possible.

The success of the service went beyond their wildest imagination.

More than two hundred people showed up for the event, which was covered by several representatives of the local press. Most important, dozens of surviving family members and friends came to lend a face to their loved ones who were eradicated so savagely by Coral Watts.

Among those in attendance: Jane Montgomery, Elizabeth Montgomery's mother, Keri Whitlow (formerly Murphy) and Lori Katt (formerly Bukowski), who were Suzi Wolf's best friends, Harriett Semander and JoAnna Nicolaou, mother and sister of Elena Semander, Laura Allen, mother of Anna Ledet, Larry Fossi, husband of Meg Fossi, Elizabeth Young, mother of Emily LaQua, Marie O'Bryant, sister-in-law of Carrie Mae Jefferson, Lori Sword, best friend of Suzanne Searles, Beverly Searles, mother of Suzanne Searles, Maricela Gracia, niece of Yolanda Gracia, and Myra Gracia, daughter of Yolanda Gracia. Myra was only six months old at the time of her mother's death.

Also in attendance were some key players in the case:

retired police officer Don Schmidt, the man who arrested Watts, Ira L. Jones II, the assistant district attorney who came up with the plea bargain for Watts, Detective Jim Ladd, the officer who helped elicit Watts's confessions, and survivor Lori Lister.

The gathering started off in a somber tone as people filtered into the church hallways. They ambled over toward several tables that were set up as memorials for the victims. For many, this was their first time to meet the other survivors. It was also the first time for them to learn more about the other victims' lives.

They walked past tables decorated with attractive boards commemorating the women. One was entitled "In Memory of All Victims" and was decorated with cheerful, explosive-looking splashes of red, white, and blue. It was festooned with blue and white stars and tiny American flags. Another board was entitled "Angels in Heaven" and contained thirteen oversized red hearts; each one represented one of Coral Watts's confessed-to victims.

Each participant would register at one of the tables and pick up a commemorative button showing their support. Another table was manned by a woman requesting signatures for a petition to keep Coral Eugene Watts behind bars. A poster board behind the volunteer was labeled with a bold black marker and entitled "Keep These Serial Killers in Jail. Please Sign These Petitions." Practically every person who showed up signed the petition.

The beginning reception allowed the participants the opportunity to mingle and get to know one another. It also gave people time to look at the displays for the girls. Each tableau had photographs, letters, or keepsakes of the girls. Elizabeth Montgomery's display had several pictures attached to a board, many that looked like professional modeling shots. There was also a photograph of Elizabeth, where she looked like actress Kristy McNichol during her *Little Darlings/Family* heyday, replete with a T-shirt emblazoned with press-on letters that spelled out "Cherokee People."

There were five photographs of Emily LaQua, three of her as a small girl. Suzanne Searles had two adult photos on display, which showcased her flaming red hair. Linda Tilley had two glamour photos, one serious and one with an openmouthed, full-bodied laugh/smile. There was a third photo of her playing in the snow. Elena Semander had ten photographs, which included a black-and-white shot of her playing field hockey, as well as many photographs with her brother and sisters. The table also displayed a poem written by Elena's brother, John, entitled "To Elena With Love," which was published in 1995 in a collection of poetry entitled *A Sea of Treasures*. There was also a letter of encouragement written by Elena for John.

After the reception ended, Andy Kahan, on behalf of the city of Houston's Crime Victims Assistance of the Mayor's Office, stepped up to the podium before the gathered crowd. The tall, thin Kahan, dressed in all-black and wearing round, wire-rimmed glasses, opened up the "Remembrance Memorial" by introducing Elizabeth Padilla and Nancy Salinas, who sang "The Lord's Prayer." The song was followed by the "Pledge of Allegiance," led by a young Boy Scout named Nicholas Pappas.

Kahan then addressed the crowd in a stentorian voice: "Families that are present here today that lost a loved one twenty years ago, we salute their bravery, their courage, fortitude, tenacity, and the humanity they have shown the rest of us." Kahan then paused. "They have taken one of the worst tragedies that could happen to a human being and have turned it into a positive, perennial focus on influencing society and, ever hopeful, that no one has to join this infamous group."

Kahan then turned his attention to retired Houston police officer Don Schmidt, one half of the team that arrested Coral Watts. Luther Domain, Schmidt's partner, had suffered a stroke and was unable to attend.

"We salute you, for without your presence at the particular time and location, there's no doubt in my mind, or anyone else's mind, that there would be more families here today, if not for your fortitude." Kahan directed his gaze at Schmidt and added, "The families, I know, thank you. I thank you. The citizens of Houston thank you. The society thanks you."

Kahan asked Schmidt to step up to the podium and accept a "Certificate of Appreciation" for his efforts in capturing Coral Eugene Watts. Schmidt, the good guy dressed in all-white, seemed embarrassed by the attention. He shook hands with Kahan and tentatively walked up to the lectern. The once-slim, dark-haired police officer, now paunchy and sporting a head of white hair, quietly spoke to the audience. "My heart goes out to you," he addressed the families of the women killed. He then modestly stated, "I'm glad where I was and I'm glad what I did"—he paused—"I just did my job." He lifted the letter up a bit above his head and nodded, then just as quietly slipped away.

Kahan returned to the podium and also to the focus of the morning's memorial: a remembrance of the victims. He asked that Marie O'Bryant, Carrie Mae Jefferson's sister-in-law, come forward and speak about Carrie. The tall, striking woman, dressed in a purple-and-white silk blouse and purple blazer, walked onto the podium platform. The elegant woman spoke of all the important events that Carrie missed out on: her children's graduation, her daughter's wedding, the birth of her grandchildren, family reunions, and Christmas.

"We have missed the potential of what Carrie may have been," O'Bryant continued, "for we were blessed to be a part of who she was. The love she gave. The strength she shared. The laughter she brought into our lives.

"However, we were deprived of what she could have become. The experienced and wise older woman who could have shared the keys to life's riches. The loving and tender mother who could have fully groomed her daughter into the rites of womanhood. The maternal grandmother who could have shared with her grandkids some insight into how deep their roots extend.

"All of this was stolen by a man with no remorse or love for innocence or sanctity. To me, it is simply unfair that a man that has stolen so many lives has the right to consider freedom at the expense of the pain and suffering of the victims' survivors and the victims' families whose lives will forever be a shadow of what they could have been."

After O'Bryant spoke, Kahan returned to the podium. He mentioned Elena Semander's name as another one of Coral Watts's victims. He then mentioned his friendship with Elena's mother, Harriett Semander. Kahan spoke of Harriett's unannounced efforts in coordinating the "Call to Action." He also thanked her for her ten years of friendship and her dedication to the cause of keeping Coral Watts behind bars. Kahan then asked JoAnna Nicolaou, Elena's youngest sister, to come and speak on behalf of her sister.

For those who knew Elena, it had to be a shock to see her sister. JoAnna was the spitting image of her oldest sister. The thirty-five-year-old former Houston Oiler cheerleader was now a mother of three children, but had kept her dancer's figure. She looked almost exactly like Elena from the hair, to the nose, to the eyes, to the size.

The seemingly nervous JoAnna stepped up to the gathering of microphones and pulled out her typed notes. She then comfortably slipped into the role of public speaker as she recalled several memories of her sister. She had asked those who had known Elena to give her their memories of times they spent with her.

JoAnna first read a letter from Elena's cousin Karen Pappas, who was also with Elena the night before she died. Karen wrote about how she and Elena grew up together and how Karen believed Elena was her own big sister. She wistfully reminisced about playing dolls with her cousin and how she would be the voice of Barbie, Elena was the voice of Skipper, and how they used to alternate doing the voice of Ken.

JoAnna then read portions of a letter from their brother, John Semander. He wrote of barely being able to remember his sister, but a few things came back to him. He remembered being outside in their humble backyard when Elena would pull open the back door and scream out loud how much she loved the Houston Oilers football team during the 1979 or 1980 play-offs. He also remembered how his oldest sister was playing basketball with him in the family driveway and that she broke her leg.

JoAnna also read a letter from Georgia Vionis, the choreographer of the Houston Greek Festival dance program the year before Elena died. She raved about Elena's "great smile and talent," and how Elena was always so patient with the young kids and eager to teach them. She was amazed at how much life the twenty-year-old girl had packed into such a short period of time. Georgia considered Elena to be "one of God's children."

JoAnna read another letter. This one was from a lifelong family friend, Chrissy Jelson. She, like Karen Pappas, considered Elena to be an older sister. She described Elena as "graceful, gracious, beautiful, and strong." She remembered how Elena once wore a purple paisley scarf in her hair and how beautiful she looked. Chrissy went home to find a scarf just like Elena's. She also recalled how, when she was young, she realized she needed glasses, but was too embarrassed to let her parents know because she thought they would look dorky on her. When she told Elena, Elena handed Chrissy her sunglasses and told her how good she looked and that glasses were "cool." Chrissy immediately told her parents that she needed eyewear and that "glasses are okay. Elena Semander said so."

Finally JoAnna read a letter from her older sister, Maria, who could not make the trip from her home in the South Bay region of southern California. Maria wrote, "It's been twenty years since I held Elena's hand singing and laughing at a Diana Ross concert. Twenty years since I graduated high school without her there. Twenty years since Elena was taken from life. "It seems like an eternity. Sometimes, it feels like just yesterday.".

Maria's memories continued: "As a typical stuck-up teenager, I was lucky. I had an older sister who was loving, cool, and, most importantly, accepting. Elena looked after me as her younger sister but she treated me as her friend.

"Most of my friends had older sisters who didn't want us tagging along, but Elena was different. She took me to cool parties and places and she covered up for me when I was in trouble. Well, sometimes. And she showed me how to embrace life and people."

Maria also wrote about Elena's love of water, music, and sports.

JoAnna concluded by stating that Elena was with God and part of His bigger plan.

Andy Kahan then acknowledged Watts's final murder victim, Michelle Maday, and her family, who were unable to attend.

Next up was Larry Fossi, widower of murder victim Meg Fossi. Larry quickly and succinctly acknowledged how much he missed his wife; however, he turned his attention to the legal matter of Watts's impending parole release.

Fossi spoke of the absurdity of Watts's mandatory release. He asked the assembled crowd how this could happen. How could Coral Watts be released in 2006?

"I'll tell you how," the slim, well-spoken lawyer answered, "because some elected Texas judges made this happen." Fossi talked about former judges Charles F. Baird and Michael Charlton, who both sat on the Texas Criminal Court of Appeals in 1987, when it was determined that Watts would receive his good-time credits. Fossi spoke of how Baird and Charlton made parole a mandatory right for all criminals, even though such law did not exist in either the Texas Constitution or the Constitution of the United States.

Fossi sighed as he became more worked up. The angry widower spoke of how Baird actually claimed that "it felt good, it felt wonderful" to create such a new law. He also pointed out that neither Baird nor Charlton would be around when Watts would be released in 2006.

Fossi asked the crowd, "Is Mr. Baird here today? I don't think so. How about Mr. Charlton? I seriously doubt it." He then mentioned how the judicious thinking of such staunch anti–death penalty advocates, such as Baird, was going to allow convicted murderers to walk the streets of Texas, the United States, and the world.

Fossi spoke of how Baird and other anti–death penalty advocates complain that the problem with the death penalty is that an innocent person may be executed. Fossi pointed out that not one innocent person had ever been executed in the state of Texas, but that statistically, over time, such a tragedy would inevitably occur. He added, however, that had Watts been captured and sentenced to die in Michigan early on, at least twenty women would not have been killed.

"It would probably take centuries before Texas made twenty mistakes and put twenty people to death. It took Watts, of course, only a few years."

Fossi implored the crowd to take a stand against such lawmakers. He asked them to reject lawmakers who created new laws that were to the detriment of the well-being of the state of Texas's citizens.

"Let us not be afraid," Fossi concluded, "to stand up for what is sensible and what is right."

The crowd erupted in applause as Fossi left the podium.

The remainder of the testimonials continued on a more personal level. Keri Whitlow quoted lyrics from Lynyrd Skynyrd's "Freebird" to describe her best friend, Suzi Wolf; Lori Sword spoke of how she met Suzanne Searles in college at Drake University; Elizabeth Young spoke of how wonderful a caregiver her daughter Emily LaQua was, at such an early age; and Maricela Gracia, Yolanda Gracia's niece, struggled to speak of her loving aunt, but was literally supported by Yolanda's grown-up, gorgeous daughter, Myra Gracia.

Laura Allen, the mother of Anna Ledet, spoke fondly of her oldest daughter. The elegant woman, dressed in a finely pressed black business suit and bejeweled with pearl earrings, was the symbol of strength and tenacity in the face of tragedy and despair. The gracious mother spoke in glowing terms as she remembered her daughter. She mentioned how Anna had completed all of her medical-school studies just one day before she met Coral Watts and was murdered by him. She decried that "the world was deprived of great gifts and great healing" with the murder of her daughter.

Allen had come to a different conclusion about Watts than had many of the other participants in the memorial. She reminded everyone that "the grief, the sorrow, the anxiety always will be with us." She stopped, looked up at her fellow friends—who also had lost a loved one to a serial killer—and earnestly stated, "I'm going to say something that may be unpopular with some of you. As a Christian I'm called upon to forgive. If I do not forgive, I can never be forgiven." What she said next ran counter to many in attendance. "So after about two-and-a-half years, I was at Holy Communion in Episcopal Church and about three people down from me, receiving, it was as if a voice screamed in my head, 'I forgive. I forgive.'"

Allen, however, clarified her position. "I have forgiven the act, but only God can forgive the sin. And that forgiveness does not mean"—she stopped and emphasized again—"does . . . not . . . mean, I want Watts released. I want him to stay in that prison or any other prison where they put him all his mortal life."

Allen then directly addressed the families who had lost a loved one. "With all of you, I share what we've been through, what we still go through, for life holds many things for us. And I want you to know, I'm so glad to be here with you.

"Again I have been honored to be with you."

The crowd again burst into applause and several dabbed their eyes with tissue.

The mission of the remembrance came to fruition with the presence of Joe Tilley, father of Watts's first Texas victim, Linda Tilley. The congenial man from Temple, Texas, drove in with his wife and Linda's mother, Carol Tilley, Linda's sister, Lauren, and Lauren's son and Linda's nephew she never knew, Max.

The calm and collected Tilley stood behind the phalanx of microphones and began to speak. He gripped the lectern firmly with his left hand and spoke. "Having journeyed from the far country of Arlington"—he chuckled—"we had absolutely no knowledge that there was a group such as this, with the dedication you have, and obviously have had, and the work that you've done to bring some justice to the occasion." He looked admiringly at his fellow mourners. "You all have done tremendous work up to this point." Tilley took three- or four-second pauses before resuming his speech. "And you have an awful lot of work, and hopefully myself and we included, will be able to work with you effectively toward preventing this happening again."

Tilley spoke of how he and his family got lost on the way to the memorial earlier that morning. It "called to mind the need for having a good road map wherever you go and having the ground plowed and the way well-marked," he added. "That will lead you to an eventual victory"—he stressed the final with a finite punctuation—"in what you seek [as] evidenced by your effort here this morning."

Tilley continued with what he described as his own personal thoughts. "I might suggest to you that what we work for and what we seek so earnestly, here, now, has nothing to do with punishment, nor vindication, but it has to do with protection." He added, "I would further suggest to you that the object of the work of this group and other groups has nothing at all to do with Coral

Eugene Watts, and it has nothing to do with a broken or bent criminal justice system." Tilley believed, "Instead, I would suggest to you that what we face here, at this time and place, is confrontation with pure evil." Many nodded their heads in agreement.

"And I don't think any of us here would confront the adversary without the tools that are necessary to accomplish the task." Tilley brought his message home when he concluded, "I will further suggest to you that the work we do and the *war* that we do is not with flesh and blood, but with the principalities and powers of the air." He finished with, "And I would suggest that the guidance, with the help of God, in the pursuit that is undertaken here today, and no doubt will be successfully concluded, will have to do with the—not the forgiveness, because we know that forgiveness cannot be bestowed when forgiveness is not sought"—in direct contradiction to Laura Allen's belief—"and we know that Coral Eugene Watts has vowed to do again what he so very effectively did so many times. And to spiritualize the attack, enlist the aid and the protection of God, then we cannot but be successful in this effort.

"I thank you."

Joe Tilley was followed by Lori Lister, who survived Watts's final attack on May 23, 1982. Lister, now remarried and known as Lori Baugh, came to the stage with her son, Blake, sixteen, and daughter, Cher, thirteen, in tow. She stated that she wanted them behind her because she would break out into tears if she had to look at them as she spoke of the suffering she had endured after the attack by Coral Watts.

Baugh recalled how, for the first four years, after Watts attacked her, she hid in her closet with a gun in her hand, sweating. She also mentioned how she would see Watts's face everywhere out in public, even though she knew he was locked up in prison.

Baugh also talked about how she would read the papers about Watts's victims and the photos of the girls and how she was supposed to have been the next photo. She was shocked at "how little each article said of these girls." She also thanked the families in attendance for bringing a part of their loved ones back to life at the gathering. "I was so proud and glad to hear about your loved ones. They were very special people."

Baugh also expressed her disgust with the fact that Watts was scheduled for release in 2006. She believed that the Texas criminal justice system was more concerned with the rights of criminals than with the rights of the criminals' victims. "I'm in denial," she stated, referring to Watts's impending release. "Something has to be done. I'm hoping against all hope that something will be done."

Baugh concluded, "I'd like to see an end to this."

After a closing prayer by Father Brendan Pelphrey, Andy Kahan reminded everyone why they had come this day. Not only to remember the victims, but to manage somehow to keep Coral Eugene Watts behind bars. Then, with a chilling reality, Kahan stated that there were only 1,370 days until Watts would be released.

To drive the impact home of the murderer's deeds and the negative impact he had—not only on the victims, but their loved ones as well—Kahan asked all of the surviving family members and friends to come to the stage. Forty-three people of all ages, races, and sizes ventured forward together. The ceremony ended with the plaintive wails of bagpipe player Keegan Bratsch, of the Houston Police Bagpipes Band.

Tears mingled with smiles.

One week later, the purpose of the memorial was finally realized. Michigan assistant attorney general Donna Pendergast opened up her morning paper. She came across an article that covered the services held in Houston. The name Coral Watts immediately rang a bell for her. Pendergast had been a college student at the University of Michigan during the late 1970s when Watts allegedly had killed several women in the Ann Arbor and Detroit areas.

Pendergast got on the phone and contacted Andy Kahan. She informed him that she had no idea that Watts was going to be released and she immediately asked what she could do.

Pendergast, along with the Michigan State Police (originally conceived on April 19, 1917, as a mounted precursor to Homeland Security) created a task force entirely devoted to finding evidence in old cases to use against Coral Eugene Watts. Their goal was simple: to prevent Watts from being let loose among the minions and avoiding the inevitable slaughter.

"He is diabolical," Pendergast stated. "There really is no other word for him. He is a killing machine and he has told a sergeant from Houston, Texas, that if he gets out, he will kill again.

"A battle plan needs to be drawn, but it sends shivers up my spine because if we don't come up with a case here in Michigan, he will walk out the door on May 8, 2006, and there's nothing anybody can do about it."

Michigan State Police lieutenant Charles Schumacher informed the media that the Watts case was their top priority. "When you are dealing with a serial killer, especially one that may present a danger again, it is something important, something we want to do our best work on." That work included looking back on more than a dozen cases, including the Lena Bennett strangulation murder in Harper Woods.

The lieutenant hoped that the advent of new crime-fighting technology might somehow connect Watts to any of these old cases. "Perhaps we could find some DNA under fingernails in some of the victims, or perhaps some hair was found in a victim's hand or something like that that we may be able to connect to Watts," presumed Schumacher.

Pendergast also stated that "he hasn't received immunity in the other Michigan cases, not the ones in Ann Arbor, not the single case in Kalamazoo, not in any Detroit cases. So, that could be the luckiest thing that happened to us."

It would take an awful lot of people to create that luck.

CHAPTER 44

With Coral Watts's release on the horizon, Texas officials also scrambled to figure a way to keep him behind bars. One of their best bets was the case of Emily LaQua, Watts's youngest known victim. Police officers, and Watts, mistakenly assumed her body would be located in Harris County, thus making him eligible for the plea bargain, along with the other women's cases. LaQua's body, however, had been discovered in a metal culvert ditch off Interstate 10 in Brookshire, Texas, which is located in Waller County, whose officials would not offer a plea bargain to Watts. LaQua's murder, subsequently, was not part of any deal offered to Watts.

There was a major flaw in the LaQua case. Key evidence, including Emily's clothes, had gone missing over the years. The authorities had no idea where to locate them, thus making it impossible to use something other than Watts's confessions.

In lieu of potential prosecution in the LaQua case, the Texas authorities also had to turn over every stone to see if there had been a case that they had missed—one that Watts had not confessed or struck a plea bargain for.

Kahan stressed the importance of the search. "Either

we do something now, or he gets released." Kahan also added the commonly mistaken assessment that "we will have the dubious honor of being the first state to legally release a serial killer in this country's history."

In reality, there were at least two previous serial killers, both females, who had been released. Fourteen-year-old Caril Ann Fugate, along with her boyfriend, Charles Starkweather, went on an eight-day killing spree from Nebraska to Wyoming, slaughtering eleven innocent victims, including Caril's parents and two-year-old baby sister. Fugate and Starkweather would later inspire such films as *Badlands, Natural Born Killers,* and *Starkweather.* While Starkweather was executed on June 25, 1959, Fugate was paroled in June 1976. Some argue that she is considered a "spree killer," instead of a serial killer.

Another female serial killer who was legally released was Terilynn Wager, who, according to author Wilton Earle, murdered nine people before she turned fifteen. Since she was a juvenile at the time of the killings, she was sentenced as a minor and released when she was eighteen.

Watts, however, would be the first male serial killer to be released from prison.

Harris County ADA Ira Jones, who assisted in the plea bargain for Watts, added, "It's not over."

Many of the victims' surviving family members, who could not attend the "Call to Action" memorial service, expressed outrage at Watts's mandatory release. "I can't imagine that the prison system would let him out," proclaimed Judy Wolf Krueger, Suzi Wolf's older sister. "They plea-bargained my sister's life away." She added, "The people in the United States should be outraged that this man is getting time off for good behavior after murdering thirteen women for which he was not punished."

Krueger held out little hope that she could do anything to help keep Watts behind bars. "I don't know what we'll be able to do in the next four years. I don't think there will be any healing that goes on if he becomes a free man."

CHAPTER 45

November 7, 2002, was Coral Watts's forty-ninth birthday. It was also the day of his fifth parole hearing since he had been imprisoned back in 1982. Watts sat once again before the board members of the Texas Board of Pardons and Paroles to learn his fate. Watts was denied parole once again. Chairman Gerald Garrett stated, "The parole review process is complete. The parole panel recommended against parole." Garrett and two other board members voted unanimously to keep Watts incarcerated.

When asked about Watts's parole review, Andy Kahan stated, "That was about as big a no-brainer as you will ever see. I wish I could say I was shocked. Parole has always been a moot point in this case. The imminent issue still is his release."

Watts was scheduled for release on May 8, 2006.

On November 8, 2002, Donna Pendergast stepped up to the plate. The Wayne County Assistant District Attorney officially opened a probe into the Harper Woods murder of Lena Bennett, the sixty-three-year-old waitress whose nude body was found hanging in her garage on Van Antwerp Street.

"We're reprocessing every piece of evidence that was found in the room," informed Pendergast, who led the investigation. "There's a possibility of finding DNA or some other evidence with technology that wasn't in existence in 1980."

When asked about the differences in the murder victim and the modus operandi, Andy Kahan stated, "This would be an anomaly, but it could be before he perfected the art of killing. This was very early in his killing career."

Simultaneously with the Michigan probe, Texas officials petitioned the Texas Department of Corrections for a sample of Watts's DNA.

The walls seemed to be closing in on Coral Eugene Watts.

The Michigan State Police Department retrieved the evidence in the Bennett case. They began by conducting DNA testing on a broomstick and a belt. Unfortunately, unlike television crime dramas, such as *CSI*, results would not appear overnight or at the snap of fingers. In the reality-based world of crime fighting, DNA results take months to retrieve.

State police lieutenant Ted Monfette stated, "We really don't know what we have until we look at everything. We don't want to charge Mr. Watts with a crime he didn't commit, because that means the person who did it is going to walk free, but we're looking for something to connect one of these crimes so we can take Mr. Watts to trial."

It seemed as if any person in the state of Michigan who

wore a badge was on the cold-case trail of Coral Eugene Watts.

One of those officers was Sergeant Tom Seyfried, of the Ann Arbor Police Department. He, along with another task force, had been investigating the murders of Shirley Small, Glenda Richmond, and Rebecca Huff. The team was not able to connect Watts to any of the evidence, but they continued to look at different aspects to find a match.

"We're not going to make a case unless he confesses," Seyfried declared. "We don't have any witnesses or any evidence. As far as I'm concerned, this case is done."

Paul Bunten, the former Ann Arbor felony investigator, who was now the police chief of Saline, Michigan, located just over nine miles southwest of Ann Arbor, believed that Watts might get tagged for the Bennett murder.

"This looks like Watts," Bunten affirmed. "She was followed home. He attacked her when she pulled her car into the driveway. That's his MO.

"The only thing different is the broomstick. Watts buried some of his victims and drowned others. He didn't much care how they died."

The cavalcade of cold cases marched onward during the week of November 20, 2002, when Southgate police turned over the Lilli Dunn murder to the Watts task force. Dunn, twenty-eight, was taken from her driveway at 3:00 A.M. on July 31, 1980. Her body was never located. Southgate detective lieutenant Joseph Walsh stated, "This case could be unrelated, but I really don't think so. It fits the profile, MO, and timeline of Watts exactly."

By March 2003, the Coral Watts cold-case task force encompassed police officials from Ann Arbor, Detroit, Flint, Kalamazoo, Southgate, and Windsor, Ontario. The total number of cases that were looked at mushroomed to over 115.

For five months the task force attempted to find one iota of evidence to tie Watts to any of the numerous murders. So far, there search had been fruitless.

"The amount of work is incomprehensible," Donna Pendergast revealed, "but we want to make sure there is no stone left unturned to keep this monster behind bars."

Larry Fossi had his doubts about the ability of the Michigan officials' efforts to corral Watts. "I think it is a long shot that in cases that old, with as little physical evidence evidently as remains, that they'll be able to do it, but I'm glad they're making the effort."

Andy Kahan praised the Michigan officials for their efforts. "There's a lot of promising prospects in Michigan," Kahan noted. "Their entire state is galvanized to prevent his release."

The same could not necessarily be said of their Texas counterparts.

About the only case that seemed to have any potential was the Emily LaQua murder in Waller County. Brookshire police chief Joseph Prejean stated, "I just refuse to believe he's gonna be turned loose." The chief made sure his department contributed by submitting what little LaQua evidence they had to a state laboratory for DNA testing.

Most authorities, however, assumed the LaQua case to be a long shot. Many believed that Watts assumed the confession of the murder of Emily LaQua was also under the aegis of a plea bargain. It might be one obstacle too large to overcome.

CHAPTER 46

On January 13, 2004, Kalamazoo County police officials announced that they might charge Coral Watts with the 1974 murder of Gloria Steele. Dan Weston, chief of Kalamazoo's public safety department, stated that charges could possibly be made against Watts as soon as February or March of that year.

Weston refused to divulge what evidence he had against Watts. He did mention, however, that he traveled to Houston in September 2003. He did not elaborate.

The thought that Coral Watts could be brought to justice for murder brought happiness to several people affected by his actions. Among them, Judy Wolf Krueger, who opined, "Anything we can do is better than putting him back on the street."

Kevin Ford, who was Gloria Steele's sister's boyfriend at the time of the murder, stood outside the Ecumenical Senior Center, on the 700 block of North Burdick Street, outside of Kalamazoo, alongside his friend Hazel Brophy, passing out petitions to keep Watts in prison. Ford would later say, "It hurts my heart to know here's a guy who killed all these women [and he's] getting out of prison."

Ford added, "I have this vengeance now. It's not sorrow. It's a feeling that we have to get this guy, this coward, this woman-killer. We have to keep him in prison. Hopefully, he's changed his ways, but we don't need someone to die to figure out if he has."

Dr. Debbie Somerset, of Grosse Pointe Woods, who taught Anna Ledet at the University of Texas at Galveston Medical Branch, and also lived only a few blocks away from her, wistfully recalled her student's murder. "I still think about it all the time. Frequently I walk the dog and think, 'You know, you think you're safe, but this could happen to you. Anytime, anyplace.' It's infuriating to think Watts someday could be out there, out free."

When Andy Kahan heard about the Kalamazoo authorities' intentions possibly to pursue charges against Watts in the murder of Steele, he added, "This is our best and only hope [of] keeping him in. It will be total euphoria when Watts is charged." Kahan seemed relieved when he said, "We've never let go of this case, never stopped believing and never stopped pressing for twenty years."

Others held their hopes in check. Elaine Embrey, a retired registered nurse from Bay City, Michigan, and Suzi Wolf's cousin, was skeptical. "Until he's been tried for murder and convicted, we're just holding our breath that everything will go as we hope it will."

Guarded optimism peppered with a dash of hesitancy seemed to be the dish of the day.

Judy Wolf Krueger was amazed still at how few people knew of Coral Watts. "There are still people that I talk to that don't know about the issue here in Saginaw, and it's received a fair amount of publicity." Just in case, Krueger wanted to remind everyone that "he's murdered thirteen women and he's coming out of jail.

"I would dearly love to be able to shout it from the

rooftops that this man is a killer," she continued. "They should be aware of this, they should be outraged, they should be writing their congressman, the president."

Evocations of Peter Finch's climactic "I'm mad as hell and I'm not going to take it anymore!" speech from the movie *Network* spring to mind.

Elaine Embrey agreed about the necessity of spreading the word about Coral Eugene Watts. "All we can do is say that we've done our best to get the word out, and one thing we do know is that we have brought this to the awareness of the whole nation." Indeed, Embrey, along with Krueger, Harriett Semander, Keri Whitlow, Andy Kahan, Kevin Ford, Hazel Brophy, and many others had beaten the bully pulpit until its nose was bloody about the travesty of the imminent release of Watts.

But Embrey and Krueger knew their work was far from over.

"If this guy, by some technicality, gets out," declared Embrey, "he's going to have so many people watching him that we'll be safer than we were before."

CHAPTER 47

On January 15, 2004, Joseph Foy and his second wife, Laura, sat on their couch in their home in Westland, Michigan.

Foy zoned out in front of the television as he wound down from the previous night's work at Faygo. He mindlessly flipped the channels until he skimmed across *The Abrams Report* on MSNBC. He ignored the screen as he got dressed. Suddenly he saw a familiar face, one that had haunted him for twenty-five years. Instantly he knew it was the face of the man who had murdered Helen Dutcher in the alleyway behind his home on East Bennett Street in Ferndale. The face of the man they never caught. Foy depressed the mute button on the remote control.

"Coral Eugene Watts."

The gentleman who uttered the unforgettable name was Michigan attorney general Mike Cox, who spoke with the show's host, Dan Abrams. The two men discussed the impending release of Watts.

Cox had another agenda as well. He asked the viewers if they had any tips on any murders that Watts may have committed.

Foy, who claimed he saw Watts stab thirty-six-year-old

Helen Dutcher outside his house near Eight Mile Road, known these days as the run-down area where white boy rapper Eminem sprung from, decided to call the local authorities.

Foy's claim was deemed credible because he informed authorities the night of the murder, in 1979, and even helped a sketch artist create a likeness of the attacker. He also reported it in 1982 when he saw television footage of Watts after his initial arrest. Authorities at the time told Foy that they would not need to pursue the Dutcher case, since Watts had confessed to at least a dozen other murders.

CHAPTER 48

On March 4, 2004, Michigan attorney general Mike Cox issued a statement at a hastily arranged press conference that shocked everyone. Flanked by Ferndale police detective George Hartley, Assistant Attorney General Tom Furtaw, and state police captain Annemarie Gibson, Cox announced that the state of Michigan would bring a murder charge against Coral Watts in Ferndale District Court in the Helen Dutcher case.

"This man is a killing machine who has admitted he will kill again," Cox announced before a throng of journalists. "The specter of Watts's release has haunted Michigan families, the nation, and untold victims and their families for too long."

Cox praised the numerous police officials who participated in this monumental decision. "These charges are the result of countless hours by several, persistent law enforcement agencies all intent on protecting the public. It is a credit to my staff at the attorney general's office, the Michigan State Police, the Ferndale Police Department, Texas law enforcement officials and other law enforcement agencies, that these twenty-five-year-old charges were able to be sworn out."

Cox assured all that the Watts case was number one on his to-do list. "The full resources of my office will be directed to ensure justice is delivered to the numerous victims and their families. The attorney general's office is committed to solving the most complex crimes in Michigan, protecting citizens from Michigan's most violent criminals, and becoming a home to the best practices in law enforcement."

Cox spoke about the witness Joseph Foy, but did not mention him by name. Officials planned to keep the lid on Foy's identity until it was time for a pretrial hearing, when Foy would testify.

"The witness first came forward years ago," Cox informed, attempting to dissuade the media from assuming that the attorney general merely was trying to grandstand politically by bringing down the country's most prolific serial killer. "But I don't know why it did not go anywhere at the time."

One state official, when asked about the possibility of finding Watts guilty, replied, "It's a strong case. We're not going to bring a case to lose it."

Judy Wolf Krueger could not believe what had happened. "I couldn't be more encouraged right now," she said of the indictment. "This is the result of a lot of hard work from Michigan to Texas. Coral Eugene Watts shouldn't be let out of prison."

Jeanne Clyne's widower, Michael Clyne, was relieved, but skeptical, to hear that Watts finally had been charged with murder. "I hope and pray they have enough of a case to convict him. The man is very sick. I don't know what justice means in this case. I am just concerned he is not released."

Back in Texas, the general mood was ecstatic.

"It's just a big relief," stated Melinda Aguilar, who,

along with Lori Lister, escaped Watts's final attack. "I know that he said he always went after the evil eyes, but in my eyes, he is the evil one."

Andy Kahan was elated. "It's an awesome, euphoric feeling. . . . One of the most prolific killers in our country's history has now had a murder charge filed on him." The advocate noted the absurd irony. "The only thing that gets better than that is the ultimate conviction.

"We always felt that Michigan was our best and only hope, and if Michigan didn't come through, Watts would be released."

Dianne Clements, president of Justice For All Alliance, exclaimed, "Victims did this!"

Joe Tilley, Linda Tilley's father, calmly hoped that "they can do what they think they can do. It's going to save the state of Texas from a huge embarrassment."

JoAnna Nicolaou, Elena Semander's youngest sister, spoke of the event that brought the case to national attention. "It wasn't just a memorial service," she stated, referring to the gathering at the Annunciation Greek Orthodox Cathedral, back in August 2002, "it was a call to action."

The effects rippled eastward as well. From her home in Massachusetts, Jane Montgomery, mother of Elizabeth Montgomery, spoke about the charge against Watts: "There is no need for the pain this animal has caused. He has no right to go free."

Montgomery, however, reserved her enthusiasm. "You can't assume a damned thing. I know what I've gone through, what I'm still going through. To think that some other mother might suffer the same thing is such a sickening, frightening feeling, it turns my stomach. I hope he's never released."

Attorney General Cox also announced that Watts's trial would take place in Oakland County Circuit Court, near Pontiac, Michigan. The trial would take place later that year.

Later that same day, on a smaller scale, the Kalamazoo Cold Case Unit and assistant prosecutor James Gregart also stated that they were seriously considering charging Watts with the murder of Gloria Steele. After everything that had already occurred over the years in the Watts case, Kalamazoo officials were taking no chances.

Gregart relayed that his office would "see if there is sufficient admissible evidence to initiate a criminal homicide prosecution."

Public Safety Chief Dan Weston added, "I have every confidence that the Kalamazoo County Prosecutor's Office will come to the appropriate decision, and whether they decide to issue any warrants or not, we will be happy with whatever decision they make, knowing that we have done the very best investigation possible."

Gregart was not sure how soon—or if—charges actually would be brought against Watts in the Steele case. "It will be as soon as reasonably predictable. It's at the top of our radar screen."

Harriett Semander, who had led the charge for twenty years to keep Coral Eugene Watts imprisoned, was cautious about getting her hopes up too high for the Dutcher case. "I'm very excited they're pursuing the murder charge. We've waited a long time for this." She cautioned, however, that "the thing is, he's not convicted yet."

CHAPTER 49

On April 1, 2004, April Fools' Day, Michigan governor Jennifer Granholm (D) proved that the case of Coral Eugene Watts was no joke. The governor sent an official extradition request to Texas governor Rick Perry (R), formally demanding that Watts be transferred to Michigan to face a jury in the murder of Helen Mae Dutcher.

"Today is the first step in the path to justice for the family of Helen Dutcher," announced Granholm.

Michigan attorney general Mike Cox also spoke to the press about the potential for bringing Watts to Michigan. "It is rare when a lawyer or prosecutor can say with certainty that initiating a case or filing charges in a prosecution can save lives. Today, I can."

Governor Rick Perry received the extradition request the following day, on Friday, April 2, 2004. Perry's spokeswoman, Kathy Walt, addressed the media in regard to Michigan and Granholm's request. "The governor's general counsel wants to review the paperwork carefully and make sure everything is in order." At the risk of not wanting to sound as if there might be some foot shuffling going on in the Texas Governor's Mansion, Walt quickly added, "The governor will sign it as soon as possible."

Walt informed that once the request was signed, it would be sent to Huntsville and delivered to Watts at the Ellis Unit. "Once he is served with the warrant," Walt continued, "he can fight extradition."

There was some hand-wringing going on as to whether Watts would comply with the warrant or if he would contest it. Not known for his cooperation, Watts denied all media requests. Most authorities had no idea whether or not he even had a lawyer.

The following Tuesday, April 6, 2004, Governor Rick Perry signed the extradition papers for Coral Eugene Watts. "By signing this extradition warrant," Perry stated in his official press release, "families of Watts's victims have renewed hope that he will remain behind bars for many years to come." Perry continued by thanking the Texas Rangers, the Texas Department of Public Safety's Special Crimes Unit, as well as the Harris County District Attorney's Office, in addition to the "Michigan authorities."

There were people waiting in line to get a piece of Coral Watts.

"We are not going to forget Coral Eugene Watts," promised Waller County district attorney Oliver Kitzman. Speaking in reference to the murder of Emily LaQua, Kitzman stated that "we have a viable case against Coral Eugene Watts here in Waller County if it becomes appropriate to prosecute him." The prosecutor added, "We are glad, frankly, to have Michigan come forward with what they seem to feel are cases they can make up there." Kitzman brought up another point that had some officials perturbed that Texas could not bring charges against Watts sooner: Michigan did not have the death penalty. If Watts could be charged in Texas, Kitzman alluded, then "we would have the death penalty here available to us."

Eight days later, on Wednesday afternoon, April 14, 2004, Watts made his first public appearance in more than two decades. The occasion was his extradition hearing before state district judge William McAdams.

Watts slowly lumbered into the courtroom, his legs restrained by metal shackles, his wrists with handcuffs. He looked much older, of course, and slightly disheveled. He took his time walking up to the defense table, where he was greeted by Texas State Counsel for Offenders attorney Rudolph Brothers. The legal aid attorney even assisted Watts by placing his oversized prison-issued glasses on his face so he could read Governor Granholm and Governor Perry's extradition request.

Brothers addressed the court. He informed Judge McAdams that Watts recently had undergone major surgery for prostate cancer. Specifically, Watts had tubes implanted in his ears and was also on the ass-end of exploratory nonterminal prostate cancer surgery. Brothers also informed the judge that Watts was currently on medication to "address some mental-health issues that he has." Brothers did not care to elaborate.

He did, however, inform the judge of Watts's intentions.

"He is willing to voluntarily return to the state of Michigan," Brothers stated.

Judge McAdams looked directly at Watts: "You can fight extradition. If you can't afford your own attorney (to represent him in an extradition fight), I'll appoint one to represent you."

Brothers leaned over and whispered something into Watts's ear. After a few moments, the men separated and Watts spoke to the judge. It was probably the first time that many people involved in the case actually had heard Watts's voice.

"I understand" was all he said.

Watts then informed the judge that he had chosen not to fight the extradition request. His attorney, Brothers, however, did add that Watts "is concerned that he be able to complete his medical treatment before returning to the state of Michigan."

Judge McAdams agreed to allow Watts to complete his treatment before being transferred to the state of Michigan.

Michigan attorney general Mike Cox was already gearing up for the trial. "My office is taking the necessary steps to ensure this murder trial is held in a timely and reasonable manner." The youthful-looking attorney general was not afraid to spread his plume either.

"I created the Office of Special Investigations—with seasoned and skilled prosecutors—for cases exactly like this one." He gesticulated, while apparently forgetting that it was Donna Pendergast who read about the "Call to Action" memorial service in 2002 and acted upon it.

Two people who truly greased the wheels of justice after decades of creaky starts commented on Watts's decision not to fight the extradition. Andy Kahan replied that "this is a big step in assuring that a cold-blooded killer never gets out to victimize any other person."

Harriett Semander was pleased, but still cautious. "It's not the end. He has to have a conviction," for her to be satisfied.

* * *

Early Thursday morning, April 22, 2004, Coral Watts was transported by the Michigan State Police Department from the Ellis Unit in Huntsville, Texas, to Michigan. He was delivered to Oakland County sheriff Michael Bouchard. Watts had completed his cancer treatments successfully and was ready to stand trial for the 1979 murder of Helen Mae Dutcher.

CHAPTER 50

On Friday, April 23, 2004, Coral Watts was arraigned by Judge Joseph Longo in the Forty-third District Court, located in Ferndale, Michigan. Watts ignored the large gathering of reporters as he shambled into the building.

Once inside the courtroom, Watts remained quiet. Dressed in a dark blue sweat suit, Watts listened as the judge read the charges against him. Bespectacled in thick, dark glasses, Watts aimlessly tapped his toes to a rhythm only he could hear. His manacled hands kept him relaxed as he occasionally scratched his skin.

"Coral Eugene Watts, on or about December 1, 1979, in the city of Ferndale . . . did with intent to kill, and with premeditation, kill and murder one Helen Mae Dutcher."

Since Watts had no legal representation, the judge entered a plea of not guilty of the murder of Helen Mae Dutcher on Watts's behalf.

With his head bowed down, Watts then asked Judge Longo for a court-appointed attorney. He also stated in a barely audible voice, "My legal papers were withheld from me." Quiet, yet defiant.

Judge Longo informed the defendant that he would appoint an attorney to handle his case. He also ordered that Watts remain in the Oakland County Jail without bail and set his initial preliminary hearing for the following Thursday. The hearing was expected to be postponed once Watts was assigned an attorney.

On April 29, 2004, attorney Ronald E. Kaplovitz was given the unenviable task of representing Coral Watts. Kaplovitz ran a successful legal practice that focused on immigration law and criminal law.

The preliminary examination was postponed, as expected. Kaplovitz needed more time to prepare an appropriate defense for his newest, most notorious client. The attorney claimed he just had over three thousand pages of evidence against his client dumped on his desk that needed to be reviewed. Furthermore, Kaplovitz claimed, Watts had not been receiving proper medical treatment for his prostate cancer.

"Since he has been in the county jail," Kaplovitz decried, "he has not been provided with what I believe is adequate medical care." The passionate defense of Coral Eugene Watts had begun officially.

Judge Longo rescheduled the preliminary hearing for June 2, 2004, so Kaplovitz could prepare better.

Kaplovitz made good use of his time between hearings. He made sure to fire his opening salvo in the press to question the legitimacy of Joseph Foy's claim to have seen Coral Watts murder Helen Dutcher.

"I have some serious questions about a witness who says he saw something for a few fleeting moments in a dark alley on a dark night twenty-five years ago."

Another sticking point for Kaplovitz was Pendergast's desire to file a motion to request that Watts's previous murder confessions be allowed in as evidence. Kaplovitz, of course, was adamantly opposed to such a motion.

He would have just over a month to prepare his initial arguments.

On Thursday, May 20, 2004, Judge Joseph Longo placed a gag order on all legal parties involved in the Coral Watts murder case. He ordered that certain evidence and testimony that would come forth in the preliminary hearing be concealed. Longo claimed he wanted to prevent contamination of the potential jury pool.

Ron Kaplovitz was pleased. "It's one of those situations where you have to balance the right of the public to know versus the defendant's right to a fair trial."

As the preliminary hearing crept closer, some parties refused to keep quiet. Harriett Semander, Keri Whitlow, and Andy Kahan all planned on attending the hearing.

Semander was far from relieved. "I want this burden to be lifted from me," the advocate and grieving mother declared. "You hope for closure for you, the rest of the family who's moved on, married, and given me grandchildren." The exhausted woman shook her head as she said, "They return to my home and still see newspapers spread on the table from twenty-two years ago. I know it's a long time, but how do you move on? It's my daughter."

Keri Whitlow lamented that "survivors are dealing with their own torment in surviving. This is hell on people's lives. Who wants to relive it?" But Whitlow knew the pain she would feel would pale in comparison to the pain her friend Suzi Wolf suffered at the hands of Coral Eugene Watts. She would be there, no matter what.

"You go because someone needs to represent the victims."

Two fellow victims' family members from Michigan would join them. Michael Clyne stated, "I owe it to Jeanne and all the other victims to be there. It's not curiosity, it's seeing this through."

Clyne also added that "closure is a funny word. The most important closure for me is to keep him off the streets. That's what I'm most worried about. Intellectually, I'm prepared for this [trial]. Emotionally, I won't be."

Judy Wolf Krueger would also attend the hearing. "For me, the wound never closed, and I don't know what I'd do if he's acquitted." Instead of anger, however, Krueger spoke of faith: "I've been having multiple conversations with God lately. I say, 'God, you have to help us out. Give us the wisdom, insight, and guidance to do what we can to help keep this man in prison.'"

Semander talked of a very personal, very practical plan if Watts was convicted. She said that her boxes of newspaper clippings would meet their own demise.

"I have boxes and boxes of newspaper clippings, files, and notes. It just goes on and on. I think I'll have a party and burn everything."

On Wednesday, June 2, 2004, at 9:00 A.M., the rescheduled preliminary hearing took place before Judge Joseph Longo in the Forty-third District Court in Ferndale to determine if there was enough evidence to proceed with a trial against Coral Watts. More than twenty of his victims' surviving family members or friends were in attendance in the less-than-spacious courtroom. Among them were Judy Wolf Krueger, Harriett Semander, Keri Whitlow, and two of Helen Dutcher's sisters. Andy Kahan was also in attendance.

One of the most memorable encounters was that of

Harriett Semander and Paul Bunten. For twenty-two years their lives had been intertwined; however, it was the first time they had met each other: the man who suspected Watts back in Michigan, and the mother who lost a daughter to the man Bunten suspected. A meeting under much different circumstances would have been preferable, but the officer and the mother were glad to meet one another finally.

"I'm here to see him," Bunten declared in reference to Watts. "I wish it could have been one of my cases, but I'm excited he finally may face justice."

He spoke about how he had officially been off the case for years, but that the thought of Coral Watts never left his mind. "You don't retire from something like this. It's important to me because of the number of people he impacted and the fact that it's still open and hanging there. I want to see this get some closure."

In regard to Harriett Semander, Bunten had nothing but praise: "It was tough to talk to Harriett. . . . [It] brought back a lot. Here's someone who has done so much good out of something so tragic."

The key testimony in the hearing was the unveiling of Joseph Foy, the man who claimed to have witnessed Watts murder Helen Dutcher more than twenty-five years earlier. After giving a detailed description of what he saw that night, Foy positively identified Coral Watts as the man who murdered Helen Dutcher.

During a recess, however, Watts's defense attorney, Ron Kaplovitz, disputed Foy's claim. "His whole testimony is questionable," pitched the bulldog of an attorney. "The guy tells prosecutors his memory today is better than twenty-five years ago. It could not have happened the way he said it did."

Apparently, Foy's memory was good enough for Judge

Longo. After five hours in the hearing, the judge ruled that there was sufficient evidence for Coral Eugene Watts to stand trial for the first-degree murder of Helen Mae Dutcher. Longo then ordered Watts back to his county jail cell.

Afterward, some of the survivors spoke about seeing Watts in the courtroom.

"That's the first time I'd seen him," relayed Judy Wolf Krueger. "The only time I'd seen him was in photographs and it was not frightening . . . just real emotional for me."

Harriett Semander seemed more relieved than usual. "I have this feeling that a heavy burden is being lifted off my shoulders," she declared about Watts finally going to trial for murder. "I want to never, ever have to think about him again. That will be my freedom."

Keri Whitlow calmly stated, "I'm guarded, but we're very grateful Michigan is trying to make sure he never gets out of prison to walk the streets."

Andy Kahan was just happy to see this day finally come to be. "We've come so far in less than two years when we've resurrected him and put him back on the map for all the world to see. I think it's a true tribute to what grass-roots movement is all about."

Nearly two weeks later, on Tuesday, June 15, 2004, Watts was ushered back into a heavily secured courtroom. This time it was before Judge Richard Kuhn in the Oakland County Circuit Court. Watts, adorned in the jail-issued wardrobe of an orange-and-white-striped jumpsuit, stood before the judge. Watts looked bored. Judge Kuhn did not beat around the bush. He entered a plea of not guilty on behalf of Watts and scheduled a pretrial date

for August 10, 2004, and a trial date for the defendant
of November 8, 2004.

The entire hearing lasted two minutes.

Harriett Semander prayed that everything would stay
on course. She prayed for her burden to be eradicated
finally.

Almost two months later, Coral Watts's pretrial hear-
ing came up. The day before the hearing, Monday,
August 9, on the thirty-fifth anniversary of the "Helter
Skelter" massacre of Sharon Tate and four of her guests,
Watts's attorney, Ronald Kaplovitz, argued that Watts's
prior murder confessions should not be admissible in the
Helen Dutcher case.

Randall Thompson, spokesman for the Michigan Attorney General's Office, relayed that the prosecution had
already filed a motion that asked the judge to introduce
evidence that Watts was a serial killer. "In this case, Watts
always targeted young single women of smaller stature,
he stalked them, he would get them when they were
alone, and would have no sexual assault involved." Evidence of "prior bad acts" is admissible if the acts point
to a consistent pattern that would tie the individual to the
specific crime in question.

Kaplovitz, of course, argued that such information
would be unduly prejudicial to his client. "My biggest concern is that it's going to interfere with the ability of the
jurors to focus their attention on what's really important
in this case." He added, "What happened in Texas was
dealt with by Texas courts."

Kaplovitz informed the press that he would file a
motion the next day to exclude the evidence. "I am

hopeful that the judge will exclude it or at least limit it to some extent."

On September 23, 2004, Harriett Semander and Andy Kahan made the nearly fourteen-hundred-mile trek from Houston, Texas, to Detroit, Michigan. This time it was to hear more arguments as to what the judge actually would allow into the trial. The issue of whether or not to include Watts's confessions to any prior murders still had not been decided. Another issue was whether or not, if admissions of prior bad acts were introduced, the jury could hear of the immunity deal Watts struck to avoid thirteen murder charges.

Bernard E. Restuccia, first assistant state prosecutor, was somewhat reluctant about the immunity information being released. He stated that the downside of that would be that if jurors heard he received immunity for thirteen murders, then he probably did not commit the Dutcher murder because he would have admitted that too, since he knew he would not be charged with any murders.

Kaplovitz was still upset that the judge was considering entering any of Watts's previous confessions. "The jury is going to convict him on this case, regardless of the evidence, simply to punish him for [the cases in which he was granted immunity]."

Not the most ringing of endorsements for Watts's case.

Judge Kuhn informed the attorneys that he would make his decision by October 8, 2004.

Harriett Semander and Andy Kahan vowed to return in November for the trial.

* * *

Two weeks later, on Friday, October 8, 2004, Judge Kuhn made his ruling. He would allow Watts's admissions of previous bad acts to be included in the trial. He would not, however, allow information about Watts's immunity deal that he struck with the state of Texas to be included.

Predictably, the prosecution was happy.

"Today is a major step forward in bringing a confessed serial killer to justice," Attorney General Mike Cox stated. "We are pleased the judge recognized the consistency and relevance of Watts's previous acts and look forward to presenting them in trial."

Predictably, the defense was not happy.

"Obviously, we are concerned that the information will sway the jurors," said Ron Kaplovitz. "We are hopeful we can get fair-minded jurors who can look at the evidence they have in this case."

The few remaining weeks that led up to Watts's murder trial were spiced up with the backdrop of the 2004 presidential election between Supreme Court-appointed President George W. Bush and Democratic challenger John Kerry. Also, the Laci Peterson murder trial was coming to a conclusion. The tragic, yet sadly, all-too-common spousal murder case had captured a large part of the country's attention—or at least the attention of the twenty-four-hour yell-i-vision networks.

Miraculously, the upcoming trial of possibly America's most prolific serial killer—who killed more people than Ted Bundy, Gary Ridgway, aka "the Green River Killer," John Wayne Gacy, Jeffrey Dahmer, or Charles Manson (even though he literally never did kill a single person)—was finally getting some national attention.

CBS's top-rated television news magazine, *60 Minutes,* actually decided to run a headline piece on the Coral Eugene Watts case. The segment, entitled "A Deal with the Devil," aired on Sunday, October 17, 2004. The piece was a basic rehash of the case, but was beneficial because it was the first medium that could have possibly reached millions of viewers with the information. Whether or not anyone paid attention would remain to be seen.

One week before the trial was to begin, the television network A&E, and its successful true-crime television program *Cold Case Files,* announced it would be sending cameras to the Oakland County Circuit Court to shoot some footage of the Coral Watts trial for use in a later special. Even more important, Court TV, the twenty-four-hour legal entertainment programming network, announced that it would broadcast the Watts trial live.

The case of Coral Eugene Watts finally was beginning to see some notoriety . . . twenty-two years after his initial arrest.

Inexplicably, however, the pertinence of the trial did not seem to take root with the Houston media. For some unknown reason, only one media outlet dispatched a reporter to Michigan. KTRK-TV Channel 13, the local ABC affiliate, sent Ted Oberg, a former University of Michigan graduate. Amazingly, no other local media outlet deemed the case worthy enough to cover it in person, despite the fact that this would be the first time that Watts's Texas victims, dead and living, would have their voices heard in a courtroom in a murder trial.

A further sign of the erosion of quality investigative journalism.

In the modern era of media conglomeration and consolidation, apparently the Houston media did not believe that a homegrown terrorist was worthy of news coverage.

There was probably some flooding that needed to be covered or a dog that could whistle the "Dixie Chicken" through its nose.

At least Court TV would broadcast it live, in its entirety, every day that court would be in session.

Several participants in Watts's legal life, who would not be a part of the current trial, were interviewed before his murder trial began. Charles Baird, Watts's appellate attorney, reiterated that the prosecutors John B. Holmes Jr. and Ira Jones II's last-second inclusion of the water-as-a-deadly-weapon ruling was instrumental in having Watts where he was today. "They should have informed him, long before sentencing, that they were gonna ask Judge Shaver to make a finding that a deadly weapon was used in the commission of this offense (the attack on Lori Lister and Melinda Aguilar). And they failed to do that."

Judge Doug Shaver, now retired, spread the wealth when it came to blame in the Watts case. "Almost everybody that touched this thing, you could find some fault in what they did. In almost every one of us . . . but I don't know of any way that you could ever have changed it."

Shaver also stated about Watts, "I thought he was probably the most evil person that I'd ever come across."

Andy Kahan continued to pound the bully pulpit, warning people what would be in store for their daughters, sisters, and mothers if Watts managed to elude justice one more time.

"I don't think there is any doubt in anybody's mind that if he is released, he will resume his carnage against humanity."

Kahan was doing his part to make sure that every key witness from Texas would make the trip. He already had organized a trip for surviving family members, such as Harriett Semander, Maria Crawford (Elena Semander's sister from California), John Semander (also from California), and Jane Montgomery (from Massachusetts).

In addition to the family members, three of Watts's survivors were coming from Texas to testify against him: Lori Lister, Melinda Aguilar, and Julie Sanchez.

On Sunday, November 7, 2004, on Coral Watts's fifty-first birthday, Andy Kahan prepared for the trip to Michigan the next morning. He was concerned because he knew two of the three survivors did not want to make the trip to Michigan. They did not want to face Watts for the second time, in over twenty-two years.

It was imperative that they be there.

Kahan had his work cut out for him.

"Ninety-nine percent of the public wouldn't know Coral Eugene Watts if you handed them a picture, but he's one of the most prolific serial killers in the country's history.

"Serial killers don't get reformed. This is his career—killing women randomly."

CHAPTER 51

On November 8, 2004, the day after Coral Watts's birthday, there was one present he did not want: the appearance of a group of victims' surviving family members and friends. Harriett Semander and Andy Kahan arrived in Michigan. They were joined by John Semander, Michael Clyne, Jane Montgomery, and various members of Helen Dutcher's family.

The Dutcher supporters all checked into a nearby hotel. Kahan and Semander contacted Assistant Attorney General Donna Pendergast to make sure there were no last-minute changes. Everything was fine, the prosecutor assured them. Afterward, the crew went to a local restaurant and caught up with one another and chatted about the trial.

A sense of nervous anticipation filled the area surrounding their table.

Despite the impressive display of support, Kahan had his worries. The surviving Watts victims—Lori Lister Baugh, Melinda Aguilar, and Julie Sanchez—were not scheduled to testify until the second week of the trial.

Kahan would not know until the last minute if any of the three women would hold out.

Instead, he focused on the following day's landmark event—the first murder trial for the country's most prolific serial killer.

CHAPTER 52

The following day, the families and friends of Coral Eugene Watts's victims stood waiting in the lobby of their hotel. They were accosted by a television crew from *60 Minutes*, actually the same team that filmed the original report that aired just a few weeks before. The *60 Minutes* team asked if they could film the group as they left the hotel and entered the courtroom for the first day of the trial. The group agreed and went on their way.

Outside the courthouse the group stood around, mainly several women in their sixties and seventies, mothers of many of the victims, and quietly chatted amongst themselves. The tall, looming figure of Andy Kahan peered through the maelstrom like a ray of light in a thunderstorm.

Court TV's Jean Casarez held court nearby with her black-screen-covered stage with two chairs set up, one for her and one for whomever she would be interviewing as the trial progressed.

The buzz in the air was palpable.

Republican judge Richard Kuhn, seventy-five, quietly stepped out of his chambers and into the packed courtroom. He had never seen the courtroom so packed for a voir dire, or jury selection. He was prepared to take quiet control of the situation.

The thirty-two-year judicial veteran had overseen just about every type of case imaginable. From business matters to divorces, from child custody hearings to hired hit men, from teenage killers to teenage victims, and now, a serial killer. Judge Kuhn was not about to allow a little extra attention on a case to distract him from his duties.

Kuhn, a strict constructionist, did not feel the need to create a spectacle. He believed it would be pertinent to the country to televise the proceedings; however, he was not going to use the platform to showcase his political or ideological beliefs.

This would also be one of the judge's final cases. He would retire at the end of the year, due to the state law that forbade judges from running for their seat after they turn seventy years old.

Judge Kuhn had led a storied career, beginning with two failed runs for political office in the 1960s. The first was for a seat with the United States House of Representatives. The second was for the county district attorney position. After failing to attain either position, Kuhn became a judge in 1972, where he remained for over thirty-two years.

According to the *Daily Oakland Press*, Kuhn's father, Dr. Charles Kuhn, died when Richard was only six years old. Little Richard grew up quick and learned how to become a man, way too early, from his mother, Ella Kuhn. Richard had several siblings, who pitched in and helped their mother take care of things. Mrs. Kuhn did a fantastic job raising her children, eventually churning out from her nine sons: three doctors, two lawyers, a mortician, a teacher, a county drain commissioner, and a businessman.

Richard Kuhn kept his family close throughout his life. He currently took care of his oldest brother and also held a regular Sunday dinner at his house for the surviving members of his family. Kuhn was also coming up on his forty-ninth wedding anniversary with his bride, Sally.

The Kuhns had four children of their own, including son Richard Kuhn Jr., who followed in his daddy's footsteps. Kuhn Jr. was also a district judge for the Waterford Township.

"He's a strong family man," relayed his fellow judge Gene Schnelz. "He is a steadying influence within the courtroom."

Judge Kuhn would oversee courtroom 2F. He would also keep Assistant Attorney Generals Donna Pendergast and Tom Cameron, along with defense lawyer Ronald Kaplovitz, in check.

Donna Pendergast, a former Wayne County prosecutor, made her name in the high-profile 1999 retrial of Jonathan Schmitz, in the case known as the "Jenny Jones Murder Trial." In March 1995, Schmitz and his neighbor Scott Amedure appeared as guests for a taping of Jenny Jones's talk show. The theme for the show was secret admirers.

Schmitz, a heterosexual, had no idea that his neighbor Amedure had his sights on him. In the episode Amedure spoke of a fantasy involving champagne, whipped cream, and Schmitz. Schmitz was allegedly furious and humiliated. Three days later, Schmitz blew Amedure away with a shotgun.

Schmitz was tried and convicted in 1996; however,

the verdict was overturned in 1998 due to "an error in the jury selection process." Pendergast successfully prosecuted Schmitz in the second trial in 1999.

The trial of *The State of Michigan* v. *Coral Eugene Watts* would be an entirely different beast for the sophisticated prosecutor.

CHAPTER 53

The first order of duty was to select a jury. At approximately 9:00 A.M., a prospective jury pool of more than sixty candidates was ushered into courtroom 2F. The first round consisted of one-on-one interviews between the attorneys and the potential jurors. This was conducted behind closed doors. After the brief interviews, Judge Richard Kuhn let the attorneys toss out eleven candidates. The doors were then open to the public and the media.

Coral Watts was also ushered into the room.

The defendant was dressed in black slacks, a clean powder blue long-sleeved button-down shirt, and a black pullover sleeveless sweater given to him by his family—specifically, his sister Sharon. Watts's family opted not to attend the trial, though they did support him.

"I feel bad for these people," Sharon Watts said of the victims' families, "but I don't know what I can say to change things for them or bring their [loved ones] back." She also spoke of the stress the trial would have on the Watts family. "Coral's family is as innocent as anyone else's family."

Sharon told the members of the press that she was unwilling to go on television to talk about her brother "because it won't change anything."

Coral Watts wore his prison-issued thick black glasses. He also was adorned with the Oakland County Jail regulation body cuff for the protection of the individuals in the gallery.

Watts entered the courtroom, flanked by two well-built court officers. Watts slowly sauntered over to his chair behind the defendant's table, next to his counselor, Ronald Kaplovitz. He did not, however, take a seat. Instead, he paused in front of his chair and waited for one of his personal escorts to assist him. The court officer pulled out the key to the prisoner's handcuffs and unlocked each restraint. The cuffs dangled off each side like a janitor's batch of keys. The officer then rotated the chain around Watts's waist so that the lock was readily accessible. He unlocked the waist chain, slipped it around Watts's minimal girth, and removed all of the bindings. Watts took his seat.

Surely, he felt the eyes of Harriett Semander, Jane Montgomery, and Betty Rankin, Dutcher's sister, as they tried to burn metaphorical holes into the back of his skull.

Watts seemed disinterested as the prosecution and his defense attorney whittled through the jury pool. Kaplovitz wanted to make sure that the jurors could differentiate between Watts's previous murders and confessions from the murder that occurred on the night of December 1, 1979. Pendergast wanted to make sure that the jurors believed that an eyewitness may give varying levels of information upon witnessing a horrific crime and later when the information had seeped into one's subconscious.

Eventually the attorneys completed the voir dire and settled on a panel of fourteen jurors: the regulation twelve, plus two alternates in case of emergency or other extenuating circumstances. Among the six men and eight women were an engineer, a pharmacist, and a registered nurse. The jurors were allowed to go home so that the attorneys could file motions to delay opening arguments until the following day. The reason for the delay was that some of Helen Dutcher's relatives still had not been able to make it to Michigan, but would be there the next day.

For some of those who were already there, maintaining control seemed to be a top priority. Jane Montgomery, for instance, seethed with rage when she thought of Watts.

"I'm not afraid of him," she expressed. "I'm afraid of myself." She further explained herself. "It was all I could do to keep from taking a butcher knife, cutting off both of his hands and making him sit through the rest of the trial. That would be a starting point to justice."

CHAPTER 54

On Tuesday, November 9, 2004, the starting point to justice began in earnest. Before Judge Richard Kuhn could ask the attorneys to begin their opening arguments, Jane Montgomery whispered to no one in particular, from her seat in the second row behind the prosecution's table, "God, forgive me for my thoughts."

Prosecutor Donna Pendergast, immaculately dressed in a feminine business suit, stood up and confidently strode toward the jury box. She did not carry any notes with her.

"The defendant's motive may remain incomprehensible even at the end of this trial, [but] the evidence in this courtroom will reveal his identity as the person who committed the murder of Helen Dutcher in cold blood," she said, with a none-too-subtle nod to Truman Capote's "true crime" classic.

"You'll see the most gruesome images available of a woman, literally butchered alive," the assistant attorney general declared. "Slashed, sliced, and eviscerated, carved up, and left to die in a pool of blood. Unfortunately, this was no nightmare. This was real. What you are about to hear in this courtroom will terrify you, will horrify you, will haunt your dreams for a long time to come." She drew out each word for emphasis. "Maybe for the rest of your life.

"It has all of the elements for a grade-B horror movie: terror, torture, a knife. This trial will tell the twenty-five-year-old story of the brutal and vicious obliteration of a human life.

"He spotted, targeted, and murdered Helen Dutcher in an act of brutality so diabolical, so monstrous, I guarantee, it will chill you to the bone.

"True Halloween horror.

"Helen Dutcher was chosen for murder not because she had a relationship with the defendant or any pre-existing animosity," Pendergast informed in a calm, even voice, "but simply because she was in the wrong place at the wrong time.

"The defendant's pattern and scheme was to target women who were alone"—Pendergast paused—"and Helen Dutcher fit the defendant's plan just like the thirteen other women he admitted to killing."

Pendergast began to describe, in detail, the murder of Helen Dutcher. "What is known from the physical evidence at the scene is that the defendant first had contact with and first cut Helen out in front of that establishment because blood belonging to Helen was found in the snow in the front of the building. After Helen was first cut, she was either chased, or, more likely, once you know the specifics of the defendant's pattern, forced to the alley end of that same service drive. The same alley that abuts Mr. Foy's yard. Same spot where Helen Dutcher would ultimately die, just inside the entrance, the alley entrance to that service drive, after being stabbed twelve times in the neck, the chest, and the back, but it wouldn't happen without a witness. Joseph Foy.

"At the end of this trial, when you leave this courtroom, you will leave it a changed person because you will have an understanding that evil can wear a human face." She flashed the youthful picture of Watts onto a projection screen with a PowerPoint presentation. "And you will have looked, square, into the face of evil. You will have the luxury of doing that from the jury box. Helen Dutcher had no such luxury. She looked at evil up close on December 1, 1979.

"At the end of this trial, when you've heard all of the evidence, and when you understand all of the evidence, I will ask you for a fair and just verdict based upon that evidence. A verdict that says, 'Mr. Coral Watts, it's been a long time, but justice is a concept that never gets old.'"

Coral Watts seemed uncomfortable throughout Pendergast's opening statement, especially as she described the various murders he confessed to committing. He appeared to twitch his shoulders, and his face seemed to jerk involuntarily. To ease the tics, he constantly rubbed his large hands over his face.

Once Pendergast completed her opening, Judge Kuhn turned his attention to defense attorney Ron Kaplovitz. The attorney sauntered over to the jury box.

"Your role," he addressed the members of the jury, "as I said, will be passive for most of the time, but at the end you will have the full responsibility as to what's going to happen in this case. And at the end of this case, when I ask you to return a verdict of not guilty, you're not gonna like it. You're not gonna want to do it. It is not something that's gonna come easy for you to do. And the reason it's not gonna come easy for you to do is no matter what I do, no matter what I say, you're gonna hate this guy. You hate him already, right now, there's no doubt about that. I understand that. And I sympathize with that and I sympathize with the victims and the families in regard to all the other cases involved, there is no doubt about that."

Watts's defense attorney warned the jurors of his client while pointing directly at him with his finger. "But I'm gonna to ask you to set aside that hatred, I'm gonna to have to ask you to look at this case harshly and fairly to determine what exactly happened on December 1, 1979, because that, in fact, is what is actually important in this particular case. No matter what you think, no matter what you want, the role that you play, that I play, the prosecutor plays, and the judge plays is to ensure that Mr. Watts has a fair trial. And no matter how horrific, how much you hate Mr. Coral Watts he must have a fair trial. It is a perversion of justice if Mr. Watts, is convicted of this case, if, in fact, the evidence does not support that he committed this crime. No matter what you think, no matter what you want to do with Mr. Watts, you have to follow the law and you have to look at the evidence in regards to whether or not Mr. Coral Watts is the person who killed Helen Dutcher."

Kaplovitz then began to attempt to discredit the state's key witness, Joseph Foy.

"You will hear a great deal of inconsistencies and uncertainties. It will become clear to you that while somebody murdered Helen Dutcher, and there is no doubt about that in my mind and there should be no doubt about that in your mind, there really is no significant evidence to establish that, in fact, Mr. Watts was the person who committed this crime."

Kaplovitz also tried to lessen the blow of the 404 (b) evidence of Watts's prior bad acts and his confessions that detailed those acts. "The evidence in this case clearly establishes he committed those murders and the reason he confessed to them is that he did them." Kaplovitz laid it out very clearly that his client was no angel. "But the issue here is, did he kill Helen Dutcher? He confessed to those cases, but to this case, Coral Watts pleaded not guilty.

"The issue isn't that Helen Dutcher died. The issue is who killed her, and the prosecution can't establish beyond a reasonable doubt who killed her. If someone else did this crime, they would have done it the exact same way."

Both Pendergast and Kaplovitz presented their arguments with clarity and succinctness. Their professionalism was broadcast live on Court TV with their opening arguments. Unfortunately, the twenty-four-hour "Investigation Channel" had other plans. Instead of sticking with around-the-clock live coverage of America's most notorious serial killer that no one knew about, the executives at Court TV opted to cover the Scott Peterson murder trial. Of course, the jury had been in deliberations for five days and the Redwood City, California, courtroom was completely empty; however, Court TV brass believed that incessant nattering nabobs of negativism were more compelling than the Watts case.

The Watts case would not be covered live from gavel to gavel. Instead, the country's premier trial network showcased endless yapping from talking heads Lisa Bloom, Kimberly Guilfoyle Newsom, Nancy Grace, and Fred Graham, discussing the finer points of "jury watch" in the Peterson case and what the jurors may or may not be deciding. The network decided that feeding the American masses a story about a distraught couple and a tragic spousal murder was more important that the most dangerous serial killer in the United States and the fact that he could be set loose on the streets.

Despite the screwed-up priorities of Court TV, the trial continued on.

The first witness for the state was Betty Rankin, Helen Dutcher's sister. She was one of six Dutcher relatives who made it to the courtroom in Oakland County. She was also the relative who identified her sister's body in the morgue.

The second witness up for the state of Michigan was Barbara Neph, a waitress at Alfie's, where Dutcher dined on her last meal. Neph testified that she served Dutcher a cup of coffee late that night. The waitress also testified that she saw Dutcher place some coins in the diner's jukebox. She also testified that she believed Dutcher may have been a prostitute. The night Dutcher's body was discovered she was wearing a three-piece business suit, not the usual outfit for a low-rent-district hooker.

Next up for the state was Ferndale police officer Carl Eberhardt, who arrived on the scene first and interviewed the witness, Joseph Foy. Eberhardt testified that he only interviewed Foy for approximately two or three minutes. He also stated that during the brief interview with Foy the witness did not say that he saw the killer's face, or specifically, his eyes. In fact, Foy did not say whether or not he even saw the crime actually being committed.

On redirect examination, Officer Eberhardt reiterated that the interview was only a couple of minutes long and that it would not be unusual for a witness to be unable to recall every minute detail immediately after the crime occurred. Many times witnesses are still in a state of shock or denial after they have witnessed a horrifying act.

Officer Eberhardt also spoke of the fact that police were ready to reopen the Dutcher case back in 1982 when Joseph Foy saw Coral Watts on television in regard to his plea bargain and subsequent sentencing for assault and burglary. Eberhardt informed the jury that all of the files on the Dutcher case from the 1982 reopening had been misplaced.

Eberhardt, however, was not allowed to testify as to *why* Watts was not charged for Helen Dutcher's murder back in 1982. No mention of the plea bargain and Watts's upcoming release could be spoken in front of the jury.

A second Ferndale police officer, Detective George Hartley, took the stand after Eberhardt. He reiterated how he wanted to reopen the case in 1982. He also mentioned the lost case files from that same year.

Oakland County deputy chief medical examiner Kanu Virani, who had worked on thousands of autopsies, including one of Dr. Jack Kevorkian's assisted suicides in which he determined the man did not suffer from terminal cancer, as was suspected by Dr. Kevorkian, conducted the autopsy on Helen Dutcher.

With oversized autopsy photos of a nude Helen Dutcher as his backdrop, Dr. Virani discussed the twelve stab wounds inflicted upon her body. He informed the jury that Dutcher's killer stabbed her in the heart three times, four times in her lungs, and that her jugular vein had been slit open. There were also stab wounds to the victim's back.

The fifth witness before the lunch break was Dr. Steven Lorch, from Michigan State University, who was a crime scene specialist on the night of Dutcher's murder. Lorch testified that he arrived at the murder scene after Dutcher's body already had been removed. His job was to collect blood samples and tire track marks.

* * *

When asked about the difficulty of testifying at her sister's trial, Betty Rankin stated, "It's very hard, but it will be nice to have it over with."

Sandy Anglebrandt, Dutcher's good friend, was upset by the talk of Dutcher as a prostitute. "She never told me if she was or she wasn't (a prostitute). It doesn't matter to me."

Anglebrandt fondly remembered her best friend. "She smiled. She hurt. She cried. She was a human being. I knew the good part of Helen. I don't care about the rest."

Outside the courthouse, after the day's testimony was completed, Jane Montgomery, Elizabeth Montgomery's mother, was asked how she dealt with everything. She told a reporter that it was no more painful than the knowledge that her daughter had been dead for more than twenty-three years.

"It's something that never leaves you," she said of the memory of her daughter's death. "You can't say, 'How do you feel about hashing it all up again?', there's no such thing. It's always there."

CHAPTER 55

On Wednesday, November 10, 2004, all of the key courtroom players returned to fulfill their roles. Defense attorney Ronald Kaplovitz, adorned in an olive green, shoulder-pad-heavy suit, sat next to his client, who was dressed the same way as the day before. Assistant Attorney General Donna Pendergast was dressed elegantly in a tan blazer and skirt with a low-cut eggshell blouse and white hoop necklace.

Before her, sitting patiently in the witness stand, was Joseph Foy, the state's star witness, and one of the key reasons why everyone was in the courthouse in the first place. Foy seemed uncomfortable dressed in his light blue button-down oxford shirt and designer dark blue tie. His cleanly shaved dome gleamed under the fluorescent lights in the courtroom.

"Will you tell the members of the jury where you lived in December of 1979?" Pendergast asked as she stood behind the wooden lectern located directly behind the prosecution's table. Harriett Semander and Jane Montgomery sat directly behind Pendergast on the second row.

"[At] East Bennett, Ferndale, Michigan," Joseph Foy responded.

"And [the address on] East Bennett, where is that, well, first off what type of residence was that? An apartment, a house?"

"Uh, single-family house."

"All right. Where does that house fall on the block? Middle of the block, end of the block?"

"It's on the corner, which would be the, uh, nearest east corner of Eight Mile and Woodward."

"All right. Would your house be the first house off of Woodward?"

"Yes, it would be," Foy stated as he craned his neck in circles trying to work the kinks out.

"All right. Where was your house situated in relation to H&M Cleaners?"

"Directly behind the east of it."

"Did your house have a back door?"

"Yes, it did."

"And what you refer to as a back door, did it actually go to the backyard or did it go out to the side?"

"It actually went to the back porch."

"Did you have a porch outside your back door?"

"Yes, I did."

"And is there an alley behind H&M Cleaners?"

"Yes, it ran parallel to Woodward."

"All right, and this alley that ran parallel to Woodward, would that have run down the side of your house, down the side of your backyard?"

"Correct," Foy answered.

"All right. Briefly describe, if you would, for the members of the jury, what H&M Cleaners, how it was situated, what kind of building it was."

"H&M Cleaners was a cinder block building. It was the second building north on Woodward with a drive-through running along the south side of it," Foy recalled while look-

ing up and to his right, as if reaching up for the answers
that were stored away from long ago.

"When you say 'drive-through,' you mean like a driveway to drop off laundry?"

"Correct."

"All right. Did that driveway lead from Woodward to
the alley behind Woodward?"

"Yes."

"From your back porch, if you were to walk out on your
back porch, do you have a clear view of that driveway?"

"Yes, I did."

"Did H&M Cleaners face Woodward?"

"Uh, yes," Foy recollected.

"Were you home the night of December 1, 1979?"
Pendergast asked as she turned over a sheet of paper in
her legal notepad.

"Yes, I was."

"Who was home with you on that night?"

"Uh, my wife, Paula, and her two children."

"Did something unusual come to your attention in the
evening hours?" Pendergast queried.

"Uh, yes. My, uh, dog was barking quite violently."

"And what did you do when you noticed your dog
was barking violently?"

"I got up, we were watching TV. I got up, looked out
the alcove window that was directly to the alley."

"All right, when you looked out that alcove window the
first time, what did you notice?"

"I noticed a car sitting there," Foy stated as his upper
right lip curved upward in a slight grimace reminiscent
of the Joker's.

"Was it a vehicle that was familiar to you?"

"No."

"And what, roughly, [was the] general description of the vehicle that you observed?"

"Tan Pontiac."

"Had you ever seen this vehicle in the alley before, that you could recall?"

"No."

"Where exactly was this vehicle in the alley?"

"There was a custodial building that actually sat on the north corner of Woodward," Foy recalled while holding his right hand forward, "and they used it as a shipping van parked at a bay door, but it was just south of the shipping van."

"So the shipping van was in the alley?"

"Yes."

"And you were familiar with that van?"

"Yes."

"What did you watch this vehicle do?"

"Actually, nothing. It just sat there."

"For how long?"

"I really can't say how long. A minute maybe."

"What happened next?"

"It pulled away and I went [and] checked [it] out."

"When you say the vehicle 'pulled away,' it pulled away out of that alley?"

"Yes." As Foy testified, Coral Watts seemed to fidget and fiddle with some documents he had before him. He moved around so much that Ronald Kaplovitz actually grabbed his hand and silently motioned for him to stop.

"Okay, and did you see where it went out of that alley?"

"Kind of toward Woodward."

"It didn't drive to a service drive, did it?"

"No," Foy said as he shook his head.

"Okay. So it pulled out of the alley onto which street?"

"It backed up and turned down Bennett, which would

be west, because Bennett was a one-way street heading west." He used his right hand to mimic the movement of the car.

"All right. Now that area where the vehicle was parked, can you describe for the members of the jury what kind of lighting there was back in that area?"

"It was actually a well-lit, not a well-lit area, but a very . . . it was lit. It had a two-story billboard on top of the custodial building that had floodlights. I had a side-porch light that I kept on during the night and there was two floodlights that point directionally down above the shipping van."

"Okay. So behind the building in that alley area you recall two floodlights?"

"Right."

"All right, and then you said there was a billboard? Where was this billboard?"

"It was on top of the custodial building which was right where the shipping van was in a two-story building. It had lights coming down and shining up on it."

"And is that billboard still there today?"

"Yes, it is."

"All right, now you said you had a light on at your house that you kept on at night too?"

"Yes, the side-porch light. I'm sorry, side door." He grimaced again, almost as if he had a wad of chewing tobacco in his mouth and was swishing it around from his bottom lower lip to his right cheek.

"So your porch is in the back?"

"Correct."

"And, in fact, in terms of the lighting conditions, from the back of your house and the alley area, did you conduct activities at nighttime in your backyard?"

"During the summer I used to have a lot of people

come over and we'd play volleyball at night. We didn't need any lights on us just because of these lights that were back there."

"Okay. Now you said on the corner was actually a cleaning building?"

"Yeah, it was a janitorial-supply company."

"All right. So H&M Cleaners is actually the second house off the corner?"

"Second building."

Pendergast smiled at the mild, unintended correction. "After you saw the vehicle pull out, can you tell the members of the jury something unusual that came to your attention after that?"

"I went back down and started watching TV with the wife again."

"Was your wife awake or asleep?"

"Asleep. A few minutes later, my dog—well, my dog was barking constantly because it was a high-traffic area. But, again he started barking real violently again and so I got up, looked outside."

"Will you tell the members of the jury when you looked outside the second time, what, if anything, did you see?"

"I seen the same car back that was parked, farther north this time."

"Okay. Where exactly in the alley area was the car parked?"

"It was parked at the northern point of the custodial building and directly behind H&M Cleaners."

"All right. Did you notice if anyone was in this vehicle or not?"

"I couldn't see anybody in the vehicle. No."

Watts seemed to calm down and appeared bored. He nonchalantly pushed his glasses farther up the bridge of his nose and rubbed the sides of his face. His boredom was apparent.

"All right. Did you observe anything other than that this vehicle had returned and was once again parked in the alley?"

"I looked and I noticed two people standing at the outer edge of the driveway, drive-through, of the dry cleaners."

"At the end of the drive-through that's closest to the alley?"

"Correct."

"Describe the people that you saw."

"I seen a Caucasian female and an African American male," he recalled as he pulled on the right side of his dress-shirt collar.

"All right. I want to back up for just one moment before I talk about that. This vehicle, you said it was a, what color Pontiac?"

"Uh, tan."

"All right. When you looked out a second time and observed two persons in the alley under the service drive, what did you do next?"

"I was standing in my alcove and I watched him push, ummm, I'm not too sure I want to . . . to get a better view, I went up to my landing, which was in between the first and second floor and got a better view."

"All right. This Caucasian female, you said, and a black male, where was the female positioned?" Pendergast questioned.

"She had her back against the custodial building."

"Okay, and where was the black male in relation to her?"

"He was standing front of her, facing her."

"When you first looked out, could you tell what was going on?"

"Not really, there was body movement by both people and I seen a lot of vapor, 'cause it was cold that night."

"Did you, I mean, what did you think was going on when you first looked out?"

Watts's attorney, Ron Kaplovitz, raised his voice: "Objection. Speculation."

Judge Kuhn agreed. "Sustained."

"All right, after you looked outside, did something cause you to go to another window?"

"I was, I was concerned. Something just didn't seem right, so I went to my bathroom window."

"All right. And is your bathroom window on the same side of the house?"

"Yes, it is."

"And what did you do at the bathroom window?"

"Looked out again and I seen mostly the same thing, a lot of body movement and vapors."

"What did you do next that you recall?"

"What I sort of remember is going back down the same viewpoints I had just went up, just to keep an eye on what the situation was going on," Foy replied.

"And did you see anything different at this point?"

"Nah, it was basically the same thing. A lot of body movement. A lot of vapors."

"When you say 'body movement,' what do you mean by 'body movement'?"

"Shuffling. Just shuffling back and forth, like this." He reenacted by shuffling his own feet behind the witness stand. "Just shoulder movement."

"What did you do next?"

"From there I went to, I went out of my alcove through my living room, through my dining room, and out to my kitchen and I looked through that window because it was a more straight-on view."

"Okay, straight-on view into that service drive?"

"Yes."

"All of these locations that you recall going to, were they all windows that were on the same side of the house?" Pendergast inquired.

"Yes, they were."

"All right. And when you looked out of that kitchen view, what did you see at that point?"

"Basically, same thing, and I only stayed there for a brief, a very brief time and, uh, went out to my porch. I went out my back door to my back porch."

"Tell the members of the jury, when you walk out onto your back porch, do you have a clear and direct view into that service drive?"

"Yes, I did."

"Tell the members of the jury what you saw when you went out onto your back porch."

"I walked onto the back porch, kept the back door open and the screen door open, I held it open, and while I was watching, same body movement was going on. At this point I seen the black male raise his hand and bring it down from the top to down, like a downward motion." He graphically demonstrated by raising his hand up and slicing downward with it.

"One time?"

"One time." He nodded.

"After you saw the black male do that, can you tell the members of the jury what happened next?"

"I yelled to my wife, not in these exact words, 'Call the police! Call the police! Hey, call the police!' And I just kept trying to keep an eye on what was going on."

"What happened after you yelled in to your wife to call the police?"

"The black, the woman came out of my view."

"When you say, 'came out of [your] view,' what do you mean?"

"She dropped to the ground." Watts still looked nonplussed.

"All right. What happened next?"

"I went around." Foy began to choke up on the stand. "The black male started walking away from the scene toward his car."

"Okay, and was his car . . . do you need a minute? Do you want some water?"

"Yeah, please." One of the courtroom assistants handed him a tiny Dixie cup–sized paper cup with water. Maybe enough for two gulps. He took his sip and resumed. "Okay."

"So, you said the black male began walking toward his car?"

"Correct."

"Was that car in a position where it was actually closer to you than the area where you had seen the black male and the white female together?"

"Yes," Foy asserted.

"As the black male was walking toward his car, how was he in relation to you?"

"I had a view, he was, at all the time that he was walking, he was walking directly close to me, so I had a view of his left side."

"All right. Did you get a frontal view at some point?"

"Yes, I did."

Watts calmly watched Foy as the testimony was revealed. He had his left hand on the left side of his face, with his index finger pointed up beside his cheek, his middle finger under his nose, and his thumb holding up his chin.

"Can you tell the members of the jury the entire time he was walking toward his car, was he walking toward you?"

"Yes."

"Okay, and what were you doing?"

"Just watching him."

"Tell the members of the jury, was there anything unusual about his behavior, demeanor, as he was walking toward you?"

"Yes. This man was in no hurry," Foy testified in bewilderment. "He just, like, he just dropped off his laundry," he stated while shaking his head back and forth. "He had just walked casually back to his car, no hurry, and it was like nothing ever happened."

"All right. As this individual is walking toward you, did you get a clear and direct view of his face?"

"Yes."

"What, if anything, did you observe when you looked at him?" Pendergast questioned.

"When he walked around the front of his car to his driver's door, he had to stop to open his door, I noticed that he had something long in his hand, which I thought could either be a knife . . . and we both locked glances," he recalled as he looked at the jury.

"You both what?"

"We both locked glances with each other."

"Was there anything significant about locking glances with him?"

"We held it for what I thought was eternity. But he, he was cold. He had no feeling in his eyes. He was just dark," Foy stated exasperatedly.

"Objection," Kaplovitz proffered.

Judge Kuhn responded, "Sustained."

"Okay, what significance struck you about his face?"

"Again, no emotion."

"All right. Did you notice anything about his eyes?"

"Evil."

"Objection. Speculation," Kaplovitz interjected.

"Well, it's his impression. The court will let it stay," Judge Kuhn overruled.

"Now, I know it's been twenty-five years later, and I know we've had another court proceeding, do you think you would recognize the same person years later if you saw him again?"

"Yes, I would."

"Okay. Now I'd ask that Mr. Watts take off his glasses at this time."

Coral Watts removed his glasses even before the judge could respond. He seemed annoyed by the request and glared at Joseph Foy. His wide, penetrating eyes resembled a shark's eyes right before a feeding frenzy. Many observers in the courtroom believed that if Watts could have killed with his eyes, Joseph Foy would have been his first male victim.

"Mr. Foy, do you see the person that you saw that night in this courtroom today?" Pendergast asked.

"Yes, I do," Foy stated, even though it looked like he was in the last place on earth he wanted to be.

"Okay, and would you please point to him and describe what he's wearing?"

Foy, who had avoided looking directly at Watts during the majority of his testimony, shivered and twitched as he gazed in the direction of the defendant.

"The gentleman over there, blue vest (actually, black vest), blue shirt, glasses," he said as he pointed at Watts.

"Does he look the same today as he did then?"

"Eyes do."

Watts placed his glasses back on his face and resumed his chin-resting-on-hand position.

"All right, now, just so the jury understands, at some point later, did you make identification?"

"Yes, I did."

"All right, so the identification of the defendant isn't based on something twenty-five years later?"

"Not at all."

"You indicated that you locked glances with the defendant, what happened next?"

The witness took his second and remaining gulp of water from the Dixie cup. "The defendant got into his car."

"From the time he got into his car, the entire time he's walking toward that car, was he walking closer and closer and closer and closer?" The assistant attorney general stepped out behind the podium and comfortably leaned against its left side.

"Yes, he was."

"All right. How did he come around his car and get into his car?"

"Like I said, he came around the hood of the car, to the door, stopped, we looked at each other, he got into his car and started it up."

"And he had something which you believed to be a knife in his hand?"

"Correct."

"By the way, did you speak with a sketch artist the next day and have her draw composites?"

"Yes, I did."

"And did you tell her about that night?"

"Yes. Basically, an overview of what happened that night."

"All right. After the defendant got into the car, he did what?"

"He started the car up and actually sat there and let it warm up."

"Okay. What happened next?"

"After what seemed forever, he started to back down the alley with his lights out." Foy gave his Joker smirk. "And in no hurry."

"What did you do?"

"Once the car was out of view, I jumped down off the porch, and by this time my wife had came to the back porch and I started heading toward the fence."

"The fence, in your yard?"

"Yeah, separating the alley and my yard."

"And did you go over to the body?"

"Not at that point, no."

"Why not?"

"Scared," Foy admitted.

"I'm sorry."

"Scared."

"Now I'm gonna jump ahead. You indicated that you met with a sketch artist the next day?"

"Yes."

"And what did you do when you met with the sketch artist?"

"I tried to help her as much as I could with the description of the male, the black male that night."

"And did you tell her about going to a number of areas and making a number of observations?" the prosecutor questioned.

"As well as I could, yes."

"All right. Do you remember if you told her if he had a knife?"

"Yeah, I believe I did."

"Did you tell the sketch artist that you'd be able to identify him again if you saw him?"

"Definitely."

"And that was back in 1979 correct?"

"Yes."

"The day after the murder."

"Yes." Foy sighed as he somehow managed to squeeze out a third sip of water from the Dixie cup.

"So you said you were scared, you went into your yard, but you didn't go over. What happened then?"

"I believe that's when the patrol car showed up."

"What happened after the patrol car showed up?"

"The patrol car pulled into the alley and he got out of his car and I said, 'I think there's a body sitting, laying over there,' and that's when I hopped the fence and we both headed toward the body."

"What happened next?"

"We walked up there, he shined the light down and he shook the body and said 'Okay.' He started getting excited. He goes, 'I want you to go sit in the back of my patrol car,' and he led me back to his car."

"Mr. Foy, from the moment that you looked out the second time and saw this black male, this white female, this car parked in the alley, did you ever see any other person in the vicinity of the alley or the service drive?"

"No."

"Earlier, when you looked out the first time, did you see any other person in the back alley or service drive area?"

"Not at all."

"You said when you walked over and the officer shined the light, just roughly, what did you see?"

"I see the body laying there; with a large pool of

blood." Foy squirmed around in his chair. The memory made him uncomfortable.

"Did you see any injury?"

"Uh, no. Not that I remember. I just, ahh, looked and that was it."

"And you did the sketch the next day . . ."

"Yes."

". . . or the sketch artist did it with your information?"

"Yes."

"Did you ever look at a lineup back then?"

"Not that I believe. No."

"For the next two years, following that incident this night, did you ever look at a lineup?"

"No." He shook his head.

"Did you ever identify a subject?"

"Prior to '82?"

"No, for the next two years?"

"No."

"I want to direct your attention to roughly two years after this incident. In 1982, did something pertaining to this night in 1979 happen?"

"Uh, yeah. I was, uh, working at Faygo at the time and I came home and, you know, I would usually turn the stereo on, keep the volume on the TV down and my wife had just cooked dinner and I was just watching, listening to the music, eating, and the only thing that was on was the *Nightly News.*"

"What happened next? The *Nightly News* was on. . . ."

"I seen a, they had a story on, I seen a black male being led into the courtroom. As soon as he was into the courtroom, I looked at my wife. 'Paula! Paula! Here's that man that killed that woman in Ferndale!' She came running in there," he related his story in an excited manner to the members of the jury.

"And Paula was your wife at the time?"

"Correct."

"Are you currently married to her?"

"No, I am not." He smiled at the jury and began to chuckle.

"Mr. Foy, when you saw that footage and said, 'Paula, Paula, come here. Here's that guy that killed that girl,' were you referring to the girl the night of December 1, 1979?"

"Yes, ma'am." He nodded.

"And had you heard any information about this individual when you made your identification?"

"No, 'cause I had the volume down."

"Did you know that he was from Michigan?"

"No." He emphatically shook his head.

"Did you know that he had lived in Michigan at the relevant time?"

"No." He shook his head.

"Did you know whether or not he was a suspect in any Michigan incident?"

"Nope. Just seeing his face and I knew it was him," he said, and continued to shake his head.

"You said as soon 'as it came on the screen,' did this strike you instantly?"

"Instantly."

"What did you do after you viewed the image?"

"Uh, that's when I turned it up and watched the news program."

"That was the *Nightly News?*"

"Yes."

"Did you do anything after making your observation and telling your wife that this was the guy?"

"Yes, like I said, it was around five o'clock, six o'clock, somewhere around there. Right away I called the Ferndale police and at that time the desk person told me that detectives had gone home and all that, and they told me to call back in the morning."

"Did you call back in the morning?"

"Yes, I did."

"Do you recall, for sure, who you talked to?"

"No. It could have been [Detective] Sullivan, it could have been [Detective Robert] Geary, it could have been any of them."

"After you contacted them the next day, the Ferndale Police Department, what happened?"

"I went in and again we talked about it and they said they were gonna hand it, the case, over to the Oakland County prosecutor."

"Was there any other activity relating to you that you remember of?"

"They kept in contact with me on a phone basis and they kept telling me to be prepared to go down to Texas to pick Watts out of a lineup," Foy offered.

"And then did anything ever happen after that?"

"No."

"Now I wanna move ahead to January of this year, 2004. Once again, did something pertaining to this case occur?" Pendergast asked as she leaned on the lectern.

"Yeah. I got home from my part-time job and I was sitting there listening to the wife telling me about her day and I'm just flicking through the channels and listening to her at the same time and came across a news thing with Watts's face again, and I was like, 'What's he doing on TV?'"

"All right. And this clip that you saw, what show was this on?"

"*The Abrams Report.*"

"And when you saw that Mr. Watts was on TV and you

made this identification, was this footage similar to what you had seen back in 1982?"

"Basically, yeah, it was him being led into a court-room."

"And were there other segments of footage that you had saw that you had seen before in 1982?"

"Yes, ma'am. You mind if I get some more water? This is kinda small," Foy stated as he lifted up the tiny Dixie cup.

Ron Kaplovitz doubted that Joseph Foy could so quickly identify Coral Watts on a television newscast back in 1982. On cross-examination, Kaplovitz wondered aloud, "A man walks through a courtroom door, one second, that gives you enough time, he's the guy?"

"That's all I needed," Foy confidently retorted.

"He's the guy?" Kaplovitz asked again.

"Yes."

"One second?"

"Yes."

"The same person whose eye color you couldn't tell? Is that right?"

"Yeah."

"And on that video, you didn't even have time to see whether or not he had a full beard or not?"

"I don't . . . it was the eyes, it was his face. In his eyes I could tell it was him."

"So, you're saying to me, I just want to make sure that I understand this and make sure the jury understands this too. You're sitting at your couch. You just got home from work. You sat down on your couch. You flipped on your TV. You see this video, and, instantaneously, you're able to recognize the person's eyes of someone you haven't seen in two-and-a-half years?" Kaplovitz countered.

"Yes."

"That's what you want us to believe?"

"Yes."

"Okay."

"And if you ask the question again, I'll tell you 'yes' now," Foy defiantly replied.

And on and on, it went. Kaplovitz was determined to paint a negative picture of Foy, who was determined to convince the jury that he saw what he said he saw.

The first, most important day of testimony came to a conclusion. Outside the courthouse Jane Montgomery was asked if seeing Watts being tried finally for murder made everything easier.

"This never gets easier," declared Montgomery, "but we're hanging in there. You know what's going to help is taking a killer off the street so he can never taste freedom or touch another woman again."

CHAPTER 56

On Thursday, November 11, 2004, the courtroom was dark for Veterans Day.

The day after, Friday, November 12, 2004, the trial against Coral Eugene Watts continued. If you planned on watching the trial on Court TV, however, you would have been in the dark as well. On the same day that Joseph Foy's wives testified that he told the truth each time, and sketch artist Barbara Martin confirmed that Foy gave a vivid description of the man who killed Helen Dutcher soon after the attack, the Scott Peterson trial verdict came back.

The majority of the so-called "news" channels, including Court TV, switched their coverage to watch a bunch of people standing outside a courtroom listening to a broadcast of the verdict. The fact that a highly respected sketch artist displayed a sketch that *so* closely resembled Coral Eugene Watts—the worst serial killer in the history of our country—was overshadowed by the latest "trial of the century."

In Ferndale, Michigan, however, it was "Joseph Foy Credibility Day."

Barbara Martin testified about her procedures for

completing a composite sketch of a suspect. She then indicated that Foy sat down with her for more than two hours and described the man he saw murder Helen Dutcher. She informed the court that she believed the sketch she drew was indeed a sketch of Coral Watts.

Martin's testimony was followed by former Ferndale police officer Lieutenant John Marshal, who spoke about why no charges were filed against Watts back in 1982 for Dutcher's murder. He indicated that Michigan authorities acquiesced to Texas. They believed that Texas had plenty of cases to keep Watts behind bars for the rest of his life.

"The case in Texas was such we felt there was no need to do so. It was not because of the credibility of the witness."

CHAPTER 57

The following Monday morning, Andy Kahan was concerned. First, one of the jurors was dismissed by Judge Richard Kuhn. Apparently, one of the jury members discussed the case with an assistant prosecutor from Wayne County, who informed Donna Pendergast, who informed Judge Kuhn. The judge released the juror immediately.

Kahan was also concerned about Julie Sanchez. He knew that the woman who had been brutally attacked by Coral Watts on the Southwest Freeway, back in 1982, feared this trial. Not only had Sanchez never flown before, she also had never spoken about the attack in over twenty-two years. Kahan hoped she could overcome these fears and make the flight to Michigan.

On Monday, November 15, 2004, Kahan's fears subsided. He received word that not only would Lori Lister Baugh and Melinda Aguilar testify, so would Julie Sanchez. It was a day for Watts's Texas survivors to exact some revenge on their monster.

Julie Sanchez was up first. The five-foot-tall woman quietly walked to the witness stand. Her head was bowed down and her long, straight black hair covered most of her face and eyes like Sadako from the Japanese horror film *Ringu*. The hair, in reality, was not her own. Sanchez donned a wig while in Michigan.

The slightly heavyset woman, dressed in a gray business suit with a black blouse, took her place in the witness-box. She identified herself, swore in, and sat with her head down as Judge Kuhn informed the jurors that the ensuing testimony fell under the purview of 404 (b) evidence of Coral Watts's "prior bad acts."

Assistant Attorney General Thomas Cameron stood directly behind the wooden lectern. He wore a blue-gray suit, white button-down shirt, and maroon tie. He seemed pale, thin, and had the beginnings of a receding hairline. In a monotone voice, he questioned Sanchez, "I want to draw your attention back to January 17, 1982. Do you remember that day?"

"Yes," she calmly replied.

"Back on that day, did anything unusual happen?"

"Yes."

"All right, I'd like to talk to you about that something unusual that happened. Drawing your attention back around six-thirty in the morning, back on January 17, 1982, could you describe what kind of day it was?"

"It was a very cold day."

"Was it bright out or was it overcast?" Cameron asked.

"It was bright." Sanchez nodded as she rubbed the tips of her fingers together. "It was daylight."

"Okay, was it still a bit dark out?"

"Not real dark out."

"Okay. Back around that time, at six-thirty in the morning, were you alone in your car?"

"Yes."

"Could you tell the jury what happened?"

"I was driving on the freeway and I had a blown tire."

"Did you say a blown tire?" Cameron inquired.

"Yes. And I pulled over to fix the tire," Sanchez replied. She already began to appear disgusted and angry at the memory.

"Was this on a residential street or on the freeway?"

"No, it was on the freeway."

"Did you pull off to the side of the freeway?"

"Yes."

"After pulling off to the side of the freeway, what did you do?"

"I got out of my car. I went and opened my trunk. I got my jack out and I left my car," Sanchez recalled as she slightly tilted her head to her right and toward the jury box, without actually looking at the members of the jury. She consciously kept her eyes averted from her nemesis, Coral Watts.

"When you say [that] you left your car, you left the car with your jack?"

"With my jack to change my tires. I took my spare"— she paused—"and I put it to the side." She instantly bowed her head down and stared at her hands.

"At this point did you see someone unusual?"

"Yes, I saw a man"—she hesitated as she furtively glanced in Watts's direction. Watts was not too concerned. He had his left hand underneath the right side of his jaw and was immersed in his own world of note-taking— "coming from behind me." Her voice began to crack under the pressure of the pain of the memory. "I stopped doing everything that I was doing and I just stared at him and thinking he was gonna offer me some help." Her cracked voice began to turn into audible sobs at each pause. "But he didn't. He walked by and I could not see him anymore; then I feel like I was safe. And I got on my knees . . . ," she stopped, bowed her head down again, and began to sob even more. She rubbed her teary eyes, with her left hand and began to sob some more. She then clenched her hands into fists and placed them on her eyes with, her head still down.

"Ma'am, there's some water by you, if you need it," Cameron offered.

Sanchez lifted her head, nodded, and wiped her nose with tissue. "I got down on my knees and I took off the first [lug] nut off the tire." Again Sanchez bowed her head. "And I was gonna take the second one, I was attacked from behind me." She sniffled. Then she began to shake and cry harder as she recalled, "I feel the knife cutting my throat from my left side to the middle of my neck. At that point I tried to get loose, I turn around and tried to scratch his eyes, but he wouldn't let me go. Instead of that, he pushed the knife all the way down in."

Sanchez began to break down on the witness stand; however, Judge Kuhn let the questioning continue.

"When he did that, I feel like he was, he was cutting bones or cartilage or something." Sanchez continued to sob, but she was looking up at Watts with more frequency. "It was so painful, but I was still trying to fight back.

"Then he cut me the second time, all the way around to the middle of my neck." She paused for nearly ten seconds. "At that point I was getting loose from him, he smashed my face against the car, and I feel like he was pushing my nose all the way down into my face." She continued her tears for at least thirty seconds.

The silence overwhelmed.

"At that point I tried to run away from him, crawling. But I couldn't get out. I was in so much pain I didn't have the strength in my body. I was losing too much blood. He starts trying to stab me. I had cuts all over my back. But he didn't went deep down, 'cause I have a lot of clothes on me because it was very cold. And the second time I fall down and he stabbed me in between my legs and I kept crawling. I told him, 'Let me go.'"

Julie Sanchez's young adult daughter sat in the audience matching the tears of her mother.

"Did something happen that interrupted the attack?" Cameron asked.

"Yes." She sniffled and nodded, her head still pointing down.

"And what was that?"

"My husband's car pull over, and when he saw the car, he let go and then start running. And my husband saw me, he was in shock, he got real nervous. And I told him, 'He cut me! He cut me! I'm gonna die! I'm gonna die! I'm not gonna make it!'" Sanchez's tears were even more forceful.

She brushed back the thick black hair of her wig and continued. "And he said, 'Who did it? Who did that?' He tried to follow him and I told him, 'There's no time! If you follow him, I'll die. Get me to a hospital.' I got in the car and he had a good chance to turn around and see me."

"When you say he had a 'good chance to turn around and see me,'" Cameron inquired, "who are you talking about?"

"I'm talking about the man who attacked me."

"Did you see the man who attacked you turn around as he was running away?"

"Yes, he had stopped complete, turn around, and look at me . . . and smile. He was laughing," Sanchez stated of the audacity of Coral Watts. "He was just laughing at me!" she practically screamed out. "And then, he keep on running. And when we were on the feeder going to the hospital, I told my husband, 'I'm not going to make it to a hospital.' I told him he had to stop at the gas station and ask for help. 'Get an ambulance so they can do something about it.' My husband, he didn't speak no English. I make a strong effort to get out of the car and asked the guy in there to call an ambulance because I was dying. My body started going in shock and I was shaking so bad and I was feeling so weak. I feel my skin was gonna froze from shaking so much," she stated as she rubbed her face, her head bowed down. Her sobs became physical for everyone in the gallery.

At least thirty seconds passed before Cameron said, "Mrs. Sanchez? I want to back up for just a minute, okay? You said you were taking the nuts, or the lug nuts off of the tire that was flat on your car. Do you remember that?"

"Yes."

"You said that you had retrieved a spare tire from the trunk, and I think you said you leaned it against the car, is that right?"

"Yes."

"You said at that time you saw a man approaching you. Was he approaching you from the front or was he approaching you from behind?"

"No, he was approaching from behind," she said as she regained her composure.

"It seems as though you were paying special attention to this man. Why were you watching him so closely?"

"Because he never spoke. He never make an effort to help me. And I was scared because I was by myself on the road. Like I said, I was waiting for him to say, to offer some help. And I even think to myself, if he offers some help, I'm gonna say, 'No, thank you. My husband is coming to take care of me.' And he never did. It was real strange that he never did. He just walked by me."

" 'He' being this man from behind?"

"Yes."

"Could you, did you get a good look at his face?"

"Yes. He walked right in front of me."

"Could you describe what race he was?"

"He was a black man."

"When he walked by you, did you look at his face?" Cameron posed to the witness.

"Yes."

"You said, later on he came back to you, do you remember that?"

"Yes."

"When he came back to you, were you standing or were you on your knees at the time?"

"I was on my knees."

"When he came up on you, did he come up on you from the front or again from behind?"

"Again, from behind. From the front, behind me. He came back again. He was coming from behind, he passed by me, and he returned, behind me."

Watts continued to ignore Sanchez as she testified.

"Did you see him either walk or run up to you?"

"I was on my knees. I thought he was gone for good. But he [*sic*] was seconds, it was seconds before he was behind me. I can hear his breath right on my ears from when he was running." Her demeanor became more erect as she recalled the attack. Her voice became more firm.

"Did you say you could feel his breath on your ears?"

"Yes."

"Was this when he was close on you?"

"Yes, that's when he cut me the first time." The anger and resentment became evident in Sanchez's voice.

"The first time he cut you," Cameron continued, "did he stab you or did he slice your neck?"

"He went like this," Sanchez stated while bringing her right hand in front of her neck, as if she held an imaginary knife and slit her throat.

"For the record, that's a slicing motion?" Cameron confirmed.

"Yes."

"And the slicing motion, where was the slicing motion on your body?"

"In my neck." She pointed below her chin.

"Okay. Do you still have a scar from that?"

"Yes, I do."

"Have you recently had surgery on that?"

"Yes, I had surgery on this part"—she motioned to the left side of her chin—"because people always ask me, 'What happened to you?'" Sanchez again looked down, as if embarrassed. "And I didn't want to keep repeating . . . anything."

"You just used your left hand and made a motion to your face. You actually made a motion to your cheek. Is that right?" Cameron queried.

"It was from right here"—the victim pointed to the middle of her left jawbone—"all the way right here," she recalled as she pointed underneath her right earlobe. "And then from here, he push it all the way inside." She began to cry with the memory of the vicious attack.

"For the record, you're pointing to your left cheek; you're drawing a line, a continuous line across your throat."

"He came all the way across; from right here he pushed the knife deep down; then he went like, that's when I managed to move, and then he came the second time. He cut my neck all the way around and he also cut half of my ear, right here it was cut." Sanchez lifted the hair over her right ear and pointed to where Watts sliced her.

"Okay. For the record, you're indicating your right ear was cut?"

"Yes." She tugged on her lobe, as if it were the Carol Burnett signature "good night."

"Okay. And is that where the slicing motion ended, at your right ear?"

"The second time, my ear."

"All right. You mentioned that there was more than one cut. Was that the first cut you just described?"

"The first one was from this side to the middle of my neck. The second one, it was from right here all the way to the middle of my neck. And from there, that one, he"—she began to sob loudly—"he push my, my face against the car. And then that's when he starts trying to stab me in my back and everywhere."

"Did he stab you in your back?"

"He cut my clothes a couple of times, but, like I said, you know I had so much clothes on me that I guess that probably helped."

"So, as I understand, you were stabbed a total of three times? Once, the slice across your neck. The second one pressed against your neck, the stab wound to your neck just below your right ear, and then the third wound was to your thigh, or your groin area?"

"In my groin area."

"Ma'am, how tall are you?"

"Five. Five feet tall."

"Okay. How much did you weigh then?"

"About one hundred eleven, twelve."

Cameron then asked Sanchez to act out the attack on him. He walked up to the frightened witness, stood before her, then turned around in front of her so that his back faced her front. He then asked her to show the jury what exactly Coral Eugene Watts had done to her.

The petite woman stood up in her witness seat, grabbed Cameron around the neck, and said, "He grabbed me like this." She mimicked sliding the knife all the way across Cameron's neck. "And the first cut went like this and he push it all the way inside and then he hit like this, and then he cut the rest of my neck and my ear."

Sanchez released Cameron and continued, "Then he grabbed my head." She paused and grabbed Cameron by the hair on the back of his head with both hands. She began to sob heavily as she pretended to smash the young prosecutor's head. "And he just went like this into the car." Sanchez broke down in tears and looked at the floor. She would not bring herself to look at the man who had tortured her all those years ago.

After she regained her composure, Sanchez testified that several months later she saw Coral Watts on television, just as Joseph Foy had done. She stated that she told a friend of hers that Watts was the man.

"Did she encourage you to go to the police?" Cameron asked about Sanchez's friend.

"After, it took a couple of days. She encouraged me, just about every day to come forward."

"And did you go forward and explain to the police that the person who attacked you was the same person you saw on television?"

"Yes."

"Okay. And is this the same person that was later identified as Coral Eugene Watts?"

"Yes," Sanchez stated emphatically as she nodded her head.

"Did it take a very long time to recognize the perpetrator's face on television when you saw?"

"No. No," Sanchez responded.

"Why not?"

"Because I look at him real good when I turn around. I think if I look at him real good when he was passing by me."

"Is that a face you'll ever forget?"

"No. Never, because he's always in my dreams." Sanchez withered from strength to tears.

"I have no further questions," Cameron informed the judge. He soon changed his mind. "Ma'am, just a few more questions, okay? When you did report this to the police, you appeared at the police station, is that right?"

"Yes."

"And did they give you what's called a photo array, or number of different photographs, a pile of photographs?"

"They gave me a pile of photographs, like this."

"All right, for the record, you're indicating a pile of photographs that looks maybe ten to twelve inches high."

"I would say a stack of this much."

"Okay. And were you asked to go through those photographs?" Cameron questioned.

"Yes."

"Were you asked to go through those photographs to determine whether the person who attacked you, if you could identify that person?"

"Yes."

"And did you identify that person?"

"Yes."

"Did you identify that person as Coral Eugene Watts?"

"Yes," Sanchez affirmed.

"All right, you mentioned also that your husband was at the scene back when you were attacked?"

"He got there before, when everything had already

happened. He didn't know anything, that it was happening. He just pull over."

"You were driving earlier that day, following each other."

"I was following my husband. Yes, he was driving to a mechanic to fix his car and I was right behind him so we both can return and leave the car there. That's when I had the blowout tire."

"Very good. Thank you."

Coral Watts never bothered to look at Julie Sanchez.

Judge Kuhn immediately turned to defense counsel. "Mr. Kaplovitz."

Ronald Kaplovitz, dressed in a blue business suit and wearing his black-framed glasses, began to speak to the witness as he sat up from his chair and walked over to the wooden lectern. "Mrs. Sanchez, my name is Ron Kaplovitz. I'm gonna ask you a couple of brief questions. You indicated that you were able to pick Mr. Watts out when you saw him on television, is that correct?"

"Yes."

"And you saw him on television a couple of days . . ."

"No."

". . . a couple of weeks afterwards?"

"No." She defiantly shook her head and spat out the word.

"Month afterwards?"

"No."

"What, sometime later?"

"No."

"When did you see him on TV?"

"Like I say, I was taking a shower, I came out of the shower, the TV was on, and there he was."

"On TV?" Kaplovitz asked.

"On TV," Sanchez replied.

"How long after the incident"—Kaplovitz slowly enun-

ciated the last word and seemed slightly irritated—
"where he attacked you, how, how, how long a period of
time had elapsed? Weeks, days, months?"

"Months."

"Now you happen, unfortunately, to see and have
dealings with Mr. Watts, up close and personal, is that a
fair statement?"

"I guess."

"I mean, he was as close to you as Mr. Kramer (actually Mr. Cameron) was when he approached, when he
had you show the jury what happened."

"He was right here."

"Right. Right next to you. You saw him . . ."

"Yes."

". . . face to face?"

"Yes. Right here."

"Okay," Kaplovitz continued. "Now, when he, you
were, you were following your husband to take his car to
the mechanic's shop?"

"Yes. No, not a mechanic's shop. One of his friends.
One of his coworkers was gonna fix his car."

"When he attacked you, did you start screaming for
help?"

"I screamed, 'Oh, God!' and everything, you know, that
he did to me . . . I could hardly talk. I could hardly
scream anymore."

"But you did scream when it happened?"

"My first words was 'Oh, God!' until he got right here
and he went deep down and I could hardly talk."

"The whole contact with him on the attack, approximately, how long did it take? I mean, can you give me a
guesstimate—seconds, minutes?"

"I would say minutes."

"Okay. Now, your husband's car pulled up, is that right?" Kaplovitz asked.

"Yes."

"And as soon as that happened, Mr. Watts ran away?"

"He let go."

"He let go?"

"Yes."

"And he ran away?" Kaplovitz confirmed.

"He ran away."

"He went to his car?"

"No, he was on foot all the time," Sanchez clarified.

"Okay, and he just took off, running?"

"He just took off, running."

"All right, he didn't stick around?"

"No."

"Okay. Were you working at that time?" Kaplovitz inquired.

"Yes."

"Okay. Where did you work at?"

"I worked at the same place where I work now, NASA. Johnson Space Center."

"NASA Jones Space Center?" Kaplovitz asked.

"Johnson Space Center."

"Oh, Johnson Space Center."

"Yes."

"Okay. Thank you, Mrs. Sanchez." Kaplovitz was done.

"You may step down, Mrs. Sanchez," Judge Kuhn informed the witness. "Watch your step."

Thomas Cameron walked to Julie Sanchez to assist her from the witness stand. The short woman seemed to grow several inches right before everyone's eyes. She had faced the essence of evil once again, and, once again, she came out on top.

Next up for the prosecution was another Texas survivor victim, Lori Baugh, known as Lori Lister at the time of the assault on her by Coral Watts. Baugh wore a gray business jacket, blue vest, and button-down white shirt. Her fashionably styled brown hair rested on the nape of her neck and she wore clear-rimmed glasses. She appeared very elegant and respectful.

Thomas Cameron again took up the direct examination. He had Baugh describe how she had been blindsided at the foot of her staircase. Her attacker did not completely knock her out and she was aware that she was in serious danger.

"He said, 'Where is your apartment?'" Baugh recalled. She tended to smile, sometimes in bewilderment, sometimes in bemusement.

"Do you remember what you were thinking?" asked Cameron.

"At that point I remember thinking, 'I'm gonna die. I want my parents to find me,' and, I don't know, I just thought he was gonna carry me off and bury me somewhere. And, but I was too weak to do anything or say anything. I remember raising my hand slightly, but I couldn't have pointed because I was too weak."

"When you say you raised your hand, is that you raised your hand in the direction of where your apartment was?"

"It wouldn't have mattered because I couldn't point and I didn't really know what direction it was"—she chuckled nervously—"but I knew it was upstairs, but I just raised my hand like this, just barely, but I just knew he was gonna carry me off somewhere and bury me." She laughed again and almost rolled her eyes up to the sky. "And I, I don't know, I just wanted so badly for my parents to find me because I was about to die. And at that point I knew he was a black man."

"What happened next?"

"He beat me up at that point and, so, I was unconscious after that."

"Okay. What's the next thing you do know?"

"I know he, the next thing I know was I woke up semi-consciously in the ambulance asking about Melinda. 'Melinda, Melinda! Is she okay?'"

"Who's Melinda?"

"She was my roommate at the time."

"Did she live with you at that time?"

"Yes, she did."

"Did she live with you in the second-story apartment you described?"

"Yes, yes."

"Why were you concerned about Melinda?" Cameron questioned.

"Because I knew she was up there. She was there that night and I was scared that he would have found the key and gone up and hurt her or killed her, because I knew that that was what was supposed to happen to me." She smiled again. "And if he had my key, he was gonna, for sure, go and find her."

"Did you learn what had happened to you?"

"I, I didn't remember for a couple of days what he had done. I remembered, it all came back to me and then, and then I did hear from everybody that he had pulled me up the stairs and my ankles were real torn up. Actually, up into my legs were all bloody and torn up and scratched from having been pulled up the stairs."

"Is this cement stairs?"

"Yes. And I had been tied with hangers and I had been submersed under a tub of water," Baugh said in a quieter voice.

"The tub of water you were submersed into, was that the tub in your apartment?"

"Yes, sir."

"You mentioned that you had regained consciousness at some point in the ambulance, is that right?"

"Uh-huh. It was still blacked out. I mean, I , I couldn't see anything, but I had woken up to yell, 'Melinda! Melinda! Where is she?' and the fireman told me, 'She's okay, she's okay," and that's when I passed out again. And the next time, the next thing I remember is in the hospital emergency room."

"Could you tell us a little bit about the injuries you had when you were in the hospital room?" Cameron inquired.

"Well, the first thing I know that happened was my tongue was swollen to the point I couldn't breathe. I, I kept having to get up on my elbows to breathe, because when you get strangled, your tongue swells and it was all black."

"Was your tongue swollen?"

"Yes, I couldn't breathe. I couldn't talk. Had to do phone numbers with my hands. I also lost the feeling on top of my hand for months on end, and I was really scared I would never regain that feeling."

"What was that a result of?"

"Having been tied with hangers," Baugh explained.

"Were those the only injuries you had?"

"No, my face was beaten up. I was all bruised. My eyes and my forehead was all scratched up. I didn't see pictures—I mean, I don't know—but I know from looking around I had some injuries on my hip and then, of course, my legs, both my legs. I tried not to look in the mirror"—she laughed again—"at that point, because it was really not a nice sight."

"Back when this occurred, how much did you weigh?"

"About one hundred fifteen."

"And how tall are you?"

"Five-seven."

"And how old were you at the time?"

"Twenty-one," Baugh replied.

"Thank you. I have no further questions." Cameron closed. Quick, but efficient.

Next up on the stand was Melinda Aguilar. Like he had been about Julie Sanchez, Andy Kahan was worried whether or not Aguilar would even make the trip. The still-tiny woman had never flown before and was not sure if she would be able to get on a plane and testify against Coral Eugene Watts. The little fighter was determined, however, to make sure she would contribute her part in the attempt to put him away for good.

The attractive Aguilar took the witness stand next to Judge Kuhn. She wore a long-sleeved white turtleneck cotton shirt, with an oversized light gray jacket with large pockets on the chest and large lapels. Her dark brown hair was stylishly streaked with blond and red strands. It was draped over her left eye, which just happened to be in the line of vision of where Watts was seated. She spoke in a pixieish, almost-little-girl voice.

Donna Pendergast asked her to describe what happened that day of May 23, 1982.

"I was shocked. I wasn't expecting to see him," Aguilar stated with no fear. "I was expecting to see my roommate and I think he was pretty shocked to find someone in there also. We just kind of stood there for a moment."

"What happened after you stood there for a moment?"

"Um, he came around and grabbed me and started,

put his arm around, put a knife," she recalled as she pantomimed placing a knife at her own throat, "and said if I was to scream that he would kill me."

"All right. Did you see where he took that knife from?" Pendergast pursued.

"From his sock in his leg."

"All right. So, is the person, you said he grabbed you. How did he grab you?"

"Kind of went behind me and grabbed me like this," she stated as she made a move that looked similar to the attack on Julie Sanchez. She brushed the hair out of her eyes and continued, "He started choking me."

"All right. And when he started choking you, did he already have a knife in his hand at that time?"

"He did everything so quick." Aguilar jerked her hand toward her throat again. "It was like all, I mean, he did everything so quick, he put the knife up to me right away, and I think kind of went, like this, and started choking me."

"All right. Did you know where your roommate, Lori Lister, was at that point?"

"Not at that point, no."

"All right. After the defendant put the knife to your neck, can you tell the members of the jury what happened next?" Pendergast asked.

"Um, he was choking me so tight that, um, I couldn't breathe, so I was afraid that, um, you know, he was gonna kill me that way, and so I pretended to pass out and I just kinda let my body loose."

"And after you just kind of let your body loose, what was the next thing you remember happening?"

"He dragged me into the bedroom and kind of laid me against the bed, and then, um, he left the room."

"All right. How big were you back then?"

"I's about, I was short." Aguilar laughed. "About eighty-six pounds."

"Eighty-six pounds. And how tall were you?"

"I'm five even, right now."

"Five foot. All right, so he dragged you and laid you next to the bed. How did he lay you next to the bed?"

"I was on my knees and he kinda laid my head against the bed."

"Did he say anything to you?"

"No," Aguilar stated as she shook her head. "I was pretending to be out. I was pretending to be out the whole time."

"All right. What's the next thing that you recalled happened?"

"He, um, left the room and I heard him open the door, and next thing I heard was, um, he was dragging my roommate, her body, up the stairs and I could just hear her body hitting every step. And then he, um, later in the living room, and I could hear the moaning . . ."

"You could hear the what?" Pendergast inquired.

"I could hear the moaning. She was moaning. I didn't know . . ."

"You could hear Lori moaning?"

"Yes. Yes," she said as she nodded her head. "And at that time after he left her there, he came and checked on me, um, and I had, I was getting ready for church, so I had my dress on the bed, and he grabbed that, the hanger off the dress and the belt, and he tied me up, really."

"How did he tie you up?"

"With my arms behind my back."

"All right. And what was actually around your arms? Was it the belt or was it the hanger?" Pendergast asked.

"Both. Hangers and belt."

"All right. After he tied you up, did he say anything to you at this point?"

"No, because I was pretending to be out still."

"Okay, so you're still pretending to be out when he bound you?"

"Yes," Aguilar asserted.

"What happened after he bound you up?"

"He went back into the living room and I could hear him, uh, getting into a closet, looking for hangers and, um, I assumed that's when he tied Lori up."

"What happened next?"

"He came back in to check on me and, um, and I was, the whole time I pretended to be out, so he checked on me and then went back out, and I don't know if he was confused because, you know, there was two of us. Then he went back out, and he came back in and, um, he started the bathwater and he came back in and checked on me."

"So, you could hear the water in the bathtub running at that point?"

"Yes. Yes."

"Did you know where Lori was at that point?"

"Um, I just assumed she was still in the living room, 'cause he had gone and started back, and he came back in and checked on me one last time, but when he did, he, um, he kinda made a, like, he kinda jumped and clapped," she said as she clapped her hands and jerked in her seat, "and made a little remark like this was 'gonna be fun.' This was gonna be exciting, and I knew at that point that he was enjoying what he was doing."

"What happened next?"

"He left the room and he left the door a little cracked, you know, he kinda shut it a little bit, and at that time I, uh, he went into the living room and I could see him dragging Lori into the bathroom, so I figured that was my time to get some help."

"Will you tell the members of the jury, what did you do in an attempt to get some help?" Pendergast queried.

"I got up and locked the bedroom door and then I went, we had a sliding door, um, in our bedroom, and so I got up and unlocked that and I went to the balcony."

"How did you do that with your hands bound?"

"I just kinda walked with the sliding door, kinda unlocked it and walked with it to open it. And then when I got out to the balcony, um, I didn't know how I was gonna get away, um, being short, and there was a fencing, the railing, um, so I decided to go headfirst. I jumped and did a somersault, and then I hit my head and my shoulder and then I landed on my knees."

"This was from the second floor?"

"From the second floor, yes."

"All right. And after you landed on the ground, what happened next?"

"Well, there's a fire station across the street, so I told myself that's where I was gonna go, but, I guess, just out of fear, I went to the left and I saw a lady sitting outside on her balcony, on the first floor, drinking coffee, and I told her that someone was trying to kill my roommate, that we needed to get help."

"Okay, were you still bound at this time?"

"Yes," Aguilar stated.

"All right, what happened next?"

"Um, they took me inside and they were trying to take the, um, hangers and the belt off, but they were having a really hard time, and, uh, I guess when they took them off, I must have gone in shock or something, because I don't remember anything after that." She jerked slightly in the witness stand. Her hair dangled back down over her left eye. "Other than, um, I had a cup of tea sitting on the couch and they told me that my roommate was fine and that I had to go outside and identify the, the person that did this."

"And did you go outside to identify the person who had done this?"

Melinda Aguilar nodded her head affirmatively.

"Okay, and who did you identify?" Pendergast questioned.

"Coral Eugene Watts."

"And where did you see him at outside?"

"In the police car."

"All right, and did you recognize that as being the same person who had been inside your apartment and had bound you up?"

"Yes," Aguilar said as she firmly nodded her head. "Yes."

"What was Mr. Watts wearing that day?"

"He was wearing a, a sweatshirt with a hood, and I noticed he had some gloves when he first came in."

"What kind of gloves, do you remember?"

"They were dark gloves. I don't, everything happened so quick."

"Nothing further, Your Honor."

"Mr. Kaplovitz?" Judge Kuhn spoke.

"Ms. Aguilar, my name is Ron Kaplovitz," Watts's defense attorney stated as he walked from the defense table to the wooden lectern. "I must say, you have my respect for your bravery."

With eyes downcast, Aguilar stated in a less-than-excited voice, "Thank you."

"Ma'am, what city did you say you lived in at the time?"

"Houston, Texas."

"Okay. And there was an area, I thought you said like the Hamley area, or something like that?"

"It's off of Hammerly Road (Boulevard, actually)."

"Oh, Hammerly Road, okay, all right. And, uh, you were on your way to go to church, is that right?"

"I was in the apartment. It was still early. I was, I had gotten up and, um, I just laid my clothes out. I had plenty of time. I was just getting ready. . . ."

"Just getting started. Did you work at that time?"

"Yes," Aguilar answered.

"Where did you work at?"

"I worked at, uh, a place called Tight Air."

"What did you do for them?"

"I was a receptionist."

"Now, you indicated that the first, sort of, indication or clue you, that something unusual was going on, was you heard a scream. Is that right?" Kaplovitz wondered.

"Yes."

"That was from outside?"

"I assume it was from outside."

"You assumed it was Lori Lister screaming, right?"

"Well, I didn't assume it was her at the time, 'cause I didn't, you know, I just heard a scream, I didn't think anything of it."

"In reflection now, you were assuming that it was her screaming when she was attacked, isn't that correct? Now?"

"Well, now, yes."

"Right, and I understand at the time you didn't know what was going on," Kaplovitz suggested.

"Right, right."

"You heard a scream from someplace coming out . . ."

". . . Right."

". . . somebody screamed outside the apartment and you were able to hear it, right?"

"Right."

"Okay, thank you. I have no further questions."

The "Texas Trio" was followed by Houston police officer Doug Bostock, who described what Watts was wearing at the time of his arrest and that Watts was driving his brown 1978 Pontiac Grand Prix.

Bostock was followed by Houston detective Tom Ladd, who read over Watts's confessions and described the crime scenes for the court. Ladd had a rather distracting habit of placing his eyeglasses on the bridge of his nose as he read from his notes and then removing the eyeglasses when he looked up at the attorneys to hear their questions.

One of the more interesting exchanges took place between Ladd and Donna Pendergast.

"What did Mr. Watts tell you he did relating to Carrie Jefferson?" Assistant Attorney General Pendergast asked the retired detective.

"He said he was driving around in his, his Pontiac. He saw Mrs. Jefferson driving, uh, a small blue car," Ladd stated as he placed his glasses on his nose. "He, again, got in behind her," he said as he removed his glasses. "He followed her to a residential neighborhood. It was a fairly long drive outside the, you know, downtown area of the city of Houston." The detective again placed his glasses on his nose. He looked down at his notes and just as quickly removed his reading glasses. "He said he saw her pull up to a curb in front of her house and there were other vehicles in the driveway, so it appeared that she probably had to park on the curb. He parked. He stopped. He saw her get out of the car. He grabbed her as she was walking to the front door of her house. Choked her down and then he put her in the trunk of her own car," he stated while holding his glasses in his hand and waving them back and forth.

"He said he would never put a complainant in his vehicle because of 'evil spirits.'

"So, he had her in the trunk of the car," Ladd continued, "he returned to his vehicle, which was parked a short distance away, retrieved his shovel. Went back, put the shovel in Carrie Jefferson's car with Carrie in the trunk, and then drove her to the location of sixteen-hundred block of White Oak Bayou, where he opened the trunk. She was still alive and fighting; he then fought with her, choked her, killed her, and then buried her."

Pendergast asked, "Did he indicate whether or not he stabbed her?"

"Yes, he stabbed her twice. One on each side of the neck," the no-nonsense detective assured her.

"Did he indicate whether or not he took any personal items with him?"

"Yes, he took a pair of burgundy pants," Ladd recalled while looking down at his yellow legal pad. "He burned them."

"Did he tell you why he buried Carrie Jefferson?"

"He said that [to] kill her spirit. He said that she was evil. He said that she had fought him so hard that he had buried her deep to prevent her spirit from getting out."

Ladd also spoke of the murder of Suzanne Searles. He stated that Watts confessed that he had choked Sue Searles and pushed her face first into a flowerpot filled with water and drowned her. He also stated that Searles was listed as five feet two inches, 120 pounds, on her missing persons report. When police unearthed her body, her decomposed corpse weighed only sixty-seven pounds.

Detective Ladd eventually was cross-examined by Ron Kaplovitz. The defense attorney honed in on Ladd's contention that Watts confessed that he attacked the women because of their "evil eyes."

Kaplovitz stood behind the wooden lectern and asked the detective, "Now, he also indicated that he selected his victims based upon their 'evil eyes'?"

"That's what he said," Ladd responded. "That was his response to the question I asked him, why he would pick one victim, you know, after he drives around all day, he sees many, many women, but yet he picks a certain woman, and so we always asked him, 'Why did you pick this particular individual?' and he'd come back and say, 'Because they had evil in their eyes.'"

"So he, he, he, saw evil in their eyes?"

"That's what he said."

"That's what he told you, right?"

"That's what he told me, yes," Ladd answered.

"So it was 'evil eyes.' Because [of] their evil eyes, right?" Kaplovitz ascertained.

"Evil in their eyes."

After calling several more officers to the stand, including Felix Bergara, Jim Ladd, Gary Fleming, and Daniel Jensen, the prosecution rested its case.

The defense only called one witness, Sergeant Tim Brown, of the Michigan State Police Department. Kaplovitz questioned Brown about the possibility that Joseph Foy could make an accurate description of his client, Coral Watts, from eighty-four feet away. Kaplovitz then had the jury step into the hallway so as to conduct a distance test. Kaplovitz wanted the jury to know what it felt like to see something from that particular distance.

After the demonstration the defense rested its case.

After the day's testimony, Andy Kahan marveled at the strength of the Texas Trio. "God, it's never left them," he said of Julie Sanchez, Lori Lister Baugh, and Melinda Aguilar. "They never thought they would have to go through this again."

Kahan discussed how the women had not wanted to fly to Michigan to face their brutalizer. He stated, however, that they knew they must.

"They don't want anyone else to suffer as they have."

Kahan singled out Aguilar for additional praise. "She's the most heroic lady I've ever met. If she hadn't jumped, they were numbers fourteen and fifteen. He was on a major roll. Who knows when it would have stopped? There are people alive today because of her actions."

CHAPTER 58

Judge Kuhn's courtroom was overflowing with spectators. Surviving family members of Coral Watts's victims, such as Harriett Semander and Jane Montgomery, sat in the audience, joined by many of Watts's surviving victims, such as Julie Sanchez and Sandra Dalpe Carlsen, to activists Andy Kahan and Dianne Clements. They were all there to witness the closing arguments of the case.

First up for the state was Donna Pendergast. The elegant assistant attorney general dressed sharp in her blue business dress, white blouse, and strand of pearls necklace. She displayed her eloquence right off the bat as she walked past the pushed-aside lectern and addressed the remaining thirteen jurors. She used no notes and stood upright and confident, but not cocky, as she spoke.

"It's been twenty-five years since the final chapter in Helen Dutcher's life was written on the blade of a knife. And yet the final chapter to this story has been written in this courtroom in a very few days. It awaits only an ending which will be written by you, the jury. After twenty-five long years, I beg of you, make sure it's the right one.

"For twenty-five years Helen's screams have been

silenced. No closure for the family, no justice. But she speaks to you now through the evidence. The evidence that points in one direction and one direction only," she declared as she turned her back to the jury box and pointed at the defendant Coral Watts. "Directly at a stalking predator with a diabolical pattern and scheme of willfully and purposefully killing women for the sheer thrill of it." Watts appeared nonplussed at the accusations being tossed his way. He simply placed his chin in his left hand and stared at a yellow legal pad on the defense table.

"And now it's time. Time to say, 'We, the jury, understand that a terrible crime was committed here. We don't understand how you could do what you did, but we know that you did it.' And the truth is, there is no understanding of the whys of Helen Dutcher's death. Only the hows. Alone, terrified, on a cold driveway, and in an agonizing manner. But, unfortunately, not quickly enough to spare her of the horrifying certainty that she was about to die.

"There is no understanding of the whys of Helen Dutcher's death because it is pure evil. And there is no understanding of pure evil, just recognition of what it is," Pendergast declared as Watts looked over for the first time, albeit briefly.

"You know, no one ever knows when the end of their life is going to come. I am sure that when Helen Dutcher woke up on December 1, 1979, she never dreamed that that was the last day of her life. If she went about her activities during the daytime hours, doing what she normally does, undoubtedly she never dreamed that those were the last hours of her life.

"As she left Alfie's Restaurant, walking toward the area where she would soon die, I'm sure she never dreamed those were the final minutes of her life.

"Surely," Pendergast said with a sigh, "when you're thirty-six years old, your world doesn't end like this: on a cold December night, isolated from everybody but a man with a knife. And then, in the struggle of your life, a struggle for your life, a struggle that ends only after you crumple to the ground"—she paused—"staring blankly at death in the face as the life drains from your body.

"The last thing that Helen Dutcher saw was the defendant. She looked at evil up close. She saw that the human face of Coral Eugene Watts is nothing more than a mask for evil so dark that your worst nightmare pales in comparison."

As Pendergast addressed the jury, she also projected images of the case on the overhead screen directly above and to the right of Watts. It was on the left of Watts from the jurors' perspective. At the same time she described "evil up close," she flashed an image of Coral Eugene Watts's eyes in a larger-than-life manner.

"You know, we see violence every day, at the show, on television. We've become so used to seeing violence for its entertainment value that we lose sight of what true violence really is. But this, ladies and gentlemen of the jury, is not TV violence," she declared as she clicked the projector to display two photos of Helen Dutcher's corpse as it lay on the morgue slab. Watts tilted his head back to get a good look at the body of Helen Dutcher.

"Unfortunately, it's not. There's nothing fictional about the plot of ground that Helen Dutcher lies in. And while we engage in our pursuits of some sort of justice, we can do it under a horrific set of circumstances, Helen Dutcher remains very dead. Robbed of her life by a man who has no conception of the value of human life. A man who kills for no reason other than the pleasure of killing. A man with his own diabolical plan and scheme. Really, a plan and scheme that almost defies comprehension. A man who sits in this courtroom today hoping for your mercy when none was shown to Helen Dutcher.

"You know, as human beings we have a tendency to want to try and understand. We relate a lot easier to things that don't threaten our views of why and how things happen. It would be a lot easier and a lot less disconcerting to think, as Mr. Kaplovitz insinuated, of this as a purse robbery gone bad. Because even though that certainly is a horrific thing, it's easier to understand. But every shred of evidence in this courtroom shows that things far more monstrous than a purse robbery gone bad to the point of murder do happen, can happen, do happen, and, in this case, did happen.

"So how do we know that the defendant is guilty?" Pendergast asked as she slowly walked back and forth in front of the jury. "Well, I'm confident that you had the opportunity to size up, listen to, hear from, and watch Mr. Joseph Foy. To size him up for what he is, a good citizen who saw a very bad thing.

"You know, it's interesting, because in this case it's no coincidence that he just happens to be the person who lives at that first house off the alley. We're not talking about somebody who comes into this courtroom and says, 'I was walking down the street and I saw a murder.' You're talking about the man who lives right there, the first house, the closest house to where the murder occurred.

"We know that Mr. Foy was home that night because we know that from his testimony as well as Paula Otto's testimony. And we know that he saw something, because he reported it to the police through his wife, as well as pointed Officer Eberhardt to the body as soon as he arrived." Pendergast paused and pointed with her index finger for emphasis. "We know that he talked to a sketch artist the very next day, and not only was able to give sufficient information for that sketch artist to compile a sketch, but also to convince her, a professional, that he would be able to make an identification again if he saw the individual. A belief that was so profound that she put it in her report. The same report where she indicated that she was of the belief that Joseph Foy had registered and recorded specific images. Her belief, a professional, he would be able to pick him out again.

"You saw that composite sketch," she reminded the jury as she displayed Barbara Martin's sketch on the overhead screen. "Put a little more hair on it and it's the defendant. Or, as good as you're gonna get with a composite sketch.

"Clearly, this is not a situation where Joseph Foy thinks all black men look alike. He got a number of features down remarkably well. The puffiness, the top of the cheeks, the eyes, the position of the ears, you heard from Mrs. Martin, the mouth. That's pretty remarkable considering when Mrs. Martin told you of the purpose of the composite sketch is to basically rule out a number of people, not to include a number of people. And Mrs. Martin told you a composite sketch is not exact. It's as best we can do under the circumstances and it rules out a number of people. But, in light of the fact that Mr. Foy got that many features down pretty well, under the circumstances, it's pretty clear that he saw the defendant.

"What else? Well, I know that Mr. Kaplovitz is going to come in here and say, 'Well, we have a picture taken six weeks before and Mr. Watts didn't have any facial hair.' And that's true. I stipulated to the admission of that picture. Actually, I think if you look at the exhibit, there is a little tuft, like he's beginning to grow a beard, but the point is, number one, Mrs. Martin never said that the composite was exact, and number two, if you look at Mr. Watts's various photographs that we've been able to compile, not only is he, is it common for him to wear facial hair, in fact, I would suggest to you, it's characteristic."

Pendergast went on to discount Kaplovitz's claim that Watts had no facial hair six weeks before the murder of Helen Dutcher.

The female assistant attorney general then talked about how Joseph Foy identified a car that closely resembled Watts's 1978 Pontiac Grand Prix.

Pendergast then came to the modus operandi of Coral Eugene Watts. "It's always the same thing. Lone female targeted, because she was there, if you recall Jim Ladd's testimony. Defendant positions himself for easy access to his victim. Defendant exits his vehicle, approaches his victim on foot. The defendant, without warning or provocation, attacks viciously in a variety of methods depending on what was convenient at the moment. The crimes are all similar.

"Let's just talk about a couple of other things that are distinctive about the defendant. What else is distinctive about the Helen Dutcher murder scene? Helen's purse is missing. Now, sure, that could be construed as a robbery, if you didn't have all the other factors.

"But what do we know about Coral Eugene Watts? One thing we know is that he likes to take personal items from his victims, and in several other cases he specifically took a purse. The case of Margaret Fossi, the woman who was stuffed into the trunk of the vehicle. The case of Alice Martell, and more than likely Michelle Maday. Instead, the defendant seemed to have some sort of bizarre fascination with purses, because you know that he also rifled through the contents of Suzanne Searles's purse, as well as Linda Tilley's purse.

Helen Dutcher's purse missing is indicative of Coral Eugene Watts."

Pendergast continued with well-maintained composure. The gallery sat in complete silence and hung on her every word. "What else seems indicative of the trademark of Coral Eugene Watts? Well, think about his demeanor and attitude as he strolled toward Mr. Foy. I mean, think about this," she said exasperatedly. "You've got a body laying about two or three feet away," she said in a considerably louder voice. "If this was a robbery gone bad to the point of murder, common sense tells you that somebody's gonna be trying to get out of there fast. Common sense tells you that it's not gonna be a slow, nonchalant stroll back to the vehicle. Common sense tells you you're gonna be hightailing it out of there."

The attorney turned to look at the defendant. "But not Coral Eugene Watts. He strolls deliberately and casually, as if he just dropped off his laundry."

The prosecutor was on a roll. "What else matches the pattern of Coral Eugene Watts at the Helen Dutcher scene? Ladies and gentlemen of the jury, might I suggest to you that the number of stab wounds itself is excessive for a robbery gone bad, not to mention the force with which they were inflicted. Twelve stab wounds severe enough to break ribs. This isn't a robbery gone bad. This is rage. This is deep-seated hatred"—she drew out each syllable—"this is Coral Eugene Watts."

Pendergast grabbed the projection clicker and turned toward the large screen next to Watts. "So how does the Helen Dutcher crime compare to the rest of them? All of the victims, female. That goes without saying. All relatively youthful. All under forty, besides Jeanne Clyne. Helen Dutcher, thirty-six. All short to average height. Slim to average build, everyone except for Phyllis [Ellen]

Tamm, who was a little bit stockier than the other ones. All alone when attacked. All occurred between dusk and dawn. Just like Helen Dutcher. Random victims." She returned her attention to the jurors. "Just like Helen Dutcher. From what we know of where she was last seen and where she ended up.

"He acted alone. In Helen Dutcher's case, we know from Joseph Foy, there was one attacker. He used a Grand Prix. The assailant was a stranger to the victim. It was a stranger. We also know he stalked or followed the victim. It would appear from circumstances of the Helen Dutcher case that something like that was going on."

Pendergast continued on the patterns and practices of murder for Coral Watts. "Mechanism of injury and death. Every one of the women, at some point, he had his hands around their neck, even if manual strangulation wasn't actually the mode of death. Ten women stabbed. All of them stabbed repeatedly, except Elizabeth Montgomery, who, I might remind you, had two dogs that she was walking. Two large dogs, which may be the reason she only got hit once. Unfortunately, for Elizabeth Montgomery, once was enough.

"All the victims, primarily left side of the chest. Another characteristic of right-handed Coral Watts. The only exception to that rule, Carrie Jefferson, who, if you'll recall, after she was taken out to White Oak Bayou, was stabbed in each side of her neck.

"Other indications that Helen's murder could, in fact, be Coral Eugene Watts, took a personal item when he had time. We know Helen's purse is missing. No evidence of sexual assault, and an attack within a previous or subsequent month. In Helen Dutcher's case, we know that Jeanne Clyne was murdered just thirty-one days before.

"We know all of these things because he admitted to

them. But don't forget, he admitted to them under a very controlled situation," Pendergast expertly skirted around the plea bargain, while indirectly alluding to it, "with his attorneys present and with the agreement that he would only talk about cases in Houston, Galveston, Austin, and Grosse Pointe. As you heard in this case, Ferndale made a considered decision not to go forward because of what was going on in Texas. They were not part of this agreement and the authorities in Texas had no reason or information or a reason to question Mr. Watts about the Ferndale case.

"Every piece of evidence in this case is consistent with Mr. Foy's identification of Coral Watts as the murderer of Helen Dutcher. And don't forget, it's a very important point, that when Mr. Foy made his identification, he had no information that Coral Eugene Watts would later confess to the Grosse Pointe murder. He had no information that Coral Eugene Watts was even from Michigan nor had lived in Michigan at the relevant time frame. Mr. Foy saw him on the TV, said, 'That's the guy who killed the girl across the alley!' not knowing that he was from Michigan, that he had been in Michigan all of this time, and certainly not knowing that he would later confess to the identical crime of Jeanne Clyne," she stated, and pointed toward the jury for emphasis.

"In terms of, in terms of Helen Dutcher matching a pattern that he exhibited with the rest of these women, always the same thing. Each and every one of them, alone, stalked, targeted, approached, murdered." Pendergast used her clicker again to show the faces of the women Coral Eugene Watts confessed to killing. All twelve faces of the beautiful women were displayed on the screen with a blue background.

"Jeanne Clynne, October 1, 1979. Thirty-one days before Helen Dutcher.

"Linda Tilley, September 5, 1981.

"Elizabeth Montgomery, September 12, 1981.

"Hours later, Suzi Wolf, September 13, 1981.

"Phyllis Tamm, January 5, 1982.

"Margaret Fossi, January 17, 1982.

"Elena Semander, February 7, 1982.

"Anna Ledet. Edith Ledet, also known as Anna, March 27, 1982.

"Carrie Jefferson, April 15, 16, I'm sorry, 1982.

"Yolanda Gracia, April 15, 1982.

"Suzanne Searles, April 25, 1982.

"Michelle Maday, unfortunately, just hours before the incident that the defendant would be apprehended on May 23, 1982.

"You know, the defense in this case has utilized a very smart strategy. But recognize it for what it is, strategy. 'You know, you're gonna hate this guy,' never mind the pattern of blood-soaked patterns of death and destruction he knew you would hear about in this courtroom. The judge has cautioned you and will caution you again . . . that you cannot use the evidence of these attacks to determine that the defendant is a bad person or that he is likely to commit a crime.

"But you cannot minimize"—she strongly emphasized each syllable of each word—"the importance of these other attacks in terms of determining whether or not the murder of Helen Dutcher was part of a plan or scheme that the defendant characteristically used. And when you look at all the different factors in this case, there can be no question." Pendergast then laid down the clicker and walked right up to the jury box.

"Ladies and gentlemen of the jury, there is an old

saying that 'dead men tell no tales.' But in this courtroom, a dead woman has spoken to you through the evidence.

"What happened to Helen Dutcher on December 1, 1979, was horrific, barbaric, savage, and even those words don't do this crime justice. And, you know what? Even you, the jury, will never be able to do justice in this matter.

"How could there be enough justice for the ruthless obliteration of a human life? How could there be enough justice for the act of savagery we now know took place? How could there ever be enough justice for the terror, panic, and pain suffered by Helen Dutcher in the last moments of her life?" she asked with her arms crossed below her chest. "And the unfortunate truth, there never could be. There never could be enough justice for the ruthless and vicious obliteration of a human life cut short by senseless violence. As jurors you are the finders of facts, the determiners of truth, and, in an effort, to somehow kind of do justice, as best we can do it, under this horrific set of circumstances.

"But might I remind you that several facts remain inescapable. The facts, and all the other facts in this case, corroborate Joseph Foy's ID. The fact that the defendant committed an identical crime, thirty-one days before. The fact that every piece of evidence points in one direction and one direction only," Pendergast stated as she pointed at Coral Watts.

"And the unfortunate truth? The unfortunate truth is that a human life has been taken, ruthlessly eliminated. And there will never be enough justice for that." Pendergast paused for five seconds.

"Never," she concluded in a whisper.

"Mr. Kaplovitz," Judge Kuhn called out to the defense attorney.

Defense attorney Ron Kaplovitz calmly and confidently strode toward the jurors. He pulled the lectern back in front of the jury box. He grabbed a tiny Dixie cup of water and placed it on the lectern. "First, I'd like to thank the prosecutors in this case, Ms. Pendergast, Mr. Cameron, for their cooperation and for their integrity. Many things happen in a case before the case begins that you don't know about, discovery, sharing of evidence, pretrial motions, pretrial hearings. They handled themselves with the utmost respect and professionalism here. Their integrity is beyond reproach and I appreciate that. Doesn't always happen in a criminal case, but it happened in this case, and it's a pleasure.

"I also want to thank you for your patience. You've been here for about five or six days of actual trial, not that long of a jury trial as compared to some that we have heard of on TV, and some that I have been involved with, but you listened attentively, you kept your minds open, and I want to thank you in advance for that.

"Also, my sympathy to the victims in this case: Ms. Dutcher, the victims in Texas, the ladies who came into court today, excuse me, yesterday, who testified about what happened to them. They're brave, courageous. The act of Ms. Aguilar is beyond belief, actually.

"In my opening statement, I promised you an experience, an interesting experience, and I have little doubt that we did not let you down in that regard. Prosecutor talks about, 'This isn't a show, this isn't a game,' she's right. This is real life, this really all happened and you're getting to experience firsthand, yourselves," he declared as he pointed at the jury with both hands, "what everybody else here is watching. Some on TV, some in person here. You are getting to experience it for real. You're part of this drama now. I hate to call it a drama because it involves a death of an innocent young lady.

"I told you you'd probably hate my client. I think that I've probably established that fact, or the prosecution has established that fact. It's not my job to make you hate my client. It's the prosecution's job. I suspect she's done a pretty good job at that and you—hate—my—client. So I, certainly we, kept our word about that. And in the end I said to you, I'm gonna ask you to return a not guilty verdict. I told you that's what I was gonna be asking you for, and in the end of this case, that is exactly what I'm gonna be asking you for. When I'm done speaking to you today, you're gonna have to make up, ultimately, your mind about that."

Kaplovitz also told the jury that the key issue in the trial was what occurred on December 1, 1979. He called it the "keep your eye on the ball."

"That's the key issue here in this case. What happened on December 1, 1979?"

Kaplovitz also talked about the possibility of a not guilty verdict, before talking about the evidence. He talked about having to make a hard decision. "You are not gonna want to do it." He flatly stated to the jury, "You are not gonna wanna come to that conclusion. But when you view your ultimate responsibility in this case, and you view the evidence that has really been presented to you, you're gonna have to come to that legal conclusion because it's what's required under the law, and even though you're gonna hate it, it's gonna be the right thing to do."

Kaplovitz flipped over a sheet of paper on his legal pad. "I'm gonna talk briefly now about the evidence in this case." Kaplovitz first returned to the idea that Helen Dutcher was a prostitute. Plenty of eyes rolled in the courtroom when the defense attorney stated that he did "not mean to besmirch her character."

Kaplovitz also did not mean to besmirch Joseph Foy's character, but he did everything to chip away at Foy's credibility.

"Joseph Foy. Joseph Foy has inconsistencies in his testimony that the prosecutor will make some excuses for.

"The car. A Ventura versus a Grand Prix. Brown, tan, the color of the car.

"The beard, well, it's not that full beard, maybe it's that partial beard.

"The purse. Didn't really ever say he saw the purse.

"It's justifiably understandable that Mr. Foy wouldn't be able to see everything; after all, it is a dark alley. But she also wants you to believe that, not withstanding the fact that he has these inconsistencies and inabilities to see certain things, was able to make a positive ID. A positive ID. 'That's the guy! I recognize him, I recognize him now, I recognized him then.'" The attorney punctuated his statements with his right hand, thrusting it toward the jury.

"Ultimately the case comes down to a credibility analysis for Mr. Foy.

"Frankly, I think Mr. Foy honestly believes he saw Mr. Watts. But we've all known people who have had honest convictions about a fact and it turns out that they're wrong. Every single one of you have been in that situation. Somebody you deal with at home, work, socially, you get into a discussion. They're certain about something. You get into a dispute with them, a debate, an argument, a conversation, and they tell you, 'This is what it is.' This is absolutely what it is. They honestly believe what they're telling you.

"Except later it's discovered, they were wrong!

"These people aren't lying. They're mistaken.

"And that has to do with the second part of credibility. The question in this case is not whether or not Mr. Foy is being honest, but whether or not Mr. Foy had ample ability to make an accurate identification.

"Accuracy, reliability. Ability to be able to make a valid identification." Kaplovitz disputed the fact that Foy could see Watts from eighty feet away.

"You'll be the ones that will have to decide whether or not you can even make an accurate identification of a person from that distance.

"There are other inconsistencies," Kaplovitz continued. "There was no sound. Prosecutor will probably tell you, 'Well, she was being stabbed, and she, her lung was penetrated so she couldn't make any sound.' She had enough time to put up a defensive wound.

"Ms. Aguilar heard the sound of Lori Lister outside screaming. Mr. Foy says he didn't hear any sounds whatsoever.

"An inconsistency. The car, the purse, the beard. All, inconsistent.

"There's one other interesting thing about Mr. Foy. It's interesting how he described Mr. Watts. How he identified him based upon his 'evil eyes.'

"'Evil eyes.' He had 'evil eyes.'

"He could recognize him because he had 'evil eyes.'

"What's so interesting and fascinating about that is we heard the testimony from Tom Ladd, came up from Texas, about how Coral Watts often picked out his victims based upon their evil eyes. The exact same wording." Kaplovitz drew out each word in exasperation.

"Now, we had a chance to see from three of the victims: Miss Sanchez, Miss Lister, Miss Aguilar. I looked at their eyes. They looked pretty normal to me. I wasn't able to see evil in their eyes. Reason I'm not able to see evil in their eyes is probably twofold: One, there is no evil in their eyes, and second of all, seeing evil in somebody's eyes is a subjective thing. It is not an objective thing.

"I can look at every single jury [member] here and I can see your eyes. Might be able to tell the color of your eyes if I got a little closer. But to say that I can see evil or goodness in one of your eyes, or sets of your eyes, that's purely subjective. That's purely my opinion. Somehow, I'm venturing my opinion as to what your eyes look like," Kaplovitz delivered with a slightly sarcastic lilt.

"'Evil eyes' is not an objective, concrete description of anything.

"It wasn't when Mr. Watts said it. It isn't when Mr. Foy said it." Again he slowly drew out the words.

"It is, however, interesting that Mr. Foy chose to use the same language that Mr. Watts used in 1982. Interesting.

"Mr. Foy, as I said to you, honestly believes he recognizes Coral Watts. Yet, if you look at the situation as to how he made this identification, we sparred a little bit, not that badly, but we sparred a little bit about whether it was a glance or a look. From eighty feet away, twenty-five years ago, I'll give him a look.

"So what Mr. Foy wants you to believe is, at night, in the dark, from eighty feet away, he had a chance to look at this person, see his eyes, and then, two-and-a-half years later, when Mr. Watts comes on TV and walks in the door, he instantaneously recognizes him," Kaplovitz said, his voice dripping in sarcasm.

"I'm sorry. That is just simply not possible. It is simply not possible," he slowly and condescendingly spat out each syllable to each word. "It cannot be an accurate description. It cannot be. What it is, is a stereotypical generalization. The story was about Mr. Watts. We know that. I stipulated to it. It was clearly Mr. Watts who was on TV about his crimes in Texas. Something to do with Michigan. Mr. Foy made a leap. He made a leap."

Kaplovitz then had the unenviable task of dealing with the 404 (b) evidence of Coral Watts's confessions.

"Certainly you can conclude there are some similarities, if you so desire," Kaplovitz stated in regard to the murders of the other women. "But those similarities don't prove anything. The last part of the instruction says, as follows, and I'm going to read it to you: 'You must not consider this evidence for any other purpose, for example, you must not decide that it shows that the defendant is a bad person or that he is likely to commit other crimes. You must not convict the defendant here because you think he is guilty of other bad conduct. All the evidence must convince you beyond a reasonable doubt the defendant committed the alleged crime or you must find him not guilty.' That's what the jury instruction says.

"Now, I'll concede he's a bad person. But the key part of that jury instruction is that not withstanding those other bad acts they cannot be the basis for your conviction. The basis for your conviction has to be evidence beyond a reasonable doubt of what occurred on December 1, 1979." The defense attorney paused for seven seconds to drive his point home.

Kaplovitz flipped over another page in his legal pad and informed the jury about their burden of proof. "We're never going to be certain what happened here. There's no way of proving at a hundred percent that this was Coral Watts. The prosecutor can't do that. Now, I know she's writing here furiously and she's going to stand up and tell ya, if she doesn't, I'll tell ya, she doesn't have to prove beyond any doubt that it was

Watts, one hundred percent sure. They only have to prove beyond any reasonable doubt. That's the law and that's correct.

"You have to start looking backwards. Okay, we know, we're never going to know for sure, so now are we gonna be able to know beyond a reasonable doubt, which would mean you would convict? Or, are we gonna have some reasonable doubt, which means you have to find him not guilty?"

Kaplovitz wrote a note on his pad and continued, "Basically, there are two types of evidence in this case. There's the evidence from 12/1/1979 . . . and then there's the 404 (b) evidence.

"The 404 (b) evidence is the pink elephant. I talked about it in my opening statement. I'll never be able to get you to get that 404 (b) evidence out of your mind because it's the pink elephant, it won't go away. But when you think about that evidence, I want you to also think about the pink elephant. Because if you eliminate the 404 (b) evidence in this case, and you had to make your decision based strictly upon the evidence about what happened on December 1, 1979, if you knew nothing about these prior bad acts, you would come back with an acquittal and it would take you no time whatsoever and you would do that because, although Mr. Foy may really believe it, his ability to give you an accurate description is simply impossible." The attorney shook his head.

"Your verdict would be not guilty if it wasn't for the 404 (b) evidence and there is absolutely no doubt about that. None, whatsoever. I know it. You know it. Prosecutor knows it."

Kaplovitz jotted down one more note, took a quick pause, and addressed the jury. "This is my last chance to talk to you. The prosecutor's gonna get one last chance to talk to you. Judge is then gonna give you, the jury, instructions. And then the case is yours. I'm done. Ms. Pendergast is done. You guys got to really get started. Not to say that you haven't gotten started already, because you've been paying attention and listening, but now you really gonna have to get started.

"You're gonna have a huge responsibility. A very huge responsibility in this case. Because you see, when this case began, it began as *The People* v. *Coral Watts*, an admitted murderer of many people. That's what the case began as. High profile, publicity, television, media, it's all there. We know that the society has this desire to want to convict. I know that.

"But what's important to you to remember is that this case has become even bigger than *People* v. *Coral Watts*. This is no longer just about trying to convict a man who's confessed to other murders. This case is fundamentally about the integrity of our jury system and of our judicial system. It has become huge. It has become huge because when you weigh the two bodies of evidence: the 404(b) versus the evidence of the incident on 12/1/1979, the evidence on that day of 12/1/79 would cause you to issue an acquittal. Yet, society wants you to issue a conviction.

"You know that the evidence is insufficient in regard to December 1, 1979. You know it is. You know it cannot be a valid, reliable identification. You know it's a stereotypical generalization. That's the description of the individual who committed this crime, on December 1, 1979."

Kaplovitz began to close his argument. "In the end integrity is all we have. The integrity of our judicial system is all we have. And as much as you might hate Mr. Watts, the integrity of our judicial system is fundamentally far more important than convicting Mr. Watts.

"You know you have to do the right thing. You have to

do the right thing in this case. And you're not gonna like it. But you're gonna have to do the right thing. And, like it or not, the right thing is to return a verdict [of] not guilty.

"Thank you."

Several heads shook in the gallery as Kaplovitz stepped away from the lectern.

Coral Watts simply rubbed his forehead over and over.

CHAPTER 59

Early in the morning of November 17, 2004, Kalamazoo assistant district attorney James Gregart held a press conference. He announced that the Kalamazoo District Attorney's Office would bring a murder charge against Coral Eugene Watts for the October 30, 1974, murder of Gloria Steele, regardless of the outcome of the Helen Dutcher case.

Just minutes later, in Oakland County, after less than two weeks of testimony, the case against Coral Watts went to the jury, a group that consisted of only twelve jurors, as one more member was booted. Apparently, a male juror went to the crime scene of his own accord, which he was not allowed to do. As a result there were no more alternate jurors left. If one more would be released, a mistrial would have to be declared.

The gallery got nervous after hearing the news.

There would be no reason for anyone to worry. After less than three hours, the jury returned with a verdict. The overflowing gallery once again waited with bated breath. Joseph Foy sat next to Harriett Semander, his hand encased in a yellow Lance Armstrong "Livestrong" bracelet. Harriett grabbed his arm as Joseph Foy leaned forward. He seemed more nervous than he had been during his entire testimony.

"Will the remainder of the jurors please rise?" the courtroom bailiff asked. "Members of the jury, listen to your verdict as recorded. You do say upon your oaths that you do find the defendant guilty of first-degree premeditated murder."

The audible sigh sounded like a rush of hot air expelled out of an expanding balloon. Backs were slapped, fists were pumped, but voices were subdued.

"So say you, Ms. Foreperson," the bailiff inquired.

"Yes, we do."

"So say you all?"

The jurors all nodded and stated in unison, "Yes, we do."

Joseph Foy buried his head into his hands. The tears of joy freely flowed.

Coral Watts, slumped in his chair, simply rolled his eyes. He was then cuffed and removed from the courtroom. As he walked past the gallery, he could not help but attempt one last act of defiance. He boldly glared at the families as he shuffled away, the sounds of tinkling metal escorting him out of the room.

Judge Kuhn then dismissed the jury. The gallery, which remained seated, burst into applause as soon as the jury left the room. Several victims' family members jumped up and cheered, hugged one another, and burst into tears of happiness.

Joseph Foy stood with his fists clenched. He smiled in victory as Maria Semander Crawford jumped into his arms. Harriett Semander, Jane Montgomery, Lori Lister

Baugh, Julie Sanchez, and Michael Clyne stood by with cautious smiles on their faces.

Julie Sanchez, who wore dark sunglasses throughout the rest of the trial after her testimony, removed her glasses. A large grin began to spread across her face.

CHAPTER 60

Less than one month later, on December 7, 2004, Coral Eugene Watts faced Judge Richard Kuhn for sentencing. The convicted felon was ushered into the courtroom, this time wearing the prison-issued orange jumpsuit.

Just as he had endured more than twenty-two years earlier, Watts received a verbal tongue-lashing from a judge. "This case cries out for the death penalty," Judge Kuhn implored. "No, it screams for the death penalty, but Michigan does not allow it."

Beth Mrozinski, Helen Dutcher's niece, gave a victim's impact statement at the hearing. She did not mince words. She first told Watts that he should be a man and admit to all of the murders he ever committed so that the victims' families could have some peace.

"Watts"—she directed her ire at the serial killer—"you have taken away and brutalized our loved ones. Our hope is that you never again see the light of day outside of prison. Hell is not even a good enough place for you."

Coral Watts took the time to speak at his sentencing

hearing. He calmly denied the charge against him. "I did not kill Helen Dutcher. That's one murder I did not do."

Watts informed the judge that he planned to appeal the sentence. He also declared he hoped that Helen Dutcher's real killer would be discovered one day.

"If I did it, I'd confess to it," he calmly stated.

Judge Kuhn sentenced Coral Eugene Watts to life in prison in the state of Michigan. Watts would not be returned to Texas.

The response to Watts's conviction and sentence was fast and overwhelmingly positive. Joseph Foy, the key witness for the prosecution, sighed. "I'm glad it's over, not for me, but for the families." Foy did not have many kind words for the man who tormented his dreams for the past twenty-five years. "He'll rot in prison until God comes and takes his soul to hell. He's a selfish coward and what he did that night will be with me every day until I die."

CHAPTER 61

On Thursday, January 27, 2005, Harriett Semander sat at a white-clothed table next to Andy Kahan and five other individuals. Their table was surrounded by thirty to forty similar tables, also filled with well-dressed individuals. The people at the other tables were there to honor Semander.

The occasion was the Crime Stoppers of Houston 2005 Annual Meeting at the plush Warwick Hotel, located in the Museum District. Keri Whitlow and Dianne Clements were also in attendance; so were dozens of judges, police officers, attorneys, and other concerned citizens. They were all there to honor the tiny seventy-one-year-old mother who had lost her child nearly twenty-three years earlier.

Crime Stoppers were there to honor Harriett Semander with the Leon Goldstein Award for the "citizen who made a significant contribution in fighting crime in our community."

After a presentation to the Harris County Sheriff's Office Robbery Division for their contribution, Master of Ceremonies Dave Ward—a longtime fixture on the local news from ABC affiliate KTRK-TV Channel 13 (the only local news station that bothered to send a reporter to Michigan to cover the Helen Dutcher murder trial)—awarded Harriett Semander for her efforts in a nearly twenty-three-year-old ordeal to make sure Coral Eugene Watts was finally charged and put away for murder.

The always modest and gracious Semander walked up to the podium and stood next to Ward. She looked out at the gathering of appreciative Houstonians and, in a barely audible voice, thanked the audience and Crime Stoppers.

Semander continued, "I dedicate this award to my oldest daughter, Elena"—Semander began to weep, but forged on—"and to the other thirteen women killed by Coral Eugene Watts." She then recited the entire list of Watts's murder victims. She then dedicated the award to Watts's surviving victims.

Semander continued stating that Watts's conviction "was the ultimate in grassroots achievement. I was told for many, many years that there was nothing we could do to stop it from happening (Watts's mandatory release). Watts's conviction is proof that you should never doubt what a small group of people can accomplish."

The audience sat in rapt attention. "There are no coincidences," Semander continued, "in Watts's case because I believe all things come together through the glory of God." Semander added that it was through God's power that "something good came out of something evil. When Coral Watts was sentenced to life in prison, heaven and earth united to celebrate the victims."

Semander concluded, "There is an old saying that 'the dead aren't buried until justice is served.' Now our loved ones rest in peace because the boogeyman has been put away."

EPILOGUE

Coral Eugene Watts: serial killer as pop culture icon?

Judy Wolf Krueger's statement about Coral Watts being less known than Ted Bundy or Son of Sam is a curious fact in this day and age of mass-media proliferation. It was inevitable that the horrific tale of America's most prolific serial killer would finally seep into America's consciousness. Or would it?

Coral Watts's tale was finally co-opted by the mainstream entertainment industry in the form of two network television top-rated shows: *Crossing Jordan* and *Cold Case.*

Sort of co-opted, that is.

In the April 10, 2005, episode of NBC's *Crossing Jordan,* entitled "Locard's Exchange," Ted Shackelford played a serial killer who was to be set free from prison despite having killed fourteen women because of a plea bargain. When asked why he killed a victim, the serial killer replied, "She had evil in her eyes." He later tells lead character Jordan Cavanaugh (played by Jill Hennessy) that "it would have been because they had evil in their eyes. Like you."

In the May 1, 2005, episode of CBS's *Cold Case,* entitled

"Creatures of the Night," Barry Bostwick also played a serial killer who was to be set free from prison despite having killed fourteen women because of a plea bargain.

One major difference between the fictional representations and the real-life Coral Watts is obvious: Ted Shackelford and Barry Bostwick are both white.

A trial date for Coral Watts in the Gloria Steele murder was set for August 23, 2005, after this book went to the publisher. On Friday, May 27, 2005, circuit judge William G. Schma ruled that Watts's confessions and information about his previous murders would be inadmissible.

Watts's latest defense attorney, Jeff Getting, asked the judge to dismiss the case against Watts. According to Getting, "The judge's decision leaves the prosecution without a winnable case. There is insufficient evidence for a finding of guilt."

Judge Schma declared he would rule on the request at a later date.

Sharon Watts, Coral Watts's younger sister, has no idea why the state of Michigan wants to try her brother for another murder.

"It makes me wonder what people's true motive is," Sharon wondered aloud in an interview with the author on June 3, 2005. "Is it truly do you want to understand what's going on because, obviously, he has some psyche [*sic*] problems. He's been peeked into this problem, this schizophrenia, displacement kind of thing, and, you know, I really don't see where anybody has tried to help him. Or other people with schizophrenia and other displacement disorders, but they're real quick to say he's a 'monster' and we should put him away."

When addressing the Gloria Steele trial, Sharon Watts professed, "I just don't understand the point. I really don't understand the point. You brought this guy back who was already doing God-knows-what for whatever and you think he probably wouldn't have gotten out of jail anyway, and to me it's just a thing that Texas decides it's spent too much money on this guy who originally originated from Michigan." Sharon Watts continued, "Okay, let's ship him back to Michigan and make it Michigan's problem.

"So now they take him and they grandstand him on the media for all they can get. As far as I'm concerned, the evidence that they had [in the Helen Dutcher trial] was nothing anyway. It was just this big thing that they had down in Texas that convicted him, as far as I'm concerned."

Watts became animated. "Okay, he did that! Fine! How come that's not the end of it? Why do you, whatcha gonna do? Take him all around Michigan and just display him?"

Sharon Watts continued to talk about her brother. "He's really not . . . well, my definition of a monster because he does have a conscience. However, he does have difficulty putting certain things in certain places and perspective. You know, that goes back to the help.

"He should be able to recognize some of those issues now. But he really doesn't. We talk with him and he still does things that are totally inappropriate and then he will have to think about. When I say he 'does things,' you know, one of his oldest, dearest friends called and got in touch with him and it just so happen, she got shot. Well, when she told him that she got shot, he thought it was the funniest thing. He's just not a normal person!"

It is for that reason that Harriett Semander will never let down her guard. Her fear that another crack may appear in the judicial system is what drives her to make sure that the man who killed her daughter will remain imprisoned until he takes his final breath. It is the reason why she will never burn all of the materials and notes and articles about her daughter Elena. She does not want to see this abnormal man hurt another human being ever again.

Don't miss Corey Mitchell's true crime classic

SAVAGE SON

Available from Kensington Publishing Corp.

Keep reading to enjoy a compelling excerpt . . .

CHAPTER 1

Wednesday, December 10, 2003, 6:00 P.M.
Whitaker Residence
Heron Way—Sugar Lakes Subdivision
Sugar Land, Texas

Nestled cozily inside their luxurious home in the tony neighborhood of Sugar Lakes, in the upscale small city of Sugar Land, Texas, just outside the crime-filled, polluted metropolis of Houston, the Whitaker family gathered for a special occasion. They were to celebrate the impending graduation the following day of their eldest son, Bart, from Sam Houston State University.

Outside, the pre-Christmas chill had finally started to kick in and the crispness permeated the neighborhood. Heron Way, the street upon which the Whitaker home resided, was bedecked with the ever-popular icicle lights. Doors were festooned with oversized evergreen wreaths, and life-sized wooden cutouts of most major Christian-based, Christmas-themed characters were erected, like a movie set for a Western.

Inside, the Whitakers huddled together in the warmth

of their lovely home, so painstakingly tended to by the family matriarch, Patricia Whitaker, known to her family and friends as "Tricia." She made sure nearly every inch of their home was covered in Christmas knickknacks— from Santa snow globes, to fake snow, to little green candy canes laid everywhere with care. But there was an even deeper devotion in this household, more than mere secular Santa–ism. Tricia and her husband, Kent, were both deeply religious people who made sure that "Christ" remained in *Christ*mas in the Whitaker household. Kent and Tricia held tightly to their faith and made sure to incorporate their devotion into their everyday lives, whether they were attending church services and functions, or simply with how they comported themselves in their daily routines and dealings with other people.

Kent and Tricia also made it a point to teach the bountiful lessons of Jesus Christ and his Holy Father to their own two sons, Thomas, who preferred to be addressed by his nickname, "Bart," and his younger brother, Kevin. Both sons were outstanding in the eyes of their parents and both had made strides toward living a Christ-filled life.

"I'm so happy," Tricia whispered to Kent. He smiled back at his lovely bride, who, at fifty-one years old, looked as beautiful to him as the day they first met. He still felt a rush of warmth in her presence, and he knew he loved her more today than he had all those years ago.

"Me too," Kent replied. "I knew he could do it."

The couple stopped what they were doing and looked up at the portrait of their family, placed over the fireplace mantel. Their twenty-three-year-old son, Bart, was ready to begin his adult life with a college degree in hand. He was brilliant, they said to one another, and now he would be able to step out into the real world and let others see his true intelligence.

"All right, Bart"—Kent Whitaker got his son's attention—"in honor of this wondrous occasion, your mother and I decided to get you something special to commemorate your hard work and dedication to finish your studies and earn that degree."

Bart stood next to the hearth and grinned. The handsome, though slightly pudgy, son beamed back in his parents' direction. He was dressed nicely in a casual pair of brown corduroy pants, a burgundy long-sleeved shirt, and preppy bowling shoes. He smiled in eager anticipation as to what it was his overly generous parents were giving him this time.

Kent handed Bart a wrapped gift, about the size of an old-fashioned small toaster oven. Bart thanked his father as he received the package. He stood near the family Christmas tree, which was already overflowing with gifts, even though Christmas was still more than two weeks away. He looked like a little kid whose parents would allow him to open one of his presents before Santa came.

Instead of diving right in, however, Bart played up the moment. He looked at the gift, held it up to his ear, and began to shake it vigorously. He smiled as he tried to guess what was inside. "Hmmmm, I'd say it's a coffee mug." His parents played along. His younger brother, Kevin, smiled as well.

"No, Bart, just open it," his mother playfully ordered.

"Yeah, c'mon, Bart. Your mother went to a lot of trouble to find this for you," his father declared. "It's not every day one of our boys graduates from college."

Bart returned the smiles and hungrily tore into the package. After he removed the wrapping and the bow, he found himself holding a green box. The outside of the box looked like the interior of a fluorescent aquarium, complete with rocky coral shelves. He knew this was no ordinary box. He also knew it was no coffee mug.

Bart flipped the box over in an effort to try and figure out the best spot where to open it. As he did, he spotted *Rolex* on the opposite side. His eyes lit up. He had always wanted a Rolex watch, but he never had enough money to purchase one of the elite timepieces.

Tricia's smile was wide enough to make every orthodontist happy as she watched her oldest boy unwrap his gift. She could not have been prouder—especially since she had always wondered about Bart and whether or not he could get his act together and be a solid contributor to the family. Now she knew that his commitment to his studies was all the proof she needed to know he was definitely on the path to a godly life and financial success. She could not have asked for anything more.

Once Bart realized what his gift was, he wasted no more time in getting to it. He opened the box, then removed another box from inside. He opened the second box and there it was: a shiny $4,000 Rolex watch. He was ecstatic. Bart had champagne tastes, and his parents never let him down.

Tricia leaned up against Kent and flashed him a loving smile. He nodded toward her and then turned to Bart. "Well, what do you think, Bart?"

Bart continued looking at the watch and then slowly shook his head to and fro. "I like it. I like it a lot." Bart smiled at his brother, Kevin, who returned the smile. "No, I love it!" Bart exclaimed.

The family spent another minute or so gawking at Bart's new symbol of success. After basking in the glow, Bart glanced at his new watch, which had the correct time already. "Hey, c'mon. We'd better get going. We don't want to be late for Pappadeaux."

The rest of the Whitaker family nodded in agreement and began to perform the "getting ready to go" shuffle of grabbing wallets, jackets, and gloves. Pappadeaux is a seafood restaurant chain that specializes in fried seafood and Cajun-style crawfish. It is owned by the Pappas family from Houston, who also own Pappas Bros., which serves steaks, Pappasito's, which serves Mexican food, and Pappas BBQ, which, of course, specializes in barbeque. There are several Pappas restaurants spread throughout the state of Texas, and they are hugely successful. The most upscale of all the Pappas' restaurants would definitely be Pappadeaux. There was one located near the Whitakers, out on Highway 59, near Highway 6, less than three miles from their home.

The four Whitakers piled into Tricia's TrailBlazer and headed out of their neighborhood.

They failed to notice the car parked on the back side street, directly behind their house.

Tricia made the short drive in very little time. The perpetually under-construction Highway 6 did not cause any problems for them, as work was being done in the opposite direction from the restaurant. In less than five minutes, the Whitakers pulled into the relatively empty parking lot, exited the TrailBlazer, and headed for the side doors of the restaurant.

No one in the family noticed the person sitting in the car who watched them as they entered Pappadeaux.

Inside the restaurant, the family was quickly seated as they had called in reservations. They perused the extravagant menus, made their selections, and gave their orders to the friendly waitstaff. Drinks were also ordered, delivered, and quaffed. It was all a very pleasant evening, with happiness and celebration the key themes for the Whitakers.

After stuffing themselves with crawfish, gumbo, and fried catfish, Kent Whitaker decided to order a celebratory dessert for Bart. A big production was made upon the delivery of the house special.

"Here's to you, Bart," Kent Whitaker toasted his oldest son. He could not contain his happiness. He had been worried that Bart would turn in the wrong direction and not make anything of himself. Thankfully, his son had proved him wrong. He was now on the precipice of greatness. "Congratulations on an amazing accomplishment. I only wish Lynne was here to share this special occasion with you." Lynne Sorsby was Bart's girlfriend. There had recently been talk of marriage proposals on the horizon.

"Thanks, Dad," Bart said, returning the salute. "I'll be talking with her later tonight when we get back home. She'll probably come over later, but she already had plans to go out to dinner with her folks."

Surprisingly, Bart had not thought to invite Lynne and her family to Pappadeaux to join his family for dinner. The whole celebration actually was thrown together at the last minute. Bart even had to call his father in to be sure he made it out to the restaurant. As a result, Lynne had already made plans that she could not back out of.

"Bart, honey, I just want you to know how proud I am of you, son." Bart's mom was beaming. "You stuck with it and now you are being rewarded for your tenacity and strong spirit. I wish you the best of luck, and know you will make a name for yourself, one day."

"Hear! Hear!" the other two Whitaker men chimed

in. All four raised their glasses for a toast. Bart smiled at his mom as he lowered his drink.

"How 'bout some pictures?" Kent Whitaker asked. The proud papa pulled out his camera and snapped several shots of the boys and their mother, Kevin and Bart together, and Bart holding up his dessert plate. A good time was had by all.

Their appetites sated, Kent asked their waiter for the check, he paid, and they exited the now-bustling restaurant. It paid to eat early in a Houston restaurant. When the Whitakers stepped outside, the parking lot had gone from relatively barren to humming with SUVs and Mercedes Benzes. This time, Kevin asked his mom to drive her TrailBlazer. She agreed and the family members piled in and drove off the lot.

None of the Whitakers noticed that the same car from earlier was still in the parking lot. Nor did they see it as it pulled out and began to follow them home.

Kevin Whitaker pulled up to the entrance of their gated community. He punched in the security code to gain access into the neighborhood. The car behind them managed to squeeze through the gate as well, without having to enter its own code. They did not notice the vehicle as they turned the corner toward Heron Way and their home.

Kevin turned right into the Whitaker driveway and pulled his mother's TrailBlazer up close to the attached garage. The family got out of the SUV, locked their doors, and shut them. Tricia was the first out and also the first to head toward the front porch and into the front-door entrance. The porch light beckoned like a shining star in the cold night.

Kevin quickly walked around the truck and scooted past his mother. He always liked to be first to the door, and the one to open it up. Kent followed behind Tricia. Bart, however, made a beeline for the street and his Yukon, which his parents had bought for him while he was at college.

"I forgot my cell phone in the truck," Bart tossed back to his family. "I need to call Lynne so she can come on over."

Kent looked over at Bart, smiled, and followed his wife.

As Kent Whitaker rounded the corner, he looked up and saw his youngest boy, Kevin, unlock the front door and enter the house. He had no idea that when Kevin went inside, there was someone standing directly in front of him. He also had no idea that Kevin smiled at the person who was standing inside their home.

Pop!

It was short, but distinct. The sound rang out clearly in the quiet neighborhood.

"Oh God, no!" Kent Whitaker heard his wife scream. He ran toward her, but he was too late. Tricia Whitaker bolted into the house to protect her baby boy. "Don't you—"

Pop!

Another crack. Nothing but silence from Tricia, then a moan.

"Help," she barely muttered.

Kent Whitaker went after his wife. He unknowingly stepped over a loose garden hose on the front porch, only to see his wife and youngest son, both lying inside the foyer of their home. Both were bleeding badly. He could not tell if Kevin was moving or not. He could see that his wife was still alive as she began to take huge gasps of air.

By this time, Bart Whitaker began to run up the

driveway to see what was happening inside his parents' home, the home he and his brother had grown up in.

"Dad!" he screamed, only to be interrupted by yet another . . .

Pop!

As Bart dashed through the front yard and hastily made his way onto the front porch, he was greeted with the ghastly vision of his father lying on his back with blood pouring out of his body. Instinctively Bart ran past his father to get inside the house. He only momentarily looked down to see his mother, gasping for air, lying in an ever-widening pool of blood. He barely caught sight of his brother farther in the house. He did not appear to be moving.

Bart sought out his target. A man dressed in black from head to toe stood near the family kitchen. Bart's adrenaline took over and made his decisions for him as he charged at the masked intruder. He grappled with the shooter and had every intention of disarming him. Unfortunately, his attempt of heroism fell short.

Pop!

The fourth gunshot crack of the night tore through the frigid air. It was much louder to Bart this time as he and the gunfire were both indoors.

The masked intruder then dropped the gun and took off running through the laundry room, which led to a door that led outside to the backyard. The man took off running by the swimming pool, leaped over the Whitakers' wooden fence, and headed for a small car parked on the street directly behind the Whitakers' home. The shooter and driver slowly drove off with the car's headlights off.

The Whitakers were left to die, writhing in their own thick pools of blood.

CHAPTER 2

December 10, 2003, 8:18 P.M.
Stanley Residence
Heron Way—Sugar Lakes Subdivision
Sugar Land, Texas

Directly next door to the Whitakers' home on the east side, their relatively new neighbor, Clifton "Cliff" Stanley, sat in his recliner in his family's living room. He was having a relaxing evening watching television.

Cliff was very fond of his new neighbors. He and his wife, Darlene, had moved into the home just six months earlier. The couple had two sons, Brandon and Dane, who had gone off to college.

Cliff's job as a vice president of a regional insurance marketing company was quite demanding and kept him very busy. Thus, he enjoyed the little time he was able to spend with Kent and Tricia Whitaker. Cliff met Tricia the day he and his wife had moved in. He described her as "just a very, very sweet person."

The Stanleys and Whitakers developed a quick, pleasant friendship. They went out to lunch together, had dinner a few times, and even made it out to the theater once on a double date. Cliff Stanley worked out of his home, so he became closer to Tricia, who was a stay-at-home mother at the time. She had previously taught at nearby Lakeview Elementary School and was acting as a volunteer there on occasion. At night, when Kent would return home from his job at the Bartlett Construction Company, the couples would "congregate out in the front yard" and catch up on the day's events.

Cliff Stanley knew the Whitakers were in for a big weekend. Their oldest son, Bart, whom he had never met, since Bart lived up north in Willis, Texas, was about to graduate on Saturday. Stanley could tell that Tricia was very excited and happy about the impending ceremony. "She was very hopeful, very upbeat and optimistic for [Bart's] future."

Cliff and Darlene sat downstairs in the back of their comfortable home, on this particular night. The couple relaxed and watched television. They were also excited to have their eldest son, Brandon, home from college for the holidays. Their son had been upstairs in his room when he peeked in on his parents in the living room.

"Was that on the TV?" Brandon asked his parents.

"What?" Cliff asked his son.

"I heard yelling and shooting," Brandon stated.

The Stanleys were watching a family show. "No, it wasn't on this TV," Cliff replied.

Brandon walked down the steps and insisted, "Then it's outside. Something's going on outside. I swear I heard a shooting outside."

Cliff and Darlene looked at one another quizzically. Cliff rose up to take a look. He and Brandon headed for the front door to see if something was going on.

When he walked out of his home, Cliff first looked over in the direction of the Whitakers' house. It was natural instinct. Look toward those you are closest with in hopes that everything is fine with them. Unfortunately, everything was far from fine at the Whitaker household.

Cliff spotted Kent Whitaker sprawled out on the concrete front porch next door. He couldn't tell whether he was dead or alive. Kent's head was pointing back toward the Stanley house in an awkward position. Suddenly Cliff saw his friend lurch sideways and mutter something.

"I'm bleeding . . ." Kent Whitaker pitifully mewled. His voice was barely audible.

"Kent," Cliff called out to his friend. "Are you okay?"

"I'm bleeding, Cliff," Kent cried out much louder. "Help!"

Cliff immediately headed in the direction of Kent Whitaker, his own safety not crossing his mind. The thought that a man with a gun might still be on the premises did not enter into his consciousness. He simply understood that his friend was in trouble and needed his help.

Cliff made his way toward Kent. As he came upon him, Cliff looked up and saw Tricia directly in front of the entryway to the house, about six feet away from Kent. She was in a kneeling position with her head on the front porch, near the slight step leading into the house. Her legs and lower body were pointed outward toward the street.

Brandon Stanley followed directly behind his father. When Cliff witnessed the carnage before him, he yelled back at his son, "Go back inside and call 911! Now!" Brandon took off back to the house to make the call.

Cliff turned his attention back to the bleeding Whitaker parents. He looked at Kent and asked, "What happened?"

Kent looked at his friend with pleading eyes and reiterated, "I'm bleeding, Cliff."

"Okay, buddy. Just hang in there. Let me see what I can do," Cliff attempted to calm his neighbor.

Cliff hustled back to his house, stormed inside, and began yelling to Brandon, "I need something to stop the bleeding! Bring me something so we can bandage Kent up!" He waited as long as he could, but his son never came out with anything to staunch the flow of blood.

Cliff tore out of his house and returned to the Whitakers. He ripped off his T-shirt and placed it on Kent's left shoulder. "Kent, hold on to this. It will keep the blood from rushing out too fast," he ordered. He could tell by the looks of Tricia that she needed his help much more than Kent. "Just hold on tight."

Cliff edged forward, closer to Tricia. She was moaning in pain, but still conscious. "What happened?" he asked her.

Tricia Whitaker looked up at him, pale and bedraggled, and said, "Someone shot us. You need to go. He could still be here." She began to moan again—only this time, it seemed more drawn out and painful than before. Cliff could sense that she was going downhill rapidly. Unfortunately, he was afraid to move her body in case her blood had already started to clot up; he didn't want to break up the clots and cause her to bleed even more.

Instead, Cliff began to pray. Tricia Whitaker continued

to moan in agony. He looked up from Tricia into the house, where he spotted someone who he thought was Kevin Whitaker. He always thought a lot of the youngest son who had returned from his first semester in college at Texas A&M University. Cliff thought Kevin was "a special kid."

It was difficult to tell if it was actually Kevin or Bart, since it was dark inside the house. There was a light on in the foyer, which provided him with his only illumination. Cliff was unsure how that person was doing; that is, until he heard a pitiful sound emanating from the victim. Cliff would later describe it as a "death rattle." It was marked by "very ragged moaning." Cliff knew that the boy, whom he could finally make out as Kevin, was breathing his final breaths.

Cliff was unable to get to Kevin because Tricia was blocking the entrance to the front door. Besides, he could tell that Kevin was very close to dead. Cliff bent his head and said a silent prayer for Kevin.

The nineteen-year-old son of Tricia and Kent Whitaker stopped breathing.

Cliff knew he needed to get assistance for Kent and Tricia. He quickly moved back and leaned over Kent to see how he could help. He took over holding the bloody T-shirt used as a bandage and held it firmly in place. He then heard the front door to his house open and saw his wife, Darlene, stick her head outside.

"Clifton, get out of there!" she shouted frantically. "The killers might still be inside their house!" She was frightened to tears and was determined that her husband not join the list of fatalities.

Cliff Stanley had not cared about the possibility of a shooter or shooters still hiding out inside the Whitaker home. Regardless, he continued holding the temporary bandage on Kent's gushing wound.

Kent then looked up at his neighbor and said, "Cliff, they really could be inside there. I don't want you getting shot."

Cliff snapped to and realized that both his wife and Kent were right. He needed to get the hell out of there. But instead of fleeing, Cliff decided he needed some protection of his own. He went to get his shotgun.

"I'll be right back, Kent."

Cliff darted up from his wounded neighbor and bolted back toward his home. He went inside, determined to find his weapon, which he did. He began to load the shotgun with bullets when his wife stepped in front of him. She was scared.

"If they pull up," she said in reference to police officers, "and they see you with that shotgun, they'll probably shoot you, too. They might think you are the one who shot the Whitakers."

Cliff knew his wife was right. He felt so frustrated. It seemed as if there was nothing he could do for his friends. He decided it was best to put down his own weapon; however, he knew he had to do something. Instead, he returned back to the Whitakers' front porch and attempted to comfort Kent.

Cliff then heard the screech of police sirens.

The whole scenario took less than ten minutes. To Cliff Stanley, it seemed like a lifetime. "Everything seemed to be moving in slow motion," he recalled.

Sugar Land police officer Kelly Gless was the first to arrive at the scene. He slowly exited his vehicle to assess the situation. He was very cognizant of the fact that the shooter or shooters might still be in the house or in the nearby vicinity. Officer Gless noticed Cliff holding a bloody shirt up against Kent Whitaker.

"Sir, could you please step away from that man?" Gless asked Cliff.

"I'm their next-door neighbor. I found them like this," Stanley assured the officer.

"That's fine, sir," Gless responded. "I need for you to step away from that man, and please stand on your driveway."

Cliff immediately complied, looked at Kent one more time, then retreated back to his yard.

More police cars pulled up onto Heron Way. The revolving lights on top of the vehicles intermingled with the red, green, and white Christmas decorations throughout the neighborhood. It looked like a spinning holiday season kaleidoscope.

Darlene came out of the house to join her husband. Cliff began to pray out loud so Kent could hear him. Cliff and Darlene clutched each other and worried about their newfound friends.

An ambulance pulled up to the location immediately thereafter. The emergency medical technicians (EMTs) jumped out of the truck and quickly examined the scene. The prognosis was grim, especially for Tricia Whitaker. One of the EMTs phoned in a request for a Life Flight helicopter. Tricia would need immediate surgical attention at the nearby Memorial Hermann Sugar Land Hospital. Her chances of holding on were slim.

Connect with Us

Visit us online at
KensingtonBooks.com
to read more from your favorite authors, see books
by series, view reading group guides, and more.

for sneak peeks, chances to win books and prize packs,
and to share your thoughts with other readers.

facebook.com/kensingtonpublishing
twitter.com/kensingtonbooks

Tell us what you think!

To share your thoughts, submit a review,
or sign up for our eNewsletters, please visit:
KensingtonBooks.com/TellUs.